The Immigrant Heritage of America Series

Cecyle S. Neidle, *Editor*

THE IMMIGRANT EXPERIENCE IN AMERICA

Edited by
FRANK J. COPPA
THOMAS J. CURRAN

TWAYNE PUBLISHERS
A DIVISION OF G. K. HALL & CO., BOSTON

Library of Congress Cataloging in Publication Data
Main entry under title:

The Immigrant experience in America

(The Immigrant heritage of America series)
Essays evolved from a 54 part television series entitled
"The immigrant in American life," produced for summer semes-
ter in 1973.
Bibliography.
1. Minorities—United States—History—Addresses, essays,
lectures. 2. United States—Emigration and immigration—History—
Addresses, essays, lectures.
I. Coppa, Frank J. II. Curran, Thomas J., 1929–
E184.A1I43   973'.04   76–8439
ISBN 0–8057–8406–3

MANUFACTURED IN THE UNITED STATES OF AMERICA

Contents

Preface

This collection of essays on the broad topic of immigration evolved from a fifty-four part television series entitled "The Immigrant in American Life" produced for Summer Semester in 1973. It was a joint venture of the St. John's University Television Center under the direction of Winston L. Kirby and the Columbia Broadcasting System. The series was well received, evoking mail from virtually every state in the country including Hawaii. The requests for transcripts of the programs were so numerous that we were encouraged to present the material in book form. In part the response was so enthusiastic because the programs were geared to a general audience and the series was aired at a time of growing ethnic awareness.

The aims of this book are the same as those of the television series from which it sprang: to explain why millions of immigrants, most voluntarily, some involuntarily, decided to leave their homes and resettle in the United States. What conditions drove them from their roots to a foreign land? How were they received in the New World? Why did America, a nation of i.nmigrants, hold so hostile a view of most immigrant groups, while professing that it was a land of refuge, an asylum for the oppressed? Was this schizophrenic reaction irrational? How did the immigrants react to this mixed reception? Why were some of these foreign-born newcomers and their descendants transformed into ethnic Americans while others were more completely assimilated? What did these uprooted people achieve, and finally what has been their impact upon the social, economic, political, and intellectual life of our nation?

In order to begin to answer these questions we have included eight essays on specific immigrant groups: the Hispanic, Germans, Norwegians, Irish, Italians, Jews, Blacks, and Asians. The essay on the Germans is the joint enterprise of the two editors with Dr. Coppa examining the European background and Dr. Curran responsible for the German role in the United States.

To complete the volume we thought it useful to include a discussion of recent immigrant legislation and specifically the impact of the McCarran-Walter Act. This forms the subject of the ninth and concluding essay in the volume.

We recognize that our treatment has ignored some groups and topics, but considerations of time and space and publication deadlines made it impossible to include all the essays presented in the television series. Twayne's "Immigrant Heritage of America Series" under the general editorship of Dr. Cecyle Neidle will publish works that deal with a number of ethnic groups that have been neglected in this book.

In doing first the series and then the book we would like to thank those members of the St. John's University History Department who offered their advice and assistance and in particular Dr. Eugene Kusielewicz. The staffs of the St. John's University Library and CBS Television were most helpful as was Cecyle Neidle, who read the work carefully and made a number of corrective suggestions. Roy Allen, the director of Summer Semester, was most understanding and proved to be a scholar as well as a technician. A special word of thanks goes to Winston Kirby who served as coordinator for the television series on immigration and provided the needed secretarial assistance to produce this work. His enthusiasm and hard work provided inspiration for us all.

F. J. C.
T. J. C.

I

The Hispanic Impact Upon the United States

By THEODORE S. BEARDSLEY, JR.
The Hispanic Society of America

WE often forget that the earliest European settlers in what is now the continental United States were not English but Spanish. As early as 1513 Florida was discovered and explored by Ponce de León, and in 1527 the first colony of Europeans was established by Panfilo de Narváez near present-day Pensacola. The colony failed, but a half-century later, in 1565, a permanent colony under Pedro Menéndez de Avilés founded our oldest American city, Saint Augustine, Florida. By this time various expeditions had been conducted by the Spaniards in the Southwest so that when the Pilgrims reached Plymouth Rock such Spanish centers as St. Augustine in Florida or Santa Fé in New Mexico were already flourishing.

Today, Spanish is the second language of the United States, and it is estimated that as many as 20 million people in this country, almost ten percent of the population, speak primarily Spanish. At most, only half of that number can be considered immigrants of the first or second generation. Before one can discuss Hispanic immigration to the United States, the patterns of Hispanic colonization prior to the annexation of Spanish territories must be established.

The accompanying map shows the ultimate reaches of Spanish domain which peaked in 1762 with the acquisition of the Louisiana territory. Almost immediately thereafter, Spanish

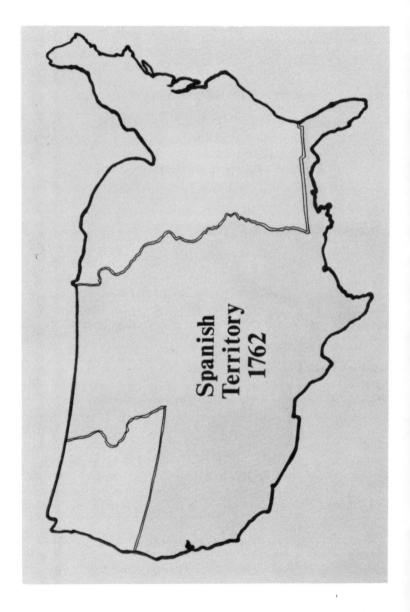

Spanish Territory 1762

territory began to recede—in 1763 the Florida territory was ceded to the British. In 1800 the Louisiana territory was returned to the French who in 1803 agreed to one of the great real estate purchases in modern history by selling the entire territory to the United States. Had Spain been able to maintain that brief consolidation of land from Florida to California the history of this country would have been very different. In 1783 Spain regained control of part of the Florida territory but lost it again, and forever, in 1821. Little remains today in modern Florida of the days of Spanish rule except for the Castillo San Marcos and other monuments carefully preserved and restored in Saint Augustine. In New Orleans, the famous main square in the old French quarter is not really French at all. It was constructed by the Spaniards. However, the stronghold of the old Spanish traditions is the Southwest rather than the Southeast.

Spanish colonization of the Southwest spilled north from Mexico first in the arc of land extending from near present-day Tucson, Arizona, northeast to Santa Fé, New Mexico, and then southwest to San Antonio, Texas. Major settlements were usually located on rivers like the Río Grande, the Pecos, or the San Antonio. Colonial Spanish life centered around military presidios, missions, or major churches. The missions, it must be remembered, constituted far more than a church or a purely religious missionary effort, but rather an entire Christian community in which the Indians were taught farming and other related skills in an attempt to create an ideal society providing for the well-being of mind, body, and soul. The founding dates of the first Spanish communities in the Southwest are very early, for example: Santa Fé, New Mexico, 1610; San Bernardino Mission, Arizona, 1629; Nuestra Señora de Guadalupe de El Paso, Texas, 1659; Albuquerque, New Mexico, 1706; San Antonio, Texas with four separate missions, 1718.

The settlement of California came somewhat later. Monterey, the first capital, was founded in 1769 as a military presidio and only lost its role of supremacy when Sacramento became the capital of the California territory in 1854. The initial Spanish colonization of California is due primarily to the efforts of one extraordinary man, Fray Junípero Serra, who became head of the missionary effort in California for the Franciscan order at the age of 56. During the following thirteen years, from 1769 to 1782, Serra personally founded nine of the major California missions starting with San Diego and including San Gabriel, San Luis Obispo, San Francisco, and San Juan Capistrano. In 1781, the Spanish governor of California established what was to become the state's largest city, now third in the entire nation: El Pueblo de Nuestra Señora la Reina de los Angeles.

Spanish Colorado, the southwestern part of the state, is a later extension by Santa Fé and Taos colonists who migrated north in the later eighteenth century in search of new farmlands. The Spanish cities of the area were not created until the mid-nineteenth century: Pueblo in 1842, San Luis in 1851, and Trinidad in 1877.

The Spanish history of Texas is perhaps the most colorful. The church community of Nuestra Señora de Guadalupe de El Paso had been founded in 1659. Throughout the rest of the century numerous missions were constructed throughout the state and in the area of San Antonio, founded in 1718, four major missions were in operation. The entire Southwest remained a part of colonial Spain as a dependency of the Mexican viceroyalty until 1821 when Mexican independence from Spain became certain. Texas was notably torn by intrigues and counterintrigues, including the illegal entry of numbers of Anglos from the north. Finally in 1836 the Republic of Texas was born with Sam Houston elected as its first president in spite of the overwhelmingly Spanish population in the new nation. After nine years of continuing Mexican attacks, which have become famous in legend and film, Texas voted in 1845 to accept statehood in the union. The northern part of the state was rather quickly anglicized with the south remaining to this day heavily Spanish-speaking. The other areas, ceded to the United States by Mexico in 1846 and 1848, were increasingly slower in gaining statehood: California in 1850, Colorado in 1875, and Arizona and New Mexico in 1912. Those dates tend to reflect the concentration of Spanish-speaking inhabitants, who were naturally reluctant to come under the total control of a culturally different, foreign nation.

The most recently published estimates for the Spanish-speaking population of the United States indicate half of that population concentrated in five states: California (over 3 million), New York (2½ million), Texas (2½ million), Illinois (over 1 million), and Florida (almost 1 million).

It is not quite the same list, however, as that of the five most Hispanic states in terms of proportion: New Mexico (38.4%), Texas (22.3%), Arizona (21.2%), California (15.0%), and Colorado (12.5%).

For various reasons the official census figures for Spanish-speaking persons in the United States are notably imperfect. In the Southwest where almost half of the Spanish-speaking population is concentrated (perhaps as many as 10 million people), large numbers have never been included in the immigration statistics for the simple reason that their ancestors automatically became citizens upon the cession of the Spanish Southwest to the United States. Illegal entry from Mexico is also a fact of life in the Southwest. Such entries are naturally encouraged and facilitated by the cultural unity of the Hispanic Southwest and northern Mexico, for the Mexican border is a political division that artificially bisects a single cultural unit.

The composition of the hispano society of the Southwest is in the Western European tradition. Maximum prestige is acquired only after some generations of relative wealth, education, and community status. Bilingualism is common among the best hispano families of the Southwest, except in a few isolated areas, and for the most part there is little social disadvantage deriving from their non-anglo heritage. For the poorer, uneducated, monolingual hispano classes, the picture is different, and it would appear that especially in the urban areas the social and economic status of the hispano citizen is little better than that of the recent immigrant, legal or illegal. Color is also frequently an important factor—in Mexico as well as in the Southwest. Social prestige tends to be linked to Spanish family origins as opposed to Indian origins, and thus by definition the poorer classes are strongly mestizo or even pure Indian. The nomadic existence of the migrant workers, *braceros,* is often detrimental to the social adjustment and to the education of the children so that, unwittingly, a disadvantaged ambient is passed on from one generation to the next. The immigration patterns, as well as we can judge, from Mexico to the Southwest, legal and illegal, tend to respond primarily to the need for unskilled, low-paid workers on the ranches and in the cities of the Southwest.

In more recent years a rather curious form of internal immigration has occurred. Substantial numbers of more or less unskilled Hispanos from the Southwest have gone to work for industry in such northern cities as Chicago and Detroit, creating Spanish-speaking neighborhoods. The social problems encountered there differ little from those of the true immigrant. At this point we must define the two major terms used to designate the representatives of our two cultures, the one Hispanic and the other Anglo-Saxon, originally English. The term *Hispano* designates primarily a person of Hispanic tradition and language, regardless of national origin, as opposed to the *Anglo*, an English-speaking American of nordic heritage, primarily Anglo-Saxon. The two terms, based on cultural heritage, are often used for racial distinctions as well.

At the moment the most popular word for the poorer, *mestizo* classes of the Southwest is the term *chicano* which apparently derives from the usage *patas chicas* ("small feet") used to distinguish persons with Indian blood from the Spaniards, *patas grandes* ("large feet"). If we define *Anglo* in its strictest terms (Nordic Caucasian, English-speaking, and Protestant) then we are quite a distance from the *Hispano* (Mediterranean Caucasian, perhaps with a mixture of Indian or Negro, Spanish-speaking, and Roman Catholic) in three crucial ways: racially, linguistically, and theologically. These are considerable cultural barriers just as strong for Hispanos as they are for Anglos. And in the Southwest we must add for the Hispanos the ever-present consideration that we have invaded *their* territory.

After the Southwest, the greatest area of Hispanic concentration in the United States is the greater New York City area. Again, statistics lack precision primarily because the Puerto Ricans (the largest national group of Hispanos in the area) are already United States citizens. It is believed that only four cities in the world have more Spanish-speaking residents than New York: Madrid, Mexico City, Barcelona, and Buenos Aires. The two major Spanish-language newspapers, *El Diario-La Prensa* and *El Tiempo-Mirador,* circulate daily to over one million readers. The internationally renowned Madrid newspaper, *ABC*, has recently found it profitable to publish a weekly New York edition.

A private study conducted in the latter sixties gives the following percentages for the Hispanic population in the New York City area: Puerto Rico (45%); Cuba (20%); Dominican Republic (8%); Colombia, Argentina, Spain, and Venezuela (4% each); Ecuador and Peru (3% each); Bolivia, Chile, and Mexico (1% each); Honduras, Nicaragua, Costa Rica, Guatemala, Panamá, El Salvador, Paraguay, and Uruguay (2% for all). New York presents, then, an almost total panorama of the hispano immigrant in the United States including representatives from almost all of the Spanish-speaking countries of the world as well as complete distribution of social levels. Beyond the usual problems of the immigrant (a person from a different culture with a different language and different customs) the Hispanos of New York also must deal with the problems of multiracial background. We can estimate the black or mulatto hispano population of New York at almost 60% and Indian or mestizo at 10%. Certainly it is a fact that the Caucasians of Cuba, Spain, Argentina, and Chile (the remaining 30%) have integrated far more successfully into the mainstream of American life.

Another large center of hispano immigration in the United States is southern Florida, with almost one million Cubans concentrated primarily in the Miami area. Apart from smaller colonies in Key West and Tampa, the majority of the Florida Cubans were overwhelmingly Caucasian and had better-than-average educations. After initial periods of difficult adjustment, this professional class has managed to reestablish itself in a satisfactory manner in a new nation in spite of the cultural and linguistic barriers. The success in the adjustment and Americanization of the Cuban immigrants has been spectacular and would appear to be a consequence of social class, race, and education as well as of personal industry—the will to succeed.

Another large center of Hispanos is the Chicago area with about the same hispano population as Florida but, on the other hand, a national-origin distribution far more similar to that of New York.

Let us take a broad look at the educational and economic

facts of hispano life in the United States. The U. S. Department of Commerce in a report published in 1971 finds that persons of hispanic origin have a notably lower level of educational attainment than other Americans especially among those 25 years old or older. In that group Hispanos average 12 years of schooling (a high school education).

Those statistics are reflected in the employment and income figures. Three-fifths of the hispano population is reported in the American labor force, about the same proportion as for other Americans. However, unemployment averages 6 percent as opposed to 3.5 percent for all Americans, and the category *white-collar job* which embraces 41 percent of the American male population only includes 25 percent of the hispano male population. In late 1969, the median income for the American family was slightly over $8,000 a year. For the hispano family in the United States, the median was only $5,600. The median income for a Puerto Rican family was slightly under $5,000, for a Mexican-American family, $5,400. Yet for the recent Cuban immigrants it was already close to $6,500.

It is clear that the interrelationship of language, schooling, racial considerations, and employment opportunity create for many Hispanos a culture of poverty. The major task of the anglo and the hispano communities, working in unison, is to break the cycle without destroying the values of hispano culture.

The Southwest of the United States has a distinct Hispanic flavor. Our folklorists, our history books, and our guidebooks are eager to tell us about it. Indeed in southern Texas one is closer to Mexico than to the United States. But curiously enough, that Hispanic tradition has two faces: it reflects the romantic characteristics of bygone days, the survival of old love songs and Spanish lace shawls—but it also represents the wrong side of the tracks, a way of life that is squalid and repugnant. In the rest of the nation the existence of hispano culture in the Southwest was largely ignored until quite recently. One Mexican-American was quoted by a national magazine as follows: "We are the best-kept secret in America."

You will recall from our previous remarks that the Southwest has the largest number of Hispanos in the United States, roughly half our entire hispano population. The official estimated distribution there is as follows: California, 3,001,830 (15% of the total population); Texas, 2,500,000 (22.3%); New Mexico, 390,000 (38.4%); Arizona, 375,000 (21.2%); Colorado, 275,000 (12.5%); Nevada, 60,000 (12.3%); Louisiana, 55,000 (1.5%); and Oklahoma, 50,000 (.2%).

Other estimates state the figures as considerably higher. It is thought, for example, that there may be as many as 6 million persons of Mexican origin in the United States. The majority of that number reside in the Southwest but at most would appear to constitute half of the hispano population of that region. In other words even without counting Indians of the Southwest, the area is characterized by a tripartite cultural division consisting of Anglos, recent immigrants primarily from Mexico, and American-born Hispanos. Such areas as Los Angeles or New Orleans also have colonies from Cuba and Puerto Rico as well as from other Spanish-speaking countries.

Perhaps the best place in the Southwest to study the different shadings of the American hispano social structure is the state of New Mexico. The oldest settlement, Santa Fé, is located in the northern hill country, considerably removed from what was to become the Mexican border. Santa Fé and the surrounding villages apparently remained in relative isolation from the other Spanish settlements in the southern part of the state and in northern Mexico and southwestern Texas. The Santa Fé trail brought exposure to anglo culture in the northern area in the earlier nineteenth century. The aristocracy, without losing their Hispanic traditions, adjusted to the process of Americanization with relative ease and success, thus remaining firmly established in the new social structure. The great influx of Anglos into New Mexico, however, came in the southern part of the state and served as a rather definitive buffer between the north and Mexico. As a consequence, the Hispanic traditions, and notably the Spanish language in northern New Mexico, have remained in nearly pristine condition, affected by anglo traditions but not by modern Mexico. The descendants of that early aristocracy felt little or no affinity at all for the recent Mexican immigrant and indeed saw their social position somewhat threatened by the very existence of *wetbacks, braceros,* and *chicanos.* This rather curious but understandable human reaction is to be found throughout the hispano culture in the United States. It has been more readily observed in New Mexico because of geographical circumstances, but it functions universally in such diverse places as Los Angeles, New York, or Florida. Thus, the older, upper-class hispano families tend to have at least adjusted to anglo culture, and throughout the nation in numerous instances their descendants have been completely absorbed to the extent of having lost Hispanic traditions and even the ability to speak Spanish. Within the older hispano communities which have Americanized without being absorbed, the recent immigrant may well find far greater hostility and discrimination than in a more enlightened anglo community.

What generally characterized the hispano communities in the southern parts of the Southwestern states is the constant contact with Mexico, including frequent visits back and forth across the border. That fact, on the one hand, stimulates immigration into the U. S. because the immigrant can adjust with relative ease into the hispano community. On the other hand, that contact works against Americanization and thus serves to maintain the gap between Anglos and Hispanos.

Various sociologists and historians have pointed to the origins of the hispano-anglo gap as being perhaps more the consequence of differences in social class rather than of different cultures and languages, the latter factors being of considerable weight in maintaining the gap. The Anglos who invaded the Southwest in the later part of the nineteenth century and who now account for the larger proportions of residents were, or have become, of the middle class. They had no counterparts in Hispanic culture, still almost feudal then, and therefore reacted negatively to the uneducated, unskilled vast majority.

Statehood brought with it, slowly, a public school system in which the language of instruction was English. Parochial schools did exist in some areas where for many years instruction was given in Spanish, and in the rural areas schooling could be avoided by resistant farmers. But increasingly the hispano children of the Southwest have been thrust into an English-speaking environment for the first time at the tender age of five or six and expected to learn to read and write in a totally foreign language. The results, as might be expected, are often disastrous, with the ever-present danger of total alienation on the part of the young.

During the Second World War the first large-scale expression of such alienation exploded briefly into national awareness. The causes of the explosion were for the most part misunderstood, and all too soon the incident was forgotten. The word *pachuco*, apparently formed on the name for the Mexican city Pachuca, became at some point around World War I the slang term in Spanish for El Paso, Texas—a city right on the Mexican border with a large Mexican-American population. Originally founded as Nuestra Señora de Guadalupe de El Paso in 1659, the settlement was a haven for the refugees of Santa Fé at the time of the Indian uprisings. One of the very oldest hispano settlements north of the Río Grande, the city today has a population of some 350,000. As a new style of dress evolved in the late 1930's, the duck-style hair and a Hispanic variant of the zoot suit, the term *pachuco* came to mean an adolescent hispano male from El Paso who dressed in that style and who behaved in a certain manner.

Some sociologists have regarded the *pachuco* as a hard-core criminal linked with border-traffic drugs. In its extreme degrees, the *pachuco* could be exactly that. But more often he was simply an alienated Mexican-American, rather ill-educated with an imperfect knowledge of English, who did bear some resentment toward anglo culture. His behavior generally did not go beyond an occasional outrageous prank, and he was far more interested in girls, the jitterbug, and beer than he was in social reform. The *pachuco* style swept across the Southwest in the late thirties, especially to urban areas like San Antonio, Albuquerque, Tucson, and Los Angeles. Along with dress, coiffure, and general demeanor, the *pachuco* life-style created something unique in the history of hispano culture in the United States. A new dialect or lingo was created, also called *pachuco*, which may well have influenced the anglo counterpart of that period, known as jive-talk. *Pachuco* is far more radical and hermetic than jive-talk, however, for it does not rely on the creation of new meanings for old words. Rather *pachuco* consists almost entirely of brand new terms whose origins are largely unknown. Again, some are definitely associated with illegal drug traffic over the border. It would appear, however, that *pachuco* was developed by adolescents as a means of excluding all outsiders, parents included, who often represented a more traditional outlook.

Except for the criminal element, which formed only a small minority, *pachuco* culture was at first looked on with the same disdain shown their anglo counterparts, the zoot suiters. But in the summer of 1943 an unfortunate skirmish between sailors on leave and *pachucos* in Los Angeles resulted in bitter attacks against not just the *pachucos* but against many Mexican-Americans in the Los Angeles area. The battle raged for days. It appears that the zoot-suit riots that subsequently broke out all over the country in such diverse places as Philadelphia, Chicago, Detroit, and Harlem were the results of the anti-*pachuco* war in Los Angeles. The Mexican Ambassador finally intervened with an inquiry to the State Department and then almost as suddenly as the trouble began, it faded into oblivion, along with the interest in the Hispanos of the Southwest.

The original *pachucos* are now parents of the present adolescent population. Styles have changed over the years and the *pachuco* dialect has also evolved, but the basic subculture continues to thrive. In many areas they are simply referred to as *chicanos*. But in El Paso, Texas, where it all seems to have begun, the term *tirilones* has emerged to designate the delinquent and criminal adolescent element of South El Paso, a district so proverbially tough that its mores and language are imitated by the hardened criminals of San Antonio and even Mexico City. A recent study of the area reveals that as many as fourteen people live in a two-room apartment which may rent for as low as $9 a month. Drug traffic and prostitution are major industries, and although some 5% of the population is officially enrolled in the schools in the area, the absentee and drop-out rate is exceedingly high. The language of the schools is, of course, English; whereas the speech of the area is border-Spanish and neo-*pachuco*. Contact with Anglos is minimal or nonexistent.

Just before the First World War Mexicans and Mexican-Americans from the Southwest began to immigrate to northern cities in the midwest where they could obtain employment in industry. The largest colonies were established in the Chicago area and in Detroit where the war industry encouraged such migration. By 1930, the Chicago colony was estimated at about 20,000. These colonies existed, and to some extent still do, in relative isolation from the mainstream of American life.

The effect of the Mexican-American migration to the North seems even more drab in the smaller locations. In some instances in the midwest as early as 1918, Mexican-American villages in barracks style were expressly created at some distance from the town for the new labor force. Children were taught, if at all, in Spanish by whoever had time or inclination to do so. Thus it was possible for several generations to live in almost complete isolation, the men going to and from industrial chores which required little use of English.

Tightened immigration quotas reduced the number of Mexicans going directly to the midwest by 1930, but those quotas did not affect internal migration from the Southwest. The Spanish-speaking population of Illinois alone now totals well over one million and that of Michigan, primarily the Detroit area, near 200,000. In all there are perhaps 3 million hispanos in the American Midwest, traditionally an anglo stronghold.

There are indications that the quality of life for some Mexican-Americans may be rising slowly. World War II brought young men of service age into much closer contact with anglo culture. For the first time in many cases, close social relationships between Hispanos and Anglos could be formed. Hispanos of necessity learned to communicate in English. And when the war was over they had the privileges of the G.I. Bill, with the opportunity to obtain further education. These circumstances appear to be reflected in various statistics. For example, the highest percentage of Mexican-Americans in 1969 who were fluent in both Spanish and English is precisely males between the ages of 35 and 55. It is also this age group which has the highest annual income. Their children, unfortunately, seem to be losing the use of Spanish. For example, the age group 16 to 24, shows only 52% fluency in both English and Spanish as opposed to over 62% for their parents' generation. This second generation also evidences a higher level of schooling, again in English, so that their economic situation will undoubtedly improve but at the cost of gradual alienation from their own culture. Many Hispanos consider the cost too high.

We have talked around hispano life but perhaps not specifically about it. What are, indeed, its characteristics that some hispano parents jealously guard and wish to see perpetuated? Perhaps old-fashioned Southwestern hispano life can best be compared to rural life in mid-America before World War II. The family is the basic social unit embracing grandparents, parents, and children with all collateral relatives included. The unit itself is institutionalized by the church, although attendance is primarily the responsibility of women a..d children. Social life centers around the traditional church festivals, with birthdays celebrated on one's saint's day. The important social events center around religious holidays, as well as weddings, christenings, and even funerals. A *fiesta* is by definition a family affair attended by babes-in-arms, young people, the middle-aged, and those with canes or in wheelchairs. A man's social life may also include a friendly glass or a game of chance at a local café where he visits with his male friends. Family ties are strong and override all other considerations. Marriages are contracted only with the full approval of the families of both parties. Formerly a man would not consider an opportunity for professional advancement, no matter how enticing, if it entailed separation from the larger family unit. The comportment and movements of an unmarried girl were vigilantly regulated by parents and brothers. World War II and the spread of *pachuquismo* began, of course, to dissipate that style of life which now seems confining to the younger generation. At the same time the specter of anglo life as a frightening antithesis, exaggerated by film and press, is hardly an attraction to the hispano parent. Divorce, wife-swapping, baby-sitters, nightclubs, legalized abortion, families separated by the distance of an entire continent, lack of church attendance and orientation— these are all anathema to conservative hispano families, who in consequence fear that contact with Anglos, including education in their schools or even use of their language, will contaminate.

By contrast, conservative Anglos may find that Hispanos make too much noise, laugh or anger too easily and too intensely, and do not seem sufficiently work-oriented. Beyond this generalization, actual contact is usually so limited that the Anglo is far more aware of the criminal element dramatized by the press. And thus, the *pachuco* who switch-blades a colleague in a drunken brawl over a drugged prostitute stands as a typical representative of hispano culture.

The passivity of the Mexican-American community for more than a century began slowly to end with the Second World War. Almost half a million Mexican-Americans served in that war, many heroically, and it has been pointed out that their numerical service record is proportionately higher than that of the anglo community. In any event, the generation of Mexican-Americans who went into military service received a liberal education in sociology. Increasingly in the 1950's and finally with some explosions in the 1960's the Mexican-American community has asked or demanded to be heard. The Second World War also witnessed the birth of the Good Neighbor Policy which, among other consequences, made Spanish the most widely taught foreign language in the American school system. Today, the American Association of Teachers of Spanish and Portuguese numbers well over 15,000, and it is estimated that over 20 million Anglos have studied some Spanish.

The past decade has been stormy, but we are perhaps closer to a *rapprochement* between anglo and hispano culture than ever before. Bilingual education is beginning to be accepted in areas where its very mention a few years ago would have created dissent. Such spectacular events as the grape boycott of 1965 attracted adherents throughout the land and served to dramatize eloquently the plight of the migrant Mexican-American workers. Perhaps even more significant is the publication of successful novels like *Chicano* by Richard Vasquez in 1970 which probes the universally human aspects of an admirable Mexican-American family striving to adjust to life in the United States. Congressmen from New Mexico, California, or Texas now have names like Montoya, Roybal, González, or de la Garza. The former mayor of El Paso, Raymond Telles, was appointed ambassador to Costa Rica. Distinguished scholars from Texas with names like Sánchez teach in such traditionally anglo areas as Wisconsin.

Indeed our universities are now discovering, many for the first time, the existence of a hispano culture in the United States. The latest annual list of new doctoral dissertations in the Hispanic field includes four concerning the Spanish of New Mexico, Texas, Arizona, and Chicago. In the entire past century only a dozen or so dissertations were devoted to the Spanish of the United States.

A great deal has already been achieved by the press in the past few years. A supposedly exhaustive study on the foreign-language press in the United States, published a few years ago, stated that the German language press was the most widespread in our country. However, a concise listing of the Spanish-language periodicals published in the United States, now in preparation, may require more than one volume in view of the thousands of titles already collected. The vast majority are local newspapers or general news magazines, but in 1967 in Berkeley, California, there was created a more serious quarterly periodical *El Grito*, "A Journal of Contemporary Mexican-American Thought," This journal has given a unified, if sometimes shrill, voice to the Spanish Southwest which the fragmented, local publications could not by definition achieve. A comprehensive bibliography on Mexican-American studies appearing in *El Grito* in 1972 lists almost 500 works, the vast majority of which were published after 1960.

Although the thought that the hispano flavor of New York City is primarily Puerto Rican is an oversimplified *cliché*, the heavy migration of Puerto Ricans to New York City is historically a very recent development. Indeed, one of the earliest distinguished European visitors to New York was Francisco de Miranda, who was to become one of the founding fathers of the Republic of Venezuela and to serve briefly as head of that nation from 1811 to 1812. In 1783, while still a colonel in the Spanish colonial army, he started a tour of the United States and stayed in New York in early 1784. His description of Brooklyn may well be one of the first: "a small place," he says, "one of some 150 little houses, inhabitated in the main by poor people."

Before the middle of the nineteenth century, almost 150 years ago, the city was beginning to acquire a Hispanic flavor. Trouble was brewing in the island of Cuba. By 1843 various political conflicts in Cuba had produced in Key West, Florida, the establishment of a revolutionary force under the leadership of General Narciso López. He was to make various landings and expeditions against the colonial Spanish government in Cuba, and as the revolutionary movement became more widespread, with the colonial government taking even stricter measures, the partisans of a liberated Cuba were forced to leave.

The successive waves of political unheaval in Cuba sent intellectuals and politicians as well as numerous middle- and upper-class professionals to New York City, where an exile class could most conveniently conduct their activities without harassment and with the advantages found in a large center. It must be remembered that Cuba is our closest hispano neighbor in the East, Havana being only some eighty miles from the Florida Keys. The increasing immigration of literate Cubans to New York City is eloquently reflected by the establishment of Cuban, Spanish-language newspapers and magazines in the city. A total of 34 different periodicals appeared between 1848 and 1872. As those figures suggest, the Cuban immigrants of this period constitute a highly literate group. Indeed several Cuban literary masterpieces of the nineteenth century were first published in New York City, written in part or entirely in New York. Cirilo Villaverde, one of Cuba's most distinguished novelists, was by 1850 editor-in-chief of the popular paper, *La Verdad*, in New York.

We have arbitrarily cut the story at 1872 only to emphasize the fact that just over a century ago New York City was already acquiring a Hispanic flavor, primarily Cuban. But Cuba's troubles were only beginning, and the establishment of 42 new Spanish periodicals, almost entirely Cuban, continued throughout the nineteenth century. Some of these journals were, of course, short-lived. But their number and their caliber are formidable. In all, Cirilo Villaverde founded two journals and served as editor for two others. In 1882 his greatest novel, *Cecilia Valdés*, was published in New York; he died there in 1892. By this time Cuba's most famous statesman and one of her most outstanding writers was also associated with New York. After 1885, José Martí founded one periodical in New York, served as editor for another, and wrote for six more up to his death in 1895.

This constant Cuban immigration to New York City created a whole spectrum of hispano social life in the city including an active Cuban theater in Spanish. In 1891 a magazine was founded to cover Spanish-language theater in New York. One view of Cuban life in the city at this time is interestingly described by Carlos Loveira in his novel *Generales y doctores* published later in Havana, in 1920. This chapter in our immigration history has gone largely unmentioned for two reasons. Firstly, the Cubans do not seem to have formed Cuban neighborhoods or ghettos; secondly, they were generally Caucasian, well educated, and professionally trained and quickly integrated into the economic life of the city. Progressively their children, educated in English, simply Americanized and passed into the mainstream of American life. The metropolitan complex and the need to earn a livelihood worked against the kind of extended family existence possible in more rural areas like the Southwest or in some areas of Florida. It is doubtful, for example, that a very large proportion of the descendants of that nineteenth-century Cuban immigration have even retained any substantial memory of the Spanish language.

Cuba finally obtained independence from Spain in 1898. The fact is immediately reflected in the history of Spanish-language periodicals in New York. In the first 25 years of the twentieth century, only 19 new periodicals were founded—most of them by American commercial firms for distribution elsewhere. A small number reflect a slowly increasing immigration from Spain and the better Cuban literary journals survive in ever decreasing numbers as the older Cuban immigrants die off or return home.

As political difficulties and dissent grew in Spain, the number of immigrants, primarily to New York City, grew throughout the 1920's. After almost a century, the torch of hispano cultural life in the city passed from the Cubans to the Spanish who by 1928 supported an active theater and a new magazine devoted to it.

Indeed, Spanish cultural and intellectual life in New York became increasingly brilliant just after the turn of the century. In 1904 the American philanthropist and scholar, Archer M. Huntington, founded in upper Manhattan The Hispanic Society of America, a research institution devoted to the arts and the humanities with one of the world's finest museums and libraries specializing in the culture of Spain. Under the Society's auspices Spain's great literary critic, Ramón Menéndez Pidal, lectured in New York in 1909. In 1915 Latin America's greatest poet, Rubén Darío, read his new antiwar poem *Pax!*, commissioned by the Society. In 1916, the world premiere of Granados' opera *Goyesca* was given at the Metropolitan Opera. In the same year occurred the marriage of Juan Ramón Jiménez, future recipient of the Nobel Prize, to Zenobia Camprubí—a girl of Spanish, Puerto Rican, and American parentage, sister of the editor of New York's outstanding Spanish newspaper, *La prensa*. In 1916, with Huntington's backing, the distinguished Spanish scholar Federico de Onís was brought to Columbia University, and in 1920 the *Casa hispánica*, Spanish House, was inaugurated there and quickly became one of the major centers of Spanish cultural and intellectual life in the city. Lectures, concerts, plays, and receptions were held frequently and included performances by such outstanding figures as Lucrezia Bori, Andrés Segovia, and La Argentinita as well as readings and lectures by Salvador Dalí, Diego Rivera, Gabriela Mistral (another Nobel Prize recipient), and the poet Federico García Lorca, whose stay in New York in the late twenties was to produce his well-known collection *Poet in New York*.

It is not surprising, then, that the tragic Civil War in Spain in the thirties should have sent to New York an outstandingly large proportion of its major professional figures. Numerically that immigration figure seems almost inconsequential, but the exceptional caliber of these immigrants, combined with the already established Spanish cultural centers, caused the Spaniards to completely dominate hispano life in the city.

The establishment of New York City as the major world center of Spanish exile life occurred prior to the explosion of Puerto Rican immigration to the city. The estimated Puerto Rican population of the United States is as follows: 1910: 1,513; 1920: 11,811; 1930: 52,774; 1940: 69,967; 1950: 301,375; 1960: 887,662; 1969: 1,600,000. The greatest upsurge in Puerto Rican immigration occurred between 1910 and 1920. This corresponds to the demand for labor, primarily in New York City, during the World War I boom. The postwar period continued to show a notable increase, although only half that of the war period. The depression of the 1930's is quite visible in the strong decline in immigration.

The figures are misleading, however, unless we compare them to the total population of New York City where the vast majority of Puerto Ricans reside. Thus, although the percentage increase of Puerto Rican immigration to the continental United States is the highest between 1910 and 1920 (almost eight times that of the preceding decade), the total number of some 12,000 persons was quickly absorbed by a city of 5½ million. Even by 1945, the Puerto Rican figure of some 75,000 only constituted about one percent of the city's total. The postwar boom in the United States created a vast need for unskilled labor, and the initiation of low-cost air transportation in 1946 from San Juan to New York resulted in a new landmark in immigration: the transportation of huge numbers of people within a brief span of time. In 1946 alone almost 40,000 Puerto Ricans came to New York, thus in one year increasing the Puerto Rican population of the city by over 50%. In the five years from 1945 to 1950, the number of Puerto Ricans in the city had grown from one percent to over four percent, and in the ensuing decade, from 1950 to 1960, came to surpass ten percent of the city's total population.

The Puerto Rican immigration to New York City is in many ways similar to the Mexican immigration in the Southwest. Both consist primarily of unskilled, relatively uneducated laborers impelled by a low standard of living at home to go elsewhere. In New York as in the Southwest, they meet with some hostility both as foreigners—that is, of a different language and culture— and usually as members of a minority racial group, Indian or Negro, mestizo or mulatto. Although their new standard of living may represent an improvement over the old, they find themselves in the same relative economic and social corner that they had left. This is true even within the hispano environment of the new locale, in New York as well as in the Southwest or even Florida. Thus betterment for these immigrants is primarily in terms of those they left behind. As their ties with home diminish, they increasingly find themselves quite understandably as unhappy and restless over their new lot as they had been with the old.

Statistics indicate a rising educational level and corresponding economic and professional improvement for the earlier Puerto Rican immigration. In 1960 the educational gap between second generation Puerto Ricans and all Americans had been reduced to a fraction, with income lagging by only $675 annually and top employment classification by only two percent. However, these figures for the second generation concern primarily those born well before the massive airlift beginning in 1946. For this earlier group of people it is evident that a climate of rising expectations was created which in all probability was a major factor in that massive airlift. However, those rising expectations seem to have peaked in the earlier generations with a tendency to diminish with the younger generation, those born in the United States. Comparable figures for the group of Puerto Rican males between the age of 25 and 34 in the year 1960 show that the two-year gap in education has widened to almost four at this age level. This younger generation of Puerto Ricans had slightly *less* schooling at this age than the entire Puerto Rican group. And in spite of the rise in job classification to over 11 percent in the category "Professional and Technical," the discrepancy in salary for this younger generation of Puerto Ricans as opposed to the national level was up to $700 annually. That trend seems to have been readily noticed in Puerto Rico. After the peak year of 1953, the immigration figure begins to slowly diminish until 1960 when it drops to almost half the figure for 1959.

We are still in the middle of the story of Puerto Rican immigration to the United States. There has been a growing proportion of Puerto Ricans who leave the New York City area. In 1940, 93% of the immigrants remained in the Northeast (primarily in the New York area but with some colonies in Boston and Philadelphia). By 1950 the proportion declined to 88.7%, and by 1960 to 84.2% A shift to the northern central section of the country, mostly the Chicago area, has occurred. Thus, that portion of the country accounted for 1.3% of Puerto Rican immigration in 1940 but 7.6% in 1960.

For the moment the Puerto Rican population of the United

States seems to have leveled off with the number of new immigrants fairly well balanced by the number of emigrants back to the island. Nonetheless some estimates of the Puerto Rican population in the United States run to 3 million. The vast majority have come here since 1946 and the oldest of their children are only now reaching the age of 27. It will be another ten to fifteen years before we can evaluate their progress and adjustment. Society at large, and more specifically our schools and then our employers, will determine the fate of the new generation of Puerto Ricans born here. Sociologists, historians, and educators all seem to agree on one point—the urgent need for successful bilingual school programs.

You will recall, of course, that the Hispanos of the Southwest are not immigrants but rather the first settlers of that area. The oldest Spanish-speaking immigrant group in the United States is that of the island of Key West which is the last of the Florida keys. It lies in the Caribbean, at the entrance to the Gulf of Mexico, only 80 miles north of Havana, Cuba, but almost 160 miles south of Miami, and contains the southernmost city of the continental United States.

Its past is especially romantic, for during the seventeenth and eighteenth centuries the island served as a base for the pirates of the Caribbean beginning with the expeditions of Sir Walter Raleigh and ending, just after 1800, with Jean Lafitte. By this time small groups of Cuban fishermen had gradually established small communities on the island. In 1823, Key West came under the flag of the United States as part of the Florida territory. The first English-speaking colonists began to arrive from the Bahamas about 1830. The closest city to Key West is Havana. Thus, when in 1843 the Cuban revolutionary movement began, it was natural that Key West should have served as a base for the Cuban revolutionaries. By 1868 Cuban immigration to the island had grown considerably, and in that year two of the major cigar manufacturing companies of Havana transferred their entire operations to Key West: lock, stock, and employees. Before the end of the century Key West was to become the world's major manufacturer of Havana cigars as well as the wealthiest and largest city in Florida. Officially, of course, the language of Key West was English after 1823. In practice the city was primarily Spanish-speaking. Indeed the mayor of Key West in 1876 was Carlos de Céspedes, one of the chief figures in the Cuban revolutionary movement and originator of the slogan "Cuba libre" ("Free Cuba"), which now survives to designate the drink also known as rum and Coca Cola.

In 1871 Céspedes founded a cultural institution unique in the hispano areas of the United States. The Instituto San Carlos, in addition to an active program of prestigious cultural and social events, inaugurated a private grade school where all instruction was given in Spanish. In an extraordinarily wise move for such early and supposedly unenlightened times, the state of Florida at the turn of the century supplied the Institute with a teacher of English so that the graduates of the Institute in the twentieth century indeed received a bilingual education. The Institute also maintains a summer program in Spanish for students of the public schools wherein English is the language of instruction.

Contact with the Florida mainland was minimal until the twentieth century. There was no overland connection with the Florida mainland until 1912 when the railroad from Miami reached Key West over an extensive series of bridges. But the distance to Miami, only a small town of 5,000 then, was a long ride of one hundred sixty miles. By contrast, the exciting city of Havana was only eighty pleasant sea miles away. The railroad was in serious economic difficulty when the disastrous hurricane of 1935 destroyed miles of rail bridges and, thus, the twenty-three-year-old rail connection with the peninsula of Florida ended forever.

By this time the American Naval Base and the fishing industry had brought anglo-Americans to the island in some number, but we are not certain at what point the Spanish-speaking population ceased to be a majority. What is more important is the unexpectedly pleasant fact that it does not seem to have mattered.

Toward the close of the century labor troubles resulted in a new transfer of the cigar industry to Tampa. By 1910 the village of Tampa had grown to twice the size of Key West, and new migration from Cuba, lessened now because of Cuban independence, was mainly to Tampa. Key West's hopes for a new revival as a tourist center did not materialize with the railroad. Finally in 1943 a highway was completed over the old railroad bed. By the late 1940's Key West did begin to attract more adventurous tourists resulting in general expansion in the city during the 1950's. Today the population of the island is about 30,000 with approximately one-third Spanish-speaking, that is some 10,000 persons. Until the Castro revolution in 1959, contact with Havana remained close; however, we must remember that substantial immigration ceased about 1900. For a century and a half the hispano residents of the island, with the help of their institutions like San Carlos and with the goodwill of the resident Anglos, have managed to preserve their hispano identity, language, and customs. At present the mayor of the city is Anglo and the chief of police Hispano. Such combinations in government as well as in private enterprise reflect the harmony of two cultures in Key West. The daily newspaper, in English, regularly includes articles in Spanish. The Spanish-language weekly regularly includes a few articles in English.

Various factors explain this exemplary situation. The original expansion of population in the earlier nineteenth century included both Anglos and Hispanos arriving more or less simultaneously. The Anglos themselves consisted of both continental Americans and colonial British from the Caribbean. No one group seems to have claimed or felt supremacy, although we must remember that as of 1823 the island was officially part of the United States. In the case of the non-Anglos, the Cubans, we must also remember that the immigration consisted almost exclusively of hard-working, literate Caucasians. Such distinguished personalities as Carlos de Céspedes or José Martí, Cuba's hero, were familiar figures in the island. Indeed cigar manufacturing was a skilled and relatively prestigious occupation in Cuba, and the workers had extraordinarily literate tastes reflected in a unique custom, the factory reader. Throughout the work day he performed for the worker audience reading novels, plays, poetry, or sometimes special accounts from newspapers and magazines. His high salary was paid by the workers themselves. Usually trained actors, the factory readers were highly respected, prosperous members of the community.

The absence of a priest or a Roman Catholic Church in Key

West throughout most of the nineteenth century resulted in the conversion of large numbers of the Cuban immigrants to Protestantism.

The immigrant Cubans were industrious, educated, and culturally inclined. By the same token, the pace of life even for Anglos in this scenic, tropical island is not the same as that of Boston or New York. Cultural shock, then, between the original anglo and hispano settlers of Key West seems to have been minimal. Indeed, there still exists a charming ballad of the nineteenth century, *Una ledi de Naso*, which recounts in a delightful mixture of English and Spanish the courting of the Lady from Nassau by a Cuban cigar maker. Intermarriage is quite common in the island so that names like Mary Valdés or Ramón Smith are typical. The old Cuban families are fiercely loyal to their Key West heritage. They are Americans not Cubans. The Anglos of the island as well as Floridians in general are in turn proud of the Hispanic flavor of the state.

We have looked at many of the sordid, unhappy realities of Hispanic life in the United States like social and economic discrimination and even mistreatment. There is, however, a happy side of the coin. In looking at Hispanic achievements in our country, we shall now concentrate mainly on the twentieth century, reminding the reader that we are skipping over a rather formidable history of exploits: the discovery of the New World by Cristóbal Colón, that of Florida and the North American continent by Ponce de León, the expeditions of Coronado and DeSoto, or the founding of the missions by Serra and many others.

We can begin with an atmosphere—the sound and the sight of the colonial Spanish Southwest. Its style of architecture has been reproduced in millions of dwellings, private and public, throughout the nation. In the 1930's a major revolution in American music was achieved. In the 1920's Caribbean music, with its heavy reliance on percussive instruments and rhythms new to our ears, came slowly to be heard occasionally in the repertoire of American dance bands. In 1932, George Gershwin gave us a more serious work, *Cuban Overture*. In 1933, the Waldorf-Astoria hotel in New York, the epitome of chic in the nation, hired a young bandleader to appear with his group in the "Starlight Roof." This young musician born in Barcelona, and raised in Havana, came with excellent credentials. He had played first violin with the National Theater Symphony in Havana and after classical concerts in New York and Europe had formed a popular Cuban dance band in California. As an ambassador of music, Xavier Cugat was a major factor in bringing to the American consciousness on a nationwide scale the existence of Hispanic music. The words *rhumba* and *conga* and, later *mambo* and *cha-cha-cha*, were to become part of American English. And their sounds were to change American music. By 1935, Cole Porter wrote "Begin the Beguine" in the Caribbean mode. The song "Ojos verdes" by Cugat's pianist, Nilo Menéndez, first became a best seller as an instrumental and then swept the nation with English lyrics as "Green Eyes."

The Cuban atmosphere invaded classical music. In 1941, Morton Gould's *Latin American Symphonette* appeared and in 1942 the distinguished composer, Aaron Copland, wrote his *Danzón Cubano.* Inspired by the Puerto Rican "problem" in New York City and cast in a modernized version of Romeo and Juliet, Bernstein created in 1957 one of America's masterpieces for the musical stage, *West Side Story,* using the sounds of Caribbean, Hispanic music now a part of national folklore. The modern American orchestra, popular or classical, includes as a matter of course *bongó* and *maracas* and uses freely the rhythms and phrasing of Cuban music.

In view of the numbers and the kinds of immigration that have occurred, as well as the attitude of Americans toward the immigrants, we should expect the greatest and most spectacular achievements in the United States to come from the Spaniards and the Cubans. Let us look first, however, at the groups theoretically far less well prepared or educated to achieve Nobel Prizes or national recognition.

Just off the press at the University of Texas is a new book entitled *Mexican-American Artists.* The author, Jacinto Quirarte, born in Arizona of hispano parentage, is an internationally recognized expert in the field of Latin American art. After treating the early architecture and church sculpture of the Southwest, Professor Quirarte first describes and illustrates the work of two outstanding Mexican artists achieved in the United States during relatively brief residence here: José Clemente Orozco's works including the outstanding murals for the New School for Social Research in New York and the extensive series at Dartmouth College. Rufino Tamayo spent ten years as Professor of Art at the Dalton School in New York and during that time completed a massive mural for Smith College now housed in their new museum. The author then proceeds to treat the work of twenty-seven notable Mexican-American artists, all of the twentieth century. As we might expect, the vast majority are from the Southwest. The rather high representation from Texas and New Mexico seems to be in part the consequence of the active art colonies in San Antonio and Albuquerque. The list is too long to enumerate, and we need only point out that these artists are nationally and even internationally known. In addition to their art, seven are also professors at American colleges and universities, and another three teach in secondary schools. One is director of the Museo del Barrio in New York City, and several others are also employed in such various enterprises as commercial art, newspaper cartoons, and military technology. About half are already supported entirely by their art. Their specializations range from oil painting through drawings, sculpture, collage, and multimedia work; their works have been exhibited as far away as China or London and displayed in distinguished permanent collections, both public and private.

The contributions of the Hispanic Southwest to American music have been primarily folkloric, especially the cowboy ballad which derived from earlier hispano ballads. These have been collected by various scholars and a representative number have been recorded by local singers. The adolescent *pachuco* subculture has produced a small body of rather fascinating popular songs which we might classify as hispano pre-rock. Outstanding figures from Spain in American music include the late Lucrezia Bori, Victoria de los Angeles, and Montserrat Caballé in opera; the conductor and pianist José Iturbi, and the composers Carlos Suriñach and Leonardo Balada. From Puerto Rico comes the noted pianist José María Sanromá as do the Metropolitan Opera's Justino Díaz and the popular and concert singer Emilia Conde. The two Spanish-language television stations in New York City regularly feature popular singers like

Myrta Silva from Puerto Rico or Miguelito Valdés from Cuba. In the past few years various outstanding hispano concerts have been presented in New York City including the premiere at Carnegie Hall of Leonardo Balada's opera *María Sabina*, portrayed by María Soledad Romero of Puerto Rico. In New Orleans, Balada's *Ponce de León* for orchestra with narrator José Ferrer from Puerto Rico was recently premiered. Cuba's outstanding composer, Julián Orbón, now resides and creates in New York City. For many years his countryman, José Echániz, was professor of music at the Eastman School of Music in Rochester.

In addition to the extraordinary collections of hispano art in the nation's museums, especially in New York, we should also note such outstanding works as the old Sert Room at the Waldorf-Astoria Hotel in New York. For some forty years this elegant meeting place was lined with murals painted especially for the room by Spain's José María Sert. A frequent resident of the city is Salvador Dalí whose portraits grace a number of this country's best drawing rooms. In Cleveland, there is a new museum exclusively devoted to his works. In Key West, Florida, the artist Mario Sánchez combines the primitive art of woodcarving with the medieval technique of polychromed wood sculpture to provide panels that give the initial appearance of oil paintings.

These notable figures and their work have given in our own time a Hispanic flavor to the culture of the United States which makes it unique and quite different from its origins, the *anglo* culture of the British Isles. The Hispanic sights and sounds that are part of our daily life, including music and even words, immediately set us apart from our anglo brothers in Europe or Australia and even to some degree in Canada.

Professor Stanley T. Williams of Yale University first published in 1955 two substantial volumes entitled *The Spanish Background of American Literature*. The wealth and depth of Hispanic influence on American letters was increasingly pervasive after 1800, beginning with such notable figures as Washington Irving, Prescott, and Henry Wadsworth Longfellow who, it is often forgotten, earned his livelihood as a professor of Spanish literature at Harvard. Twentieth-century

American literature is notably subject to Hispanic influences: Maxwell Anderson's *Night over Taos* dramatizes the emotional conflicts between Anglos and Hispanos in mid–nineteenth-century New Mexico, and Willa Cather's masterpiece *Death Comes for the Archbishop* views through the clergy, early hispano life in New Mexico. Eugene O'Neill in *The Fountain* treats the exploits of Ponce de León, and in his novel *The Bridge of San Luis Rey* Thornton Wilder re-creates colonial Perú. The influence of Spain was especially pervasive in the works of the "Lost Generation," notably Gertrude Stein and Ernest Hemingway, and predominately in the latter's novel *For Whom the Bell Tolls,* in his study on bullfighting, *Death in the Afternoon,* and in his play *The Fifth Column.*

But the history of Spanish-language letters in America is still waiting to be written. It appears, for example, that the first performance of a play in the United States occurred in 1595 in New Mexico. Captain Farfán, the author, and his company presented a new play to the recently arrived Spanish colonists on the bank of the Río Grande. Religious drama flourished in the Southwest in the seventeenth century, and various of these early plays are not only preserved but continue to be performed today. A secular literature, independent from that of Spain or Mexico, did not flourish in the Southwest until the nineteenth century, most of it published in local periodicals. This body of substantial literature awaits collecting and study.

Another especially notable and substantial body of literature in Spanish is that produced in the United States by the immigrants of the Spanish Civil War. You will recall that this immigrant group was of exceptionally high caliber, a large number cordially received by American universities. Thus a proportion of the work of two of the most outstanding Spanish poets of the twentieth century was produced in the United States. They are Jorge Guillén of Wellesley College and Pedro Salinas, professor of literature at Johns Hopkins University up to his death in 1951. Two other major figures spent briefer periods in the United States, although sufficient to cause an impact on some of their works: Luis Cernuda, and especially, Federico García Lorca in his work *Poet in New York*. The novelist Ramón Sender has resided in the Southwest for a quarter of a century.

The total number of Spanish intellectuals in our universities is considerable. In the field of Spanish literature alone it is estimated that over one hundred distinguished immigrants from Spain presently teach in major American universities. Estimates are not available for other disciplines, but it is perhaps sufficient to point out a few notable examples. The Nobel Prize in Medicine for 1959 was awarded to Severo Ochoa, professor of biochemistry at New York University, primarily for his work in the United States after 1941. One of the outstanding philosophers of the twentieth century is George Santayana, born in Madrid and for many years professor of philosophy at Harvard University. One of the outstanding mathematicians for the Apollo Space Program is Pedro Ramón Escobal, nephew of the famous eye surgeon Ramón Castroviejo who perfected in New York the technique for cornea transplant. The dean of Harvard University's School of Architecture is José Luis Sert, born in Barcelona. In little more than a quarter of a century the contributions of the Spanish immigrants have been obviously substantial.

In barely a decade the Cuban immigrants have begun to distinguish themselves in similar fashion. By the mid-sixties over forty Cuban professors were teaching in the Spanish departments of major American universities. These included, for example, the former Dean of the Graduate School of the University of Havana, also a distinguished playwright. Well over two thousand Cuban physicians have been certified to practice in the United States through one center in Miami, including the Nobel Prize Nominee Augustín Castellanos, a pediatric cardiologist.

Puerto Rican achievement has by no means been negligible. A substantial number of Puerto Ricans teach in American universities. In literature, the poets Juan de Avilés and Pablo Figueroa, and the short story writer Pura Belpré, specializing in children's folkloric tales, are permanent residents of New York City, as are painters like René Guzmán or Ralph Ortiz. Luis Quero Chiesa, writer and artist, has had a distinguished career in commercial art as well as in cultural leadership in the Puerto Rican community. The distinguished actor and director, José Ferrer, was born in Puerto Rico, as were the actresses

Miriam Colón and Rita Moreno. In city government the highest office held by a woman is Commissioner of Youth Services, Amelia Betanzos. In New York City one of the outstanding figures in politics is Herman Badillo. Various Puerto Rican cultural organizations in New York have in recent years stimulated an increased awareness of Puerto Rico's cultural heritage. These include the *Asociación Pro Cultura Hispánica-Puertorriqueña* which in addition to a program of cultural events maintains a museum and library soon to be moved to larger quarters. Founded in 1969, the Museo del Barrio maintains exhibitions of Puerto Rican art from pre-Colombian days to the present, as well as a lively program of cultural events and workshops for both children and adults. Puerto Rican theater under the leadership of outstanding performers like Miriam Colón has blossomed in New York.

Who's Who in America and *Who's Who in the East* are fairly reliable lists of distinguished persons in our society. The latest editions include ninety names in the New York City area of Hispanic origin. *Who's Who* for the South and Southwest also includes notable figures in Mexico as well, thus tacitly acknowledging the cultural unity of the American Southwest and our neighbor to the south. The distribution of birthplaces for the hispanos resident in the South and Southwest has a far more cosmopolitan profile than we might expect, quite similar to that of the greater New York City area. In spite of difficulties, which we have only been able to outline briefly, Hispanic achievement in the United States has been considerable. As educational opportunities increase for Mexican and Puerto Rican-Americans and as the second generation of Spanish and Cuban-Americans emerges, we can expect such achievement to be even more marked.

As a final consideration, it is well to emphasize again the Hispanic influences on American English. Eight of our states have Spanish names. Florida was baptized for its flowering groves as well as for the occasion of its discovery by Ponce de León at Eastertide, *Pascua Florida*. The remaining seven, as is to be expected, are states of the Southwest: California (a legendary island of plenty in Spanish folklore and literature), Nevada (land of snow), Colorado (red land), New Mexico (from *Nuevo Méjico*), Arizona (arid zone, desert), Texas (*Tejas*, land of tile roofs), and Montana (land of mountains). Over forty years ago a full fledged separate *Dictionary of Spanish terms in English* by Harold W. Bentley was published at Columbia University. Such words originated primarily in the Southwest where Spanish flows over the borders and into the United States. Given the fact that the Spanish-speaking people of the Southwest were the first European settlers there and had established a rather fixed way of life long before the coming of the Anglos, it is not surprising that the newcomers should have adopted a great many local terms. A large nucleus of these words concerns the way of life of the cowboy. Our term, cowboy, itself is only a translation of Southwestern Spanish *vaquero*. A language tends to borrow words from another language in two major ways. If possible it translates the word, as from *vaquero* to *cowboy*. Often, however, there is no possible translation and the foreign word is simply accommodated to English phonetics. *Vaquero* also came into American English in that fashion, giving us *buckaroo*. The translations, of course, are much more difficult to spot and have lost, in any event, their Spanish flavor. Thousands of accommodated words from Spanish have been adopted: tough *hombre* from *hombre, barbecue* from *barbacoa, hoosegow* from *juzgado, lasso* from *lazo, rodeo* from *rodeo,* and on and on. The cowboy terms have, of course, been given extremely wide use first by the dime novel and then by the movie western. Unfortunately they have also contributed to a distorted picture of the Southwest and, thereby, of the Hispanos. Another lexical invasion occurred with the Good Neighbor Policy and the sudden popularity in the United States of Hispano-American, and especially Cuban, music. Thus *rumba, conga, mambo, cha-cha-cha,* and *pachanga* have all become part of American English, again to some degree distorting the image of the Hispano. One of the latest terms to gain currency is *machismo,* he-man or tough guy-ism, used as the synonym, *par excellence,* for male chauvinism.

As we indicated earlier, the sights and the sounds of the United States incorporate a multitude of Hispanic flavors which set us apart from our anglo cousins either in Canada, England, or Australia. Our language itself is impregnated with Spanish words thus confirming our national heritage which includes a hispano population of over ten percent.

SELECTED BIBLIOGRAPHY

BEARDSLEY, THEODORE S., JR. "El estreno mundial de *María Sabina*: Apuntes bibliográficos," *Papeles de Son Armadans*, No. CLXXX (marzo, 1971), 321–36.

––––––. "El hispanismo universitario en los Estados Unidos," *La estafeta literaria*, Núms. 480–85 (15 nov. 1971–1 fev. 1972).

––––––. "Influencias angloamericanas en el español de Cayo Hueso," *Revista Exilio*, VII (1973), 87–100.

BENTLEY, HAROLD W. *A Dictionary of Spanish Terms in English*. New York: Octagon, 1932.

BLANCO S., ANTONIO. *La lengua española en la historia de California*. Madrid: Cultura Hispánica, 1971.

BLOCH, PETER. *La-Le-Lo-Lai, Puerto Rican Music and its Performers*. New York: Plus Ultra, 1973.

BOLTON, HERBERT E., ed. *Spanish Exploration in the Southwest, 1542–1706*. New York: Charles Scribner's Sons, 1916.

CARENAS, FRANCISCO. *Poetas españoles en U. S. A.* Madrid: Rialp, 1972.

CLARK MORENO, JOSEPH A. "A Bibliography of Bibliographies Relating to Studies of Mexican Americans," *El Grito*, V, No. 2 (1972), 47–79.

CUE CÁNOVAS, AGUSTÍN. *Los Estados Unidos y el México olvidado*. México: Costa-Amic, 1970.

CUGAT, XAVIER. *Rhumba is my Life*. New York: Didier, 1948.

ESPINOSA, AURELIO MACEDONIÓ. *Romancero de Nuevo Méjico*. Madrid: Revista Filología Española, 1953.

FERNÁNDEZ-FLOREZ, DARÍO. *The Spanish Heritage in the United States*. Madrid: Cultura-Hispánica, 1971.

FERNÁNDEZ-SHAW, CARLOS M. *Presencia española en los Estados Unidos*. Madrid: Cultura Hispánica, 1972.

FISHMAN, JOSHUA A., ROBERT L. COOPER, and ROXANA MA. *Bilingualism in the Barrio*. Bloomington, Indiana: Language Science Monographs, Vol. 7, 1971.

FODY, MICHAEL, III. "The Spanish of the American Southwest and Louisiana: A Bibliographical Survey for 1954–1969," *Orbis*, XIX (1970), 529–40.

GAMIO, MANUEL. *El inmigrante mexicano.* Mexico: Universidad Nacional Autónoma de México, 1969.

GÓMEZ GIL, ALFREDO. *Cerebros españoles en U. S. A.* Barcelona: Plaza y Janés, 1971.

GONZÁLEZ, NANCIE L. *The Spanish-Americans of New Mexico.* Albuquerque: University of New Mexico Press, 1969.

HELM, JUNE, ed. *Spanish-Speaking People in the United States.* Seattle: University of Washington Press, 1970.

"The Hispanic Society of America," *Apollo Magazine,* XCV (April 1972).

A History of The Hispanic Society of America, Museum and Library (1904–1954). New York, 1954.

ISERN, J. *Pioneros cubanos en U. S. A.* [Miami]: Cenit, 1971.

JATO MACÍAS, MANUEL. *La enseñanza del español en los Estados Unidos de América.* Madrid: Cultura Hispánica, 1961.

LEAVITT, STURGIS E. "The American Association of Teachers of Spanish and Portuguese," *La estafeta literaria,* Núm. 487 (1 marzo 1972), 30–34.

LEWIS, OSCAR. *La vida.* San Juan and New York: Random House, 1966.

LINEHAN, EDWARD J. "Cuba's Exiles Bring New Life to Miami," *National Geographic,* Vol. 144, No. 1 (July, 1973), 68–95.

LONGLAND, JEAN R. "Granados y la ópera *Goyesca,*" *Papeles de Son Armadans,* No. CXXVIII (nov. 1966), 229–55.

McWILLIAMS, CAREY. *North from Mexico: The Spanish-Speaking People of the United States.* New York: Greenwood, 1968.

MAJOR, MABEL and T. M. PEARCE. *Southwest Heritage, A Literary History with Bibliographies.* Albuquerque: University of New Mexico Press, 1972.

MANUEL, HERSCHEL T. *The Spanish-Speaking Children of the Southwest.* Austin, Texas: University of Texas Press, 1965.

NORQUEST, CARROL. *Rio Grande Wetbacks. Mexican Migrant Workers.* Albuquerque: University of New Mexico Press, 1972.

OROZCO, JOSÉ CLEMENTE. *El artista en Nueva York,* ed. Luis Cardoza y Aragón. México: Siglo XXI, 1971.

PADILLA, RAY. "Apuntes para la documentación de la cultura chicana," *El Grito,* V, no. 2 (1972), 3–46.

PEÓN, MÁXIMO. *Cómo viven los mexicanos en los Estados Unidos.* México: Costa-Amic, 1966.

PIZZO, ANTHONY P. *Tampa Town.* Miami: Trend House, 1969.

QUIRARTE, JACINTO. *Mexican American Artists.* Austin, Texas, University of Texas Press, 1973.

REYNOLDS, JOHN J. and THOMAS D. HOUCHIN. *A Directory for Spanish-Speaking New York*. New York: Quadrangle, 1971.

RIBES TOVAR, FEDERICO. *El libro puertorriqueño de Nueva York*. New York: Plus Ultra, 1970.

"Spanish-Speaking Population in the United States," *Hispania*, 55 (1972), 353.

State of California, Department of Industrial Relations. *Californians of Spanish Surname*. San Francisco, 1969.

"Teaching Spanish in School and College to Native Speakers of Spanish," *Hispania*, 55 (1972), 619–31.

TULLY, MARJORIE and JUAN B. RAEL. *An Annotated Bibliography of Spanish Folklore in New Mexico and Southern Colorado*. Albuquerque: University of New Mexico Press, 1950.

UCELAY, MARGARITA. "The Hispanic Institute in the United States," *La estafeta literaria*, Núms. 488–92 (15 marzo 1972–15 mayo 1972).

U. S. Department of Commerce, Bureau of the Census. *Persons of Spanish Origin in the United States: November, 1969 (Current Population Reports*, Series P-20, No. 213). Washington, D. C., 1971.

VASQUEZ, RICHARD. *Chicano*. New York: Doubleday, 1970.

WHITE, LOUISE V. and NORA K. SMILEY. *History of Key West*. St. Petersburg, Florida: Great Outdoors, 1959.

WILLIAMS, STANLEY T. *The Spanish Background of American Literature*. 2 vols. Hamden, Conn.: Shoestring, 1968.

From the Rhine to the Mississippi: The German Emigration to the United States

By FRANK J. COPPA

St. John's University, New York

THOMAS J. CURRAN

St. John's University, New York

DURING the reign of Charles II (1660–85) some thirteen German families arrived in Philadelphia. They were precursors of a substantial emigration from Germany to the United States. Indeed by the eve of the American Revolution there were over 100,000 German immigrants and their descendants living in the thirteen colonies. Thus the Germans were to constitute the first group that challenged the predominantly English nature of the American colonies. Subsequently, in the century and a half from 1820 to 1970, more than six million Germans found their way to America. What brought about this outpouring from the fatherland? What prompted so many Germans to come to the United States? Related to the English who speak a Germanic language and whose dynasty came from the German state of Hanover, how were the Germans received first in the colonies and later in the Republic? What contribution did they make and how did they fare in the two World Wars when Germany found herself on the opposite side of the United States? These are questions this essay will focus upon, commencing with the reasons for the massive migration.

Germany as a state is a relatively recent creation. For the greater part of the modern period, the German-speaking people of Europe did not have one centralized government. When, in the sixteenth century, the Reformation destroyed the unity of Christendom, many of the ensuing religious wars were fought on German soil, by Germans against Germans. The issue was not confined to the German world, however, and thus Germany became the battleground of Danes, Frenchmen, Swedes, and Spaniards. The havoc wrought by the Thirty Years' War (1618–48) devastated Germany for many decades: commerce declined; industry was crippled; and intellectual life sustained a deep if not mortal blow. Politically, too, Germany seemed to stagnate. The Hapsburg attempt to unite Germany was frustrated, and the country remained divided for more than two centuries. Particularism, euphemistically termed the "German Liberties," triumphed completely as the small princes preserved their petty states at the expense of unification. Thus the territory between the Elbe and the Rhine, the North Sea and the Alps, led a sleepy existence under her parochial princes.

Germany's quiet was ended by the series of events that erupted in the latter half of the eighteenth century: the enlightenment, the development of absolutism in Austria and Prussia, and most important of all, the French Revolution. Nowhere, with the possible exception of Italy, was the impact of the French Revolution as great as it was in Germany. Under Napoleon the boundaries of the German states were redrawn so that in place of some three hundred separate states, less than fifty remained. German nationalism was aroused by the French invasion. It was particularly stimulated by the humiliating defeat of Prussia and the subsequent Prussian reform movement under the inspiration of Baron von Stein. This inspiration was purchased at the price of military defeat and the disruption of an already troubled economy.

The states of Austria and Prussia had played a key role in the Quadruple Alliance that had forced Napoleon to surrender, encouraging some German nationalists to feel that the dream of unification could no longer be thwarted. After all France, their major enemy, had finally been defeated; the territorial changes of Napoleon, and particularly the elimination of many of the smaller states, had ushered in the process of unification; and, finally, middle-class businessmen had come to appreciate the benefits of a common market that unification would inevitably provide.

These possible advantages were offset by a number of factors which continued to hinder consolidation. France, although defeated, was still a major power and had much to say about the reconstruction of the postwar period, and her opposition to German unification was well known. Furthermore, the Russians who emerged from the war a dominant force in European politics, were not anxious for such unity. Nor were the English, who sought a balance of power on the continent. Meanwhile the smaller German states were determined to maintain their existence. They remained in alliance with Austria, which, unable to unite Germany herself, therefore determined that it not be united against her. They presented a formidable barrier to the idea of unification.

Consequently the old federal structure—the Bund—was reinstated under the leadership of the Austrian foreign minister, Count Metternich. Known as the "Coachman" of Europe, this astute Austrian Minister devised that the Bund, to serve his state's interests, should have a maximum influence in Germany at the cost of a minimum effort. It completely failed to satisfy the demands of German nationalists. For one thing the organization had a Diet rather than a Parliament, and it represented states rather than people. Then, too, it provided no concrete provisions for the military defense of the fatherland. Even more discouraging, there was no mechanism for the modification of this structure, no provision whereby the confederation might become a federation and eventually a federal state. Perhaps most important of all was the failure of the Bund to create economic unity at a time when some coordination was necessary to confront the severe problems facing the people of Germany.

Following the Congress of Vienna (1815), Germany, and indeed most of Central Europe, faced severe economic problems and lacked the leadership to provide solutions. The invasions and the demands of the war had left a legacy of heavy provincial and national debts, and throughout Germany the upper classes cringed at the thought of the taxes that would have to be imposed to salvage the budget. In part their hesitation stemmed from the fact that increased taxation would pinpoint the inequity of a social system in which feudalism survived and upper-class privileges continued. Despite the talk of reform the feudal nobility still remained the first order throughout most of Germany, furnishing not only the higher government officials and bureaucrats, and the most important figures in the Church, but most of the army officers as well.

As a result of Germany's economic retardation, its middle class remained small and weak. The trading and shopkeeping classes, as well as the artisan class, found their position progressively undermined. These groups were prepared to take drastic steps, including emigration and revolution, to improve their status. Finally there were farmers who constituted the majority of the population in this still preindustrial society. In addition to the feudal landlords, who were to convert their estates to a capitalist economy during this period, there were wealthy nonfeudal farmers, small freeholders, feudal tenants, and finally the agricultural laborers, who were at the bottom of the economic ladder.

This social stratification had long prevailed, but the revolutionary wars and the long period of almost continuous political reorganization had generated a sense of restlessness and had pinpointed the possibility of change throughout Germany. The economy of the countryside, the towns, and the cities was seriously compromised by the heavy concentration of the German population on a not very fertile soil. Furthermore the ending of the continental system and inadequate tariff protection could not stem the flood of cheap manufactured goods from abroad with which the artisan producers of Central Europe could not compete. In areas such as Baden, Württemberg and Rhineland Prussia, the dislocation was so serious that it proved impossible to reabsorb the soldiers who returned from the campaign against Napoleon. The governments of the various German states only belatedly recognized the danger and did not introduce any innovative or positive program to deal with it. The states did not seriously consider coordinating their efforts in dealing with the economic malaise, looking only as far as their own frontiers, and even within their own boundaries they preferred to overlook most difficulties. In Western Germany where some action was necessary, the solution favored by the various governments was to discourage marriage as well as to restrict the individual's right to raise a family. The negative approach inspired little confidence on the part of the Western Germans who saw that they would have to find their own means of survival in the difficult postwar period.

Compounding the problem in Southwest Germany was the custom of dividing the land among all the children in a family. This brought about a division of holdings into strips that were soon found to be inadequate for the families which farmed them. To cope with this land shortage some relied upon more intensive farming, others depended upon the supplementary income provided by a number of domestic industries, while still others turned to emigration as the sole means of salvation. Increasingly, artisans and farmers found that their labor could no longer provide for their needs. Emigration became a desperate necessity.

Emigrating or wandering away from one's home was not something new to the people of Southwestern Germany; some had wandered as far east as Russia or had found their way west to America by the seventeenth and eighteenth centuries. The memory carried over into the nineteenth century, providing a safety valve should the economic situation deteriorate any further. Conditions in Central Europe were far from good in the early nineteenth century. Food prices in parts of Germany had doubled within five years, and the fear of famine continued to haunt large parts of the population. Still, all would have been well if in 1816 Germany had been blessed with a good harvest. Instead, a very warm spring, a cool and excessively wet summer, a series of floods, a plague of mice, and an early winter proved disastrous for the crops.

The social consequences of the crop failure were calamitous; large parts of the countryside were rendered unsafe by hordes of thieves and beggars. The sentimental ties that held men to their villages and homes quickly snapped under the pressure of fear and hunger. Government, as before, showed itself ineffectual in confronting the disaster. Consequently Germans by the thousands spontaneously began to leave their homes, producing a great wave of emigration. Some 20,000 found their way to the

United States, while almost as many went to the Hapsburg Empire and Tsarist Russia.

This flight, ignored by a large part of the political class, was explained as the work of swindlers and fanatics by those who investigated the matter only superficially. Even the noted Friedrich List, commissioned to get to the root of the problem, failed to understand the urgency of the economic question. Heinrich von Gagern, on the other hand, quickly saw the economic problem, but proved unable to provide a solution, suggesting that the Bundestag take federal action. His call served to highlight the need for a national parliament and some sort of unification beyond the tenuous ties preserved among Germans by means of the confederation.

Fortunately, the economic situation improved with the harvest of 1817, so that the natural conditions that had done so much to provoke the emigration, now served to curtail it. Because it was short in duration the outpouring of 1816–17 was overshadowed by the more massive outpourings which followed. Nonetheless, it was extremely important because for every German who left the Reich there were hundreds of others who were on the verge of taking the same step. Furthermore the impact of this emigration was to strengthen the ties between Germany and America and fix the New World in the minds of many as a possible haven should another series of troubles commence and life in Germany prove unbearable.

For the moment emigration remained slight and was to remain so until the end of the 1820's. Then in 1830 an increasing population, political instability, and revolutionary agitation, as well as a precipitous rise in the cost of living contributed to the mid-century transatlantic migration which did not abate until the mid-1850's. As before, the emigration was most pronounced in the South and West of Germany and was largely composed of families of lower- and middle-class background. The outrageously high price of land in comparison to the income derived from it served as an incentive to sell and move elsewhere. The economic malaise of the small farmer worked to curtail his spending and therefore hit the artisan classes who relied upon his purchases. Weavers, carpenters, masons, blacksmiths, tailors— all found their incomes dwindling and were therefore encouraged to emigrate. More and more Germans looked to America as the land where they could begin their lives anew.

The promises of America were grasped by Goethe who wrote, "America, you have it better than our old continent, you have no fallen castles, no stones," adding that it was not "inwardly torn" by "useless memories and vain quarrels." Letters sent by German settlers in America to their relatives and friends in the old country also worked to create a positive picture of life in the United States. Passed from family to family, sometimes even outside the village, these missives catalogued the success of local residents in the New World and encouraged others to dream of duplicating their venture. Between the Congress of Vienna and the failure of the revolutions of 1848, some half a hundred books written by Germans who had traveled through the United States appeared on the home market. Particularly influential was Gottfried Duden's *Report on a Journey to the Western States of North America*. Like the private letters these travel books served to stimulate German interest in the New World.

If the news from America was appealing and served as a positive pull factor, conditions in Germany worked to push an increasing number of her people out. Among the causes for disillusionment and dissatisfaction were the cholera epidemics, popular disturbances, anti-Semitic outbursts, rumors of war and revolution, heavy taxes, infringements upon personal rights, including conscription, restriction of the right to marry, and the persistence of the inequitable social system. For thousands of Germans the future appeared precarious and their economic prospects dismal; this lack of opportunity in the foreseeable future served to strengthen the resolve of many to leave the old country.

In the nineteenth century large areas of Germany were as dependent as Ireland upon the potato crop to the extent that even a minimal crop failure would have grave consequences. Hence there was a widespread concern when the potato blight began to appear in different parts of Central Europe in the early 1840's. This apprehension was justified, for in 1845 the blight destroyed the potato crop throughout northern Europe, playing havoc with the already precarious Germany economy. As in 1816, in 1846 salvation from catastrophe was sought in a good harvest, but, instead, Germans were to learn that their potato crop was rotting in the dry ground while the rye crop was damaged by an early frost. Even the most optimistic souls were forced to conclude that the food situation would inevitably get much worse before it improved and that starvation was inevitable in large parts of the fatherland.

The ensuing famine could not be localized as no part of Germany proved immune to the shortage of food or the resulting astronomical prices. Peasants and farmers by the thousands fled from the countryside but found that the preindustrial cities of Germany did not have much to offer them in the way of employment. Under this situation many who had thought they would only have to venture to the nearest adjacent town found they would have to travel much further to find the security they craved. Given the widespread depression, emigration seemed the only solution for many. Whereas some 8,000 Germans entered the United States in the decade from 1820 to 1830, and some 152,000 in the following decade, over 430,000 entered from 1840 to 1850. In 1847 alone more than 100,000 found their way to the United States.

Then in January, 1848, the people of Palermo rose in rebellion against Neapolitan rule, shattering the repression of the Age of Metternich, 1815–48. This was followed in February by a revolution in Paris which drove Louis Philippe out of his capital and led to the proclamation of the Second French Republic. In March, the people of Vienna broke the power of Prince Metternich, forcing him to flee and sparking a revolution in Berlin and a spirit of rebellion throughout Germany. This revolutionary turmoil persuaded some to pack and leave home, while the restoration of 1849 forced others to emigrate. However, it would be a mistake to hold the political revolutions or the ensuing repression entirely responsible for the mid-century emigration. Political refugees were the exception rather than the rule; they were emigrés rather than emigrants. Indeed during the years from 1848 to 1850, the number of German emigrants declined from their 1847 and prerevolutionary peak, indicating that economic rather than political factors were the key to the mid-century exodus.

Likewise in the postrevolutionary period, the economic situation continued to play a decisive role as the German population grew rapidly, outpacing the quickening industrial growth. The population increase combined with poor harvests from 1850 to 1853 to stimulate a new outpouring of Germans—over half a million left in these years—which reached a peak in 1854. The greater number came from southern and western areas, long centers of emigration, although by the mid 1850's all of Germany was affected. Those who wished to stop the exodus stooped to telling exaggerated stories of American atrocities against its German-speaking minority, stressing the real prejudices of the Know-Nothings and other anti-immigrant groups and parties, and claimed that the American economy was subject to natural calamity and cyclical unemployment. Few listened to such stories, and Germans continued to cross the Atlantic in search of a better and more prosperous life. During the 1850's close to one million Germans left their native lands, and the bulk found their way to the United States. Eventually the tide of emigration ebbed as the German economy improved and the Civil War rendered life in America less attractive.

In the 1860's, the Prussian Chancellor Otto von Bismarck paved the way for the German Empire which was proclaimed in 1871. It was an answer to the prayers of German nationalists and liberals. However, not all Germans were satisfied or felt that their needs had been met, for some million and a half Germans emigrated overseas between the creation of the Empire and the mid 1880's. Of these, the vast majority once again found their way to the United States. There is still no consensus as to what caused this last outpouring. Some have stressed the dislocation of the German agrarian economy following the importation of grains from America and Russia. Others blame the building of railways which reached into Eastern Germany and facilitated the movement of masses of people from formerly remote regions. Still others point to the decline in the cost of crossing the Atlantic, while some maintain that the military conscription practiced by the new state was responsible for the flight of many of its subjects.

Whatever the reason, large numbers of Germans continued to leave the homeland and did so until 1895 when the exodus from Germany slowed to a trickle. Indeed after this time there was a substantial flow of Germans back to the fatherland. Most observers believe that the great German prosperity of the prewar decade made emigration not only unattractive but unnecessary. However by this time millions of Germans were in the New World and were to play an important role in the United States where they represented the largest immigrant group next to the English.

Most of these Germans had ventured to the United States in search of a better life, expecting that the New World would perforce have to be better than the old. Were their expectations fulfilled? Were they well received by their native American neighbors? Did they assimilate readily? It is to these matters that we now turn.

As noted earlier, the first influx of German immigrants made their way to Pennsylvania. There, Benjamin Franklin, one of the founding fathers and one of the most eminent Americans, rather than displaying a balanced attitude toward these newcomers from the German states reflected a narrow Anglo-American bias. He tended to overlook many of their positive attributes, harping upon their political immaturity, social incivility and the questionable business practices of a small minority.

In 1750, Franklin wrote to one of his correspondents that "Because of the disagreeableness of the dissonant manners of the Germans their English speaking neighbors would have preferred to move away." Again in 1753, Franklin presented the American's stereotype of Germans: "Those [Germans] who come hither are generally the most stupid of their own nation... not being used to liberty they know not how to make modest use of it. And as Holbein says of the Hottentots, they are not esteemed men until they have shown their manhood by beating their mothers, so these seem not to think themselves free, till they can feel their liberty in abusing and insulting their teachers."

But, by far, Franklin's most xenophobic and vitriolic outburst directed against the Germans can be found in his *Observations Concerning the Increase of Mankind* (1751). There he asked, "Why should the Palatine Boors be suffered to swarm into our settlements and, by herding together, establish their language and manners to the exclusion of ours? Why should Pennsylvania, founded by the English, become a colony of aliens who will shortly be so numerous as to Germanize us instead of our Anglifying them?"

The Pennsylvania legislature reacted to this alarm. In 1729, it had passed a measure which placed a duty of five shillings on each foreigner coming into the colony. In 1755 it went further by passing a bill that would prevent ships from carrying Germans into the colony. The Governor refused to sign this legislation; instead, the heirs of William Penn encouraged German immigration. The Germans were sought because they were good craftsmen and farmers and they caused the proprietor little trouble.

Others, however, viewed the Germans as a dangerous group because of their insistence on using their own language, their reliance upon German pastors, and their publication of German newspapers. Their hostility to the Germans was muted during the Revolutionary War. Then with the decline of immigration to America in the period of 1776 to 1820, the native-born Americans had the opportunity to impose upon the new nation a decidedly Anglo-American culture and tradition.

The German immigrants who came in the nineteenth century had two choices. The majority view represented by Carl Schurz, an outstanding German-American of this period, insisted that the Germans must accommodate themselves to the American way of life. The minority view was represented by Gottfried Duden, whom we have already met as the author of a popular immigrant guide. He and several others wanted to set up a German nation within the United States. This idea had the support of the New York Germanic Society which tried in 1839 to set up such a colony. It failed because most Germans did not want to establish a new Germany in America. They congregated together in the New World for social rather than for political reasons.

The native Americans developed an unfortunate stereotype of the Germans. It was based in part on their religious practices. Most Americans were not consistent churchgoers, but they nevertheless believed that the Sabbath was a day to be celebrated sedately. The Germans, especially the Lutherans, on the other hand, had their picnics and their beer gardens. They were considered by the nativists to be desecrating this holy day. Then, too, many of the Germans who came to America as a result of the potato blight, 1845–47, were predominantly Roman Catholic and were condemned as much for their Catholicism as for their Germanness. Some of these German immigrants, in demanding German-speaking clerics, antagonized both the Lutheran Synods and the Catholic hierarchy. Even their co-religionists often found this group of German immigrants quite difficult to handle.

As well as being attacked for violations of the Sabbath and their Catholicism, Germans were also accused of being atheists. The pejorative attitude of the nativists rested on a small but articulate number of Germans who had fled to the United States after the failure of the revolution of 1848. Another stereotype presented the German as a stolid beer drinker, heavy of girth and dull of mind. They were condemned at once as Protestant violators of the Sabbath, as Catholics controlled by their priests, and as atheists. Such views of the German-American dominated nativist thinking in the nineteenth century.

Hostility to the Germans became most obvious in the Louisville riot of 1855 led by the antiforeign Know-Nothings. But other factors played a role. The German-American efforts to perpetuate the German language caused difficulties. And the German government's foreign policies created suspicions of the German immigrants and their descendants.

The German-Americans congregated mainly in the Mid West, especially in Wisconsin and Illinois. There, whether Lutherans or Catholics, they were able to set up both public and parochial schools which taught in the German language. This agitated many native Americans who believed that this kind of education retarded the Americanization of the Germans. In 1890, the Bennett law was passed in Wisconsin and the Edwards law in Illinois. Both called for compulsory attendance at schools where instruction was to be given in English.

The German Lutherans were incensed at the English-language requirement. So, too, was the Catholic prelate of Milwaukee, the German-American Archbishop Francis X. Katzer, who insisted on the retention of the German language. When both laws were repealed, the American Protective Association saw these repeals as proof that a foreign Catholic conspiracy controlled these states.

Following unification, the Reich's foreign policy also caused

German-Americans some difficulties. During America's involvement in the Spanish-American War (1898), Admiral Dewey's fleet was harassed by German vessels in Philippine waters. But the greatest outbreak of anti-German hostility manifested itself during the course of World War I. During this conflict, the loyalty of the German-Americans was seriously questioned. At times, the nativists' fears reached ridiculous heights. German place names were changed or their pronunciation altered. Hamburgers became Salisbury steaks, frankfurters became hot dogs. There was even suspicion that German-Americans were putting ground glass in Red Cross bandages to thwart the war effort.

German-Americans, however, were loyal. During the years of America's neutrality, 1914–17, the German-American press tended to be sympathetic to the fatherland. Once America entered the conflict, the German-American press supported the American war effort.

Nonetheless, the nativists' attack on German-American culture continued. The German language was forbidden in many school systems. German-speaking families frequently dared not indulge in the practice. Most German-language newspapers began to publish in English. German-American societies often disbanded because mobs of one hundred percent Americans attacked their meetings. German opera was boycotted as well. It was a popular mood of indignation that transformed the old beer-drinking German into the vicious, barbaric Hun. Fortunately, with the end of the war, this hostility abated almost as quickly as it had begun.

In World War II, this agitation did not arise, though some German-Americans were accused of being pro-Hitler and pro-Nazi. It is true that some 50,000 German-Americans were members of the German-American Bund, but the overwhelming number of German-Americans were loyal to their new country. In many ways, the German-American General Dwight D. Eisenhower best symbolized their attitude.

The German-American experience was not always as dismal as during the dark days of the world wars. In the Midwest, where Germans rarely became public charges, they were by and large respected, and except for their temperance violations they were accepted as good citizens. The beer-drinking stereotype declined markedly after the Civil War. In its place, the German-Americans were pictured as hard-working, thrifty homeowners who usually made excellent neighbors, and good Americans.

What is the process by which an immigrant group becomes Americanized? This issue has occupied a good many immigrant historians. Usually the native Americans try to push the immigrants into an Anglo-American mold: English-speaking, hard-working, law-abiding, and Protestant. Large numbers of Germans refused to follow this road completely, especially in their efforts to retain the German language. The harder Americans tried to coerce them to accept the use of English, the stiffer became the German opposition.

Nonetheless, some German-Americans were speedily Americanized. One such person was John Anthony Quitman. He was born in Rhinebeck, New York. His father served the local German Lutheran Church as a minister for over a quarter of a century. Young Quitman was educated for the ministry but forsook that career and became a lawyer instead. He then moved to Ohio where he remained for a year. Then he settled in Mississippi where he married a local American girl, became a plantation owner, and never referred to his German background. He was elected to the Mississippi State Senate in 1835 and 1836 and went on to hold other public offices. In the Mexican War, he served with distinction as a Brigadier-General, then a Major-General. On the basis of his war record, he was twice elected Governor of Mississippi (1850–51). A German-American, Quitman nonetheless found it relatively easy to achieve acceptance in a completely non-German area.

Other German-Americans, while unwilling to follow Governor Quitman's pattern, were willing to accommodate themselves to the reality of life in America. They spoke English in business and a number of German-American churches even used the English language in their services. Some German immigrants who came to America after the Civil War were appalled at the changes they found in the German Lutheran and German Reform churches, where the services were held in English. But others found this pattern agreeable.

German-born Gustav Koerner's career in Illinois represents in many ways, the spirit of accommodation. Koerner studied law, passed the bar, and, for a time, became the law partner of the Irish-born politician, James Shields. Koerner himself became active in Illinois politics. But his power rested on his German-American constituency. His interest in the fatherland remained strong. In 1848, he tried to use his influence with his former law partner, now General Shields, to obtain a diplomatic appointment to Germany. Shields made a half-hearted effort, so that Koerner's bid to return to Germany at the expense of the American government was thwarted. The interest, however, was there. Remaining in Illinois, Koerner was one of the organizers of the Republican party in Illinois and became the Lieutenant-Governor of Illinois in the post-Civil War period.

By far the most prominent German-American in American political life was Carl Schurz. He had been forced to flee from Germany after the failure of the revolution of 1848. First he went to England where he spent three years. He and his bride then came to the United States. When Schurz reached America he believed that his German roots had been cut permanently.

Schurz, like Koerner, opposed the efforts to establish a New Germany in America. He insisted that he had become an American and was no longer a German. In 1859, he delivered an address at Cooper Union in New York which he called "True Americanism." On that occasion, he outlined the policy of acculturation: one did not have to be anti-German to be a true American. Schurz subsequently became a lawyer in Wisconsin. He then moved to St. Louis, Missouri, where he became editor of a German-American newspaper. Though the paper was published in German, Schurz opposed all efforts to set up segregated German communities.

The whole thrust of Schurz's career was to immerse himself in American life, especially in American politics. He was one of the most vocal supporters of Abraham Lincoln in the elections of 1860 and 1864. As a reward he was appointed Minister to Spain. But at the outbreak of hostilities in 1861 between the Union and the Confederacy, he elected to serve and was appointed a General in the Union army. After the war, he became a United States Senator from Missouri. In the administration of President Rutherford B. Hayes (1877–81), he became Secretary of the Interior. The reason for his political rise was simple enough: he was able, and he was considered to be the Republican party's German-American spokesman.

The German-American community in the United States lost much of its parochialism as a result of the Franco-Prussian War, 1870–71, which finally resulted in German unification under Bismarck. The German press reflected pride and enthusiasm for the unification of the fatherland. Shortly thereafter, the German-American Alliance was organized. It became the largest ethnic organization in America. At the turn of the century, it had over one and a quarter million members.

For the most part, the German-American community followed the path laid out by Koerner and Schurz. Some followed the example of Quitman, but, by and large, the Germans in America were unwilling to toss aside their German cultural heritage. Nor were they willing to ignore their American environment and its cultural demands. They tried to balance the two, and in the process became Americans.

How successful have these German-Americans been? What are their achievements? Whether the German-American community, or any ethnic group for that matter, has been successful, depends on what one means by success, and achievement.

Many immigration historians believe that the German immigrants have been, next to the English, the most easily assimilable and the most successful. Certainly if we measure the success of the Germans of the eighteenth century with those of the nineteenth and twentieth centuries, by examining bank accounts, home ownership, factories, breweries, then the latter Germans may be considered more successful. But if viewed from the frame of reference of the Pietist sects of the eighteenth century—the Pennsylvania Amish are an example—then the question posed by the Gospel of St. Matthew, chapter 25: "What doth it profit a man if he gain the whole world and suffer the loss of his soul," becomes relevant. Within this frame of reference, while America has given much, it has also taken a good deal.

America's impact on the Germans who ventured to the United States has produced mostly positive results as suggested above. What has been the German-American contribution to America? Certainly, the German immigrants have had a beneficial effect on education, America's celebration of Christmas and Easter, and a tremendous amount of technological innovation in publishing, transportation, and music to emphasize three particular areas. They are only a part of the inventive genius of the Germans. Naturally enough, they also have their political figures.

The Germans were among the first to set up a kindergarten in the United States. Two German groups claim credit for establishing the idea in America. One, Mrs. Carl Schurz (1855) in Missouri, the other the Poppenhusen Institute (1868) in New York. The latter group was established by a grant of $100,000 by the wealthy German industrialist, Conrad Poppenhusen. This idea became extremely popular in American education. But the German impact on American education was also felt in America's secondary schools. The German immigrants brought with them the idea of fitness of the body as well as of the mind. On the college level the Germans also had an impact. Before the Civil War, American scholars went to the German universities and there came in contact with the graduate training offered by these institutions. But this factor was more the influence of Germany on American scholars than it was the result of German immigration.

On the popular level, the German-Americans influenced the American celebration of Christmas and Easter. "Silent Night" is a German hymn. Santa Claus with his white beard and red and white suit is of German derivation. Then too, the Easter bunny and Easter eggs are of German origin. The German-American religious influence was not restricted to the celebration of Christmas and Easter. They had a profound impact on American Lutheranism and Judaism. The Lutherans in America are primarily Germans. The conservatism of German Lutheranism was transferred to the United States. The German-Jewish community brought Reform Judaism to America. Originating in Germany, it liberalized the tenets of Orthodox Judaism. It has had its greatest impact in America.

One can list literally thousands of German-American inventors, including Dr. Werner von Braun, the physicist responsible for America's space program. But who can think of American publishing without the work of the German-American inventor of the linotype machine, Otto Meyer Mergenthaler? Who can think of bridges and transportation without remembering the

supreme achievement of John Augustus Roebling and the construction of the Brooklyn Bridge? And what would America be
like without the great Steinway pianos, introduced by William
Steinway and continued to this day by John Steinway. Steinway's
concern for his workers was well known. He was an advisor to
President Grover Cleveland, and, at the end of the nineteenth
century, was one of the major German-American industrialists
and spokesmen for the German-American community.

In politics, the German-Americans had many successes.
Koerner and Schurz have already been mentioned. In 1892,
Illinois elected the Democrat, John Peter Altgeld, a German-
American, governor. Much earlier, William Havemeyer, organi-
zer of the sugar refinery trust, was elected mayor of New York
City. And, of course, the election of Dwight D. Eisenhower
as President of the United States in 1952 has brought the
German-American achievement to a culmination.

The Germans who came to this country throughout its history
have given much to the nation. They have been attacked, especially during the World War I years, but, more often than not,
they have provided America with much talent and little trouble.

SELECTED BIBLIOGRAPHY

BARRY, COLEMAN. *The Catholic Church and German-Americans.*
Milwaukee: Bruce Publishing Co., 1953.

DORPALEN, ANDREAS. "The German Element and the Issues of the
Civil War," *Mississippi Valley Historical Review*, XXIX (1942),
55–76.

FAUST, ALBERT BERNHARDT. *The German Element in the United States
with Special Reference to Its Political, Moral, Social and Educational Influence.* 2 vols. New York: Arno, 1969.

HANSEN, MARCUS. *The Atlantic Migration, 1607–1860: A History
of the Continuing Settlement of the United States.* New York:
Torchbook, 1961, pp. 220–41.

HAWGOOD, JOHN A. *The Tragedy of German America.* New York:
Putnam, 1940.

KEIM, JEANETTE, *Forty Years of German-American Political Relations.* Philadelphia: W. J. Dornan, 1919.

KOERNER, GUSTAV. *Memoirs of Gustav Koerner, 1809–1896: Life
Sketches Written at the Suggestion of His Children,* ed. Thomas

J. McCormack. 2 vols., Cedar Rapids, Iowa: The Torch Press, 1909.

SCHURZ, CARL. *The Reminiscences of Carl Schurz*. 3 vols. New York: Somerset, 1974.

SKAL, GEORGE VON. *History of German Immigration in the United States and Successful German Americans and Their Descendants*. New York: S. T. J. Smiley, 1908.

TAYLOR, PHILIP. *The Distant Magnet*. New York: Harper & Row, 1971.

WALKER, MACK. *Germany and the Emigration, 1816–1855*. Cambridge, Mass.: Harvard University Press, 1964.

WEAVER, GLENN. "Benjamin Franklin and the Pennsylvania Germans," *William and Mary Quarterly*, Series 3; 14 (October, 1957), 536–59.

WEHER, P. C. *America in Imaginative German Literature, 1815–1850*. New York: AMS Press, 1966.

WITTKE, CARL. *The German-Language Press in America*. Lexington, Kentucky: University of Kentucky Press, 1957.

————. *Refugees and Revolution: The German Forty Eighters in America*. Philadelphia: Greenwood, 1952.

III

The Norwegians in America: "Giants in the Earth"

By KENNETH O. BJORK

St. Olaf College

I

THE Norwegian immigrants came from a country largely mountainous in character, having an extremely limited area that lent itself to the cultivation of the soil. Grazing land and forests, it is true, add somewhat to agricultural possibilities, but bare mountains, lakes, bogs, and ice constitute roughly three-fourths of Norway's land surface. The population is largely concentrated in the rolling meadowland of the southeast and along an extended coast line—broken by fjords—which provides harbors and centers for trade and fishing. Coal and iron, the basic raw materials in the industrialization of Europe in the nineteenth century, are scarce. These natural conditions make it impossible for the country to support a large population, although electrification and new industries have altered the situation considerably in recent decades.

Until the nineteenth century, Norway's agriculture was largely self-contained and its rural social pattern rigidly fixed. Generally speaking, this social structure had been able to accommodate a growth in population to about 1807. From 1815 to 1865, however, the country experienced an annual human increase of 1.3 percent, a rate higher than that of Europe as a whole. Norway's population doubled from 1750 to 1850 and was to double again from 1850 to 1928. The towns, which in the past had been able to absorb a small rural surplus because of their low birth rate, could

63

no longer do so effectively without considerable industrialization as the century wore on.

The situation after 1815 was essentially this: Four-fifths of the population was engaged in agriculture. As late as 1865, two-thirds of the people were still living on the land. Industrialization was very slow. The simple social organization and inelastic rural economy could no longer meet human needs adequately. Hard times and relative poverty existed everywhere, as young people were forced to find such work as they could in the country. The number of cotters (*husmenn*), servants, and landless farm laborers increased much faster than the number of landholders (*bønder*). Needless to say, the contract terms for the cotters became more favorable to the landowners, and the wages of farm workers fell to frightening lows. Norway was ready for a social and economic explosion.

What happened was a complete breakup of the old agrarian society in the second half of the nineteenth century. This change was accompanied by economic developments in the form of expanded trade, the introduction of some industry, and therefore the creation of urban jobs. The dammed-up human reserves in the countryside provided the stuff for both internal movement and emigration—the two sides of a single coin.

The second half of the nineteenth century was a period of crises resulting from the transition from a self-contained to a commercialized form of agriculture—of producing for a market in competition with foreign countries. The first great crisis came in the 1860's, the second in the 1880's, lasting to about 1895. The 1860's were marked by mounting indebtedness, increased taxes for roads, railways, steamboats, greatly improved education, medical care and relief—all of which placed a heavy burden on the rural population, which began to decline. The decrease in number of cotters and hired hands made farming a difficult family affair. People, including small landowners, left the farms. Some districts, thanks to sawmills, shipping opportunities, and the like, were able to absorb the uprooted; others were not. From some regions, such as Telemark, almost all of the human surplus migrated. Generally speaking, the mountain people preferred America to the Norwegian towns and cities, with which they had had little contact.

The breakup of agrarian society was accompanied by a marked change in attitudes. In the early 1800's a boy had remained at home, had become a hired hand, and, on marrying and becoming a cotter, had taken such terms as he could get from a landowner—hoping to top off his limited income by logging, by clearing a tiny bit of new land, or by fishing. Later, he might go to school, then to a nearby town to become a worker—or migrate. For a variety of reasons young people were becoming more assertive, and farmers began to express themselves in politics. People read newspapers, thus becoming aware of their victimization and of the better life that was possible.

After 1830, letters written by the pioneer emigrants from Norway began to appear with accounts of economic opportunities, social equality, and local self-government in the New World. To these "America letters," written by friends and relatives, must be added the "America books" prepared by travelers and the literature circulated by railroads, land companies, states, and shipping firms.

To a people who had struggled to eke out a living from a grudging soil or had found little chance to earn a living in the towns and cities of their homeland, the accounts of almost limitless stretches of cheap, later free, land in America—and of a society that was fluid and egalitarian—were irresistible. Whole families, after giving up their meager cotters' holdings or selling their small farms, purchased tickets and prepared for the long journey to the New World. Emigration from the cities increased after 1870; many of these migrants were only recently from the country. As the years passed, increasing numbers of single persons made the decision to emigrate and found the move eased by improved transportation, cheaper fares—$23.50 to Chicago in 1884—and quite commonly by prepaid tickets sent by relatives or friends in the States.

The decision to emigrate is thus seen to be the result of both the impersonal forces of change and of a conviction that a better and fuller life was possible in America. The migration of the nineteenth and early twentieth centuries was, in a very real sense, a search for freedom at the same time that it was an escape from poverty, or relative poverty, in town or country.

The hardships of life in Norway followed the emigrants

across the Atlantic. In the holds of ships, they lived off meager supplies of food stored in their colorful chests. The journey, in the day of the sailing vessel, was often an extended ordeal, lasting for months. Steerage passage aboard steamships was often even worse, though much shorter. After arriving in New York or Quebec or at another Atlantic or Gulf port, the passengers learned of vast distances yet to be covered before arrival at their destination. In many instances, it was necessary to interrupt the journey to earn money enough to continue it. In any event, the emigrants often arrived in the Upper Midwest with little more than hope and the strength of their hands to sustain them.

The migration of Norwegians to America, beginning in July, 1825, with the tiny sloop "Restoration," was a small affair compared to that of many other countries. But the 800,000 or 900,000 who made the Atlantic crossing numbered well over four-fifths of Norway's population in the year 1801. No other European country, excepting Ireland, contributed so large a percentage of its human stock. During the last quarter of the nineteenth century, the mother country retained only forty-six percent of its natural increase.

Until 1850 the exodus was relatively small. It increased considerably in the 1850's and during the Civil War years. In 1866 it rose to over 15,000 and remained substantial until 1874. The greatest period of migration began in 1879 and continued to the early 1890's. The third major wave of Norwegian migration occurred in the early years of the present century; nearly 100,000 crossed from 1901 to 1905. The figures show a considerable migration in the 1920's as well.

Most emigrants from Norway, especially those who left before 1880, had every intention of remaining in the United States. But inevitably some of them returned to the homeland. From 1881 to 1890, nearly 6,000 made the return journey, and even more left these shores in the 1890's. The figure rose to nearly 10,000 from 1901 to 1905, and to more than 11,000 from 1906 to 1910, then fell to 6,521 between 1911 and 1915. Thereafter the number of returnees was of little importance. In all, the backtrackers totaled somewhere in the neighborhood of 50,000. But, clearly, not all emigrants either planned to remain permanently in America or found in it the realization of their dreams.

The first shipload of Norwegian immigrants—known as the "Sloopers"—settled at Kendall, northwest of Rochester, New York. Most of the families left in 1834 for the Fox River Valley in Illinois. From there settlement spread rapidly into the northern counties of Illinois (including Chicago), southern Wisconsin, northern Iowa, southern Minnesota, and later into eastern North and South Dakota. The immigrants gradually went elsewhere in these states and also into Michigan, Nebraska, Montana, and the mining and logging areas of northern Wisconsin and Minnesota. Later movements took them to the western parts of North Dakota, Montana, the prairie provinces of Canada, to the Pacific coast, especially the Puget Sound region, British Columbia, and Alaska. The vast majority, however, settled in the upper Mississippi and Missouri valleys. It is this area that has been termed "Norwegian America" by some writers. Islands or colonies also developed in Texas, Utah, San Francisco, eastern Washington, New York City, New England, and elsewhere. But the main flow was unmistakably northwestward from northern Illinois in search of land.

As a rule, newly arrived immigrant families stopped first at one of the early settlements, then moved on westward to unoccupied areas. In choosing a place of residence, they were influenced by letters from pioneers, land and railroad companies, and the advice of countrymen they met on their journey. The new settlement became, in turn, a "mother colony" from which offspring and new arrivals moved still farther westward. Often explorers went ahead of settlement, hunted out desirable farming locations, and reported back to those seeking new land. Similarly, frontier settlers wrote letters both to relatives and friends in the other settlements and to Norwegian-language newspapers, which served as a public forum in the discussion of a variety of subjects, including desirable locations.

The early Norwegian immigrant knew the value of land, and it was land he dreamed of securing in America. In fact, land ownership was the only basis of social prestige that he fully understood. With little knowledge of towns and even less of English, he preferred to settle among his kind—often with those from the same district in Norway—in the Upper Midwest, where he could continue to speak Norwegian and have at least his major associations with his countrymen. Nothing occurred to divert his interest to city life until later. Insofar as possible, he also sought to maintain the folkways of the homeland. He built a simple house of logs in Wisconsin or in the Pacific Northwest, of sod in Dakota. He might even recreate the typical *bonde* interior in his Iowa log house. The tools he brought with him in his immigrant chest were not unlike those in use on the frontier, and he learned to admire and even to prefer American tools and farm equipment. He made simple furniture, often modeled after what he had known in Europe, and, of sheer necessity, he built wagons to be drawn by oxen. He discovered soon enough that woolen clothing was ill suited to the hot summers of the Midwest, and he learned to modify his diet in accommodating himself to New World conditions. Corn (maize) replaced potatoes as a basic crop for man and beast, and wheat later became a cash product.

Whatever the location and new pattern of economic life, the Norwegian immigrant was invariably poor. His existence was one of back-breaking labor felling trees, grubbing out roots, breaking virgin soil, working the fields from dawn to sunset. And the tasks facing his wife were equally demanding and exhausting. Together they labored to create the better life they had hoped to find in America. If they succeeded in improving their lot—and a majority of the immigrants did—it was at the great price of endless toil, meager and monotonous diet, repeated setbacks from drouth, grasshoppers, and other plagues— often of extreme loneliness and disease against which there was little defense in the new settlement. If in the end they found, at least in modest measure, what they sought in this country, they also gave much in return.

II

It is commonly assumed that the Scandinavian immigrants, in contrast to those from Southern and Eastern Europe, were accepted with open arms by old-stock Americans. There is truth in this assumption, but it does not contain the whole truth. The word *Norwegian,* when spoken by a transplanted

New Englander, was not always intended as a compliment, and the word *Yankee*—often broadly defined to include the Irish as an English-speaking group—when spoken by the Norwegian once reflected distrust, dislike, and even fear. Relations between the older Americans and the Scandinavians were often strained, even bitter, especially during the early stage of settlement in any part of the country. The United States, while it did not wholly reject, also did not welcome the immigrant.

From one point of view this tension was unnatural. The Norwegians came from the North Sea area of Europe, where their occupations of farming, fishing, and sailing resembled those of the British. Their dominant Protestantism was not unlike that of the English, and its puritanical tendencies brought it close to the religion of the New Englander. The Haugean movement in Norway, which left a strong imprint on the majority of the immigrants, strongly resembled the Methodist movement in England. From an ethnic point of view, there was little difference between the old-stock American and the Scandinavian. Even their languages were similar. But these similarities, though impressive, did not automatically generate a spirit of total acceptance until fairly recent times.

The Norwegians who immigrated in the nineteenth and early twentieth centuries tended to settle closely together, although somewhat less so as they moved from early "colonies" to the Western states and provinces. They brought with them a strong sense of nationalism largely missing in the immigrants of an earlier day. In addition, they had a profound, basically rural, sense of unity which resisted exploitation of any kind. Even those who took up life in the city tended to concentrate into easily definable districts that resembled the "colonies" or "ghettos" of other immigrants. The many present-day evidences of Norwegian ethnicity are in no sense limited to the rural areas.

But when this much has been said, the fact remains that in general acculturation and assimiliation have been rapid in America—for the North European. The difficulties in the path of the Norwegian immigrant were many, but they were mild indeed when compared to those of the Italian, Slav, or Jew.

On the eve of Wisconsin's statehood, in 1846, a member of the legislative council remarked that Negroes were "as deserving of a vote and the privileges of freemen as are many of the whites, and more so as a class in this territory than are the Norwegians." They [the Negroes] were "more intelligent, more civilized, better acquainted with our institutions." The speaker had seen the Norwegians "living without what any other people would have considered the most absolute necessities of life, burrowed so to say in holes in the ground, in huts dug in the banks of the earth."

Early unprejudiced reports by Norwegian travelers support these remarks to a considerable degree. Consul Adam Løvenskjold in 1847 described his countrymen in Wisconsin as wretchedly poor, disillusioned, and plagued by sickness. Those who did not have log cabins lived "to a large extent in sod huts almost underground, with only the roofs projecting above the surface." The Norwegians took no part in politics and were apparently ignorant of it—a fact that led native Americans to refer to them as "Norwegian Indians." Ole Munch Ræder, a student of legal procedures, reported the same complaints but, like Løvenskjold, also told a story of patience and hope for improvement. He, too, stressed the fact that the immigrants were ignorant of American politics and therefore a prey to scheming politicians.

The Reverend J. W. C. Dietrichson, a pioneer church leader in Wisconsin, 1844–1850, had the same negative view of the overall condition of the early settlers, and he also referred in his writings to the expression "Norwegian Indians."

The conditions giving rise to such harsh judgments were, in addition to poverty, early confusion about American political issues and parties, the use of a fractured English spoken with a heavy accent, and a marked tendency to associate, as nearly as possible, only with people who spoke Norwegian and shared a common tradition. Justifiably, they were accused of being "clannish," but little attempt was made to understand the reasons behind this state of affairs.

Several factors contributed to misunderstanding. The early Norwegians, for example, regarded American clothing as inferior to their own and brought large quantities of their homespun clothes with them—much more so than did the Danish immigrants. While acknowledging the advantage of using American cottons in the oppressive heat of the summer and often advising later arrivals to buy such clothes after arrival in the New World, they welcomed shipments of warm woolens from the old country. They also spun yarn and knit clothing here, as they would have done in the homeland. With the passing of the years, however, they gradually adopted American wearing apparel. In recent times there is a renewed interest in national costumes, but these are worn only on festive occasions.

In their eating habits, the Norwegians, like other immigrants, were forced to conform largely to American patterns, but they delighted in preparing porridges, cheeses, and other milk products in the old manner. Until much later, the import of foreign food specialties was limited, but Norwegian-Americans gave an old-country flavor to basically American meals—and still do. Festive days, such as Christmas Eve, still call for such distinctly Scandinavian dishes as *rømmegrøt* (a thick sour cream porridge swimming in butter), *lutefisk* (made from dried cod preserved in brine), meat balls, *lefse* (a soft pancake-like speciality usually made from potatoes and baked on top of a stove), sweet soup, and the like. Such dishes, still featured at church dinners, had been the everyday food of the peasant folk in Norway, and eating them in the New World has been an important expression of their nostalgia for the homeland.

While Scandinavian eating habits aroused little or no hostility—in fact foreign foods generally have received ready acceptance in America—their love of drink certainly did. Even on a frontier where the saloon and hard drink were no strangers, excessive use of both by the Norwegians generated a measure of disgust among both old-stock Americans and pietistic countrymen. The sense of shame felt by gifted Norwegians over the drunkenness so common among "their people" was great enough to cause some of them to devote their lives to fighting this evil; a few even dedicated their considerable literary talents to the cause of prohibition.

In one other respect the Norwegian immigrants caused some resentment. Their Lutheran church—which in the long run proved to be an advantage in their being accepted as a Protestant North European group—was at first viewed as an institution having features in common with Catholicism. The

same early clergyman from Norway who gave an uncomplimentary picture of his countrymen in the Wisconsin of the
1840's—the Reverend J. W. C. Dietrichson—was a militant and
uncompromising champion of the Norwegian high church tradition. As the first minister ordained in the homeland to serve
the immigrants, he insisted, among other things, on rigid
adherence to the formal service of the Norwegian state church.
(It was rumored that he even wore his black gown while
milking his cow.) He immediately came into conflict, not only
with American traditional churches and sects, but also with
lay preachers strongly influenced by the pietistic Haugean
movement of the homeland.

When Dietrichson insisted on maintaining rigid church discipline, he was accused of papistry—and in fact was haled
before a justice of the peace. He was charged with assault and
battery for having removed from his church a drunken trouble-
maker who refused to sit in the place reserved for the excom-
municated. During the trial that followed, he was accused of
being a "pope," a "blackcoated gentleman" who had so much
power over his parishioners as to be a threat to American liberties. The jury returned a verdict of "guilty" and Dietrichson
was fined $5.00. It is reasonable to suppose that those immigrants
who remained loyal to their high church pastors were often
regarded as benighted and perhaps were pitied by members of
distinctly American congregations.

Another cause of strained relations between older Americans
and the Norwegian immigrants was the insistence of the early
ministers from Norway on creating and maintaining private
elementary schools in which religion, as well as other subjects,
was taught in Norwegian. The pastors objected to the absence
of religious instruction in the frontier "common" or public school
and let their hostility to it be widely known. Although the immigrants themselves welcomed the public schools and supported
them, the church leaders persisted in asking their members to
support and send their children to the parochial institutions.
Quite commonly the latter became only supplementary to the
publicly supported schools and were often conducted during
the summer months. If the latter were largely unsuccessful, another group that gave instruction on the secondary level met a

real need and lasted until well into the present century. They were usually called academies. Most of them faded with the universal introduction of the American high school.

The reaction to use of a foreign language is often that of suspicion on the part of Americans who speak only English. Partly because of the aggressive nationalist spirit of the Norwegians, partly because of the concentrated nature of their settlement, they continued to speak their native tongue for a long time. The language became larded with English words and expressions, but the syntax remained Norwegian. As with other transplanted peoples, the foreign language yielded very slowly to the new in the more intimate and personal areas of experience— last of all in religion. It is an interesting fact that as late as 1925 the reports of the president of the Norwegian Lutheran Church in America were written in Norwegian, and that in the same year slightly less than half of the sermons preached in this religious body were in English. There was, of course, open hostility to the use of any foreign language during World War I— and especially of a Germanic one—but the Norwegians experienced nothing like the intolerance shown the Germans, although there were unpleasant incidents growing out of overzealous patriotism.

The Norwegians in America were sometimes criticized for their liberal leanings in politics. In their opposition to slavery, they strongly supported the Union cause in the Civil War. They also identified with the Republican party, and to a considerable extent retained their affiliation with it in subsequent decades. But they were never conservative to any marked degree, contrary to the views of men like Oscar Handlin and Richard Hofstadter. In fact, they were generally progressive and at times radical in the years after 1890; in the words of one writer, they should be "ranked as one of the most consistently reform-bent ethnic groups in American society." In the New World they sought to "blend the agrarian values and institutions of the native land with the freedoms and abundance of America." Significantly, they did not, before 1915, fully understand the American ideal of rugged individualism, competitive capitalism, social Darwinism, social stratification, or the materialistic values of the Yankees they came in contact with. What they did understand was social cohesion, cooperation, the desire to develop a farm and home like their neighbor's, maybe a small business in which they dealt chiefly with their countrymen.

There were, of course, many exceptions, but more often than not the Norwegians, once they had become familiar with American ways, took a firm stand against industrial exploitation and supported reform movements aimed at maintaining a yeoman democracy in the Middle West. Thus, they were found on the side of progressive Republicanism, Populism, the La Follette movement in Wisconsin, the Nonpartisan League in North Dakota, and the Farmer-Labor party in Minnesota. While much work remains to be done on the subject of voting patterns, there can be no doubt at all that political leaders from their ranks and editors of their newspapers expressed a deeply ingrained feeling for community and a sensitivity to the needs of the underprivileged in their midst. It was said at one time that the Norwegians did not enter La Follette's camp; he entered theirs. Anti-Norwegian sentiment was inevitably expressed on many occasions in the Yankee press, thus adding an ethnic ingredient to the heated debates of pre-World War I days—and later.

From these comments it is clear that *rejection* is too strong a word when applied to the Norwegians or to the Scandinavians as a group. Nor were American stereotypes of them especially uncomplimentary or numerous. In any event, there seems to have been no widely known physical representation of the Scandinavians; cartoons of the Norwegians are hard to come by. Together with other Scandinavians, they were, of course, frequently referred to as "dumb Swedes," "herring chokers," and the like. Their fondness for snuff led to such references as "snoose chewers."

Perhaps more important was the capacity of the Scandinavians at a more recent date to laugh at themselves—their crudities of speech and manner—on the stage and in comic strips. Many Norwegians enjoyed, for example, the antics of such characters as "Han Ola og Han Per," which ran for many years in the widely circulated *Decorah-Posten.* The current Snoose Boulevard Festival revives life in the Cedar Avenue-Riverside area of Minneapolis with Scandinavian music and entertainment of a half-century ago. These events help to recall such comedians as Gus Heege, who appeared in various theaters in the early 1890's, playing "Yon Yonson" in dialect.

Although not rejected, the Norwegian-Americans were deeply conscious of having arrived in America at a comparatively late date. Seeking identity with early American life, they could and did point to the discovery of the New World by Leif Ericson about 1,000 A.D. But the saga record of this event, while reliable enough, is extremely vague as to particulars when compared to the Columbus story. Evidence of a presence in North America in more recent, but pre-Columbian, times was therefore certain to arouse Scandinavian enthusiasm and to prove convincing to perhaps a majority of them.

Late in 1898, a Swedish farmer near Kensington in Douglas County, Minnesota, reportedly discovered on his farm a stone slab lodged in the roots of a tree. He later found strange writings or symbols on one side of this stone, which, exhibited in the window of a bank in Kensington, aroused general interest. A copy of the inscription was sent to Professor O. J. Breda at the University of Minnesota, who was able, with help, to translate the writing.

The translation reads as follows: "8 Swedes and 22 Norwegians on an exploration journey from Vinland westward. We had our camp by 2 rocky islets one day's journey north of this stone. We were out fishing one day. When we came home we found 10 men red with blood and dead. AVM [Ave Maria] save us from evil. We have 10 men by the sea to look after our ships, 14 days' journey from this island. Year 1362."

If authentic, the stone's runic symbols mean that Scandinavians—Norwegians in particular—not only had explored the coasts of North America but had penetrated to the heart of the continent 130 years before Columbus and several hundred years before the French voyageurs.

Both Professor Breda and Professor George O. Curme of Northwestern University regarded the rune stone as spurious. In April, 1899, three distinguished specialists at Christiania University in Norway branded the "so-called rune stone" as "a crude fraud, perpetrated by a Swede with the aid of a chisel and meager knowledge of runic letters and English."

In 1907, despite this denunciation, a Norwegian-American farmer-historian, Hjalmar Rued Holand, visited the farm where the stone had been found, and from that time on the "rune" has been identified with his name. He wrote articles and gave lectures as a passionate champion of the stone's authenticity. When the Minnesota Historical Society published a report in 1912 favorable to the Kensington Stone, this fact, together with Holand's vigorous propaganda, generated widespread support, especially among Scandinavian Americans. Enthusiasm grew when Holand published a book, *The Kensington Stone*, in 1932. Eight years later, in *Westward from Vinland*, he elaborated the theory that the persons referred to in the inscription were members of an expedition sent out by King Magnus of Sweden and Norway under the direction of Paul Knutson in 1355. In a volume published in 1946, *America, 1355–1364: A New Chapter in Pre-Columbian History*, Holand offered further evidence for his theory by claiming that the well-known stone tower at Newport, Rhode Island, was not a seventeenth-century structure but a watch tower or fortification used much earlier by the Scandinavians. Again, in 1956, he returned to the battle, seeking to discredit his opponents with a new book, *Explorations in America Before Columbus*.

Despite the impressive list of Scandinavian linguists, archeologists, and runologists who have denounced the Kensington Stone as a hoax, Holand gathered a vast following, among old-stock Americans as well as Norwegians. Other writers have found further "evidence" for the soundness of Holand's contention or have developed theories somewhat divergent from his. Artifacts purportedly unearthed on this continent and stone carvings found in a variety of places have been submitted as proof of early Scandinavian explorations.

It is not the intention here to enter into the controversy over the authenticity of the stone, but only to point out that its many Norwegian supporters feel obligated, almost in a religious manner, to defend it. When runes are declared spurious by specialists in the Scandinavian countries or in northern Britain, that is the end of the matter. But the Norwegian-American does not give up so easily. In championing the Kensington Stone, although now far removed from the immigrant experience, he is giving expression to a burning desire for total acceptance as an American—as one whose ancestors were firmly planted on this continent long before the Anglo-Saxon arrived. A cartoon of some years ago described his sentiment: Indians, peering from behind trees at Columbus, were quoted as saying in Norwegian: "Now we are being discovered again."

III

Whether the Norwegians came in family groups—as they tended to do in the early stages of migration—or as individuals in the prime of youth, they soon found themselves to be both part of and contributors to what Fredrika Bremer once called a "Glorious New Scandinavia." This is true even if they are regarded, as once they were, merely as hewers of wood and drawers of water.

It is probable that immigrant leaders, pained or shocked into counterattack by the bigotry or ignorance of the superficial patriot, have overextolled the virtues of an imaginary "Norwegian America," a realm that took visible form in immigrant institutions but existed largely in the hearts of men—in both cases isolated by a curtain of language. But despite all exaggeration, the Norwegian immigrants created a unique press and a literature, founded churches and schools, and spoke a language that is best described as Norwegian American. These institutions, while not identical with those in the homeland, differed also from their counterparts in the New World. They symbolize a synthesis that underlies much of American history, emerging from the interplay of European heritage and American environment. Scholars have investigated aspects of the cultural transition, and the fruits of their study are valuable additions to national scholarship, but much work remains to be done, especially in the economic, social, and psychological fields.

The rural immigrant left behind him an economy that combinded small-scale cultivation of the soil with logging, fishing, sailing, and the handicrafts, in varying forms and in varying combinations. Pioneer life in America also demanded diversification and versatility, but it converted the immigrant into a producer of corn and wheat—products peculiarly associated with the frontier—subjected him to drouth, grasshopper plague, summer heat, winter cold, and frequent failure of a staple crop. In America he learned to depend more than before on cattle as a source of food and as beasts of burden. In these and other ways—in techniques of farming, in kinds of clothing, and in types of shelter—migration was attended by a many-sided transition from old-world patterns to new, from a mode of life suited to the coastal stretches of the North Sea to another that has evolved on the prairies of the Upper Midwest. It is hardly an exaggeration, therefore, to remark that it was the farmers—the most conservative social class and most bound by tradition, least given to economic experimentation or to newfangled ways—who had the first and most fundamental adjustment to make to American life.

Whatever the problems and agonies of accommodation, the transition from European peasant to American farmer was generally accompanied by economic betterment. One evidence of social advance was the growth in number and influence of a town-dwelling middle class—shopkeepers, bankers, agents, millers, managers, and operators, as well as editors, doctors, and lawyers—that quickly assumed a strategic position in the lives of the immigrant people. These townsfolk, although reinforced by urban elements from Europe, sprang for the most part from a rural background, with or without benefit of formal training, providing further proof of the fluid nature of the yeoman democracy that developed in the Middle West.

The part played by the middle class as interpreters of American life and as community leaders has been obscured by the extraordinary activity of the clergymen, and by the respect—even reverence—felt by a large part of the immigrants, especially those who arrived before about 1880, for the professional classes—first for the pastor and then to a lesser degree for the teacher, doctor, and editor. It should be remarked here that the immigrant middle class had made a fairly complete adjustment to American economic and social life by approximately 1890, that it had ties with other Americans, and that it was of necessity bilingual, an accomplishment mastered by the rural population only after considerable effort and lapse of time. It was prepared, for all practical purposes, to assume full participation in national affairs and to continue to furnish leaders among its countrymen.

To the farm and small-town middle class must be added the immigrant workers and craftsmen—especially carpenters, sailors, and fishermen—of the city. The Norwegians resembled the laboring classes of all ethnic groups and gave peculiar color and character to life in such cities as Brooklyn, Chicago, Minneapolis, San Francisco, and Seattle.

These classes and groups, both rural and urban, having made the transition from European to American life, became an integral part of the national economy and society, especially in the Middle West; yet to a certain extent they stood apart from their neighbors. They were at the same time Americans and Norwegian-Americans, citizens of an adopted country and children of the frontier, but bound to their countrymen by what has been termed "the silken bonds of love and sentiment." They were joined together by church and club, by language and press, in a union that was no less real for being lost to common sight. Theirs was a union, it is true, that was constantly dissolving in the acids of time, but it was preserved until well into the present century by new additions of immigrants from the homeland.

Nor was this Norwegian-American society more static than American life generally. As Norwegians moved from old settlement to new, from east to west, they enlarged the geographic basis of Norwegian-American life without destroying it. They made new but relatively slight adjustments to the demands of the new locale, and became in each transplanting somewhat more American—less distinguishable, that is, from the older human stock from the Atlantic seaboard or the Ohio Valley. Their basic unity and strength, however, were enhanced by newcomers who had found neither land nor opportunity in the older settlements and had joined the Norwegian-Americans in their westward trek.

In dealing with the theme of transition or Americanization, one must, of course, take a good look at the church and the immigrants' association with it. It is not improbable that the spiritual strength and energy of the settlers would have been dissipated had they not at an early date had the leadership of Lutheran ministers from Norway. These men, members of the official, therefore upper, class, had come into contact with the life and culture of the capital, Christiania, at a time when the homeland was experiencing a powerful stimulus from the forces of nationalism and a strong evangelical movement. They brought with them to the United States a deep love for the culture of Norway as well as dedication to their religious mission.

After effecting a central church organization in the 1850's, the Norwegian clergymen ruled their congregations with a kind of benevolent despotism. Their churches and homes, except for the public schools, were for a time the only centers of culture. The parsonage functioned as a community library and at times as a schoolhouse, where the children of the parish received most of their formal religious instruction and much of their other schooling as well. It was the center to which parishioners brought problems of every kind, both practical and cultural. In addition, with the majority of the immigrants united or interested in one church body—the so-called Norwegian Synod—there was created a feeling of unity or "nationalism" which class and local distinctions could not erase. The church, whatever its shortcomings, became an important basis of Norwegian-American life. The virulence of the later opposition to the clergy is a fair measure of the hold they had over the early settlers.

The immigrants apparently later wanted the substance of the churchly tradition without its many accretions, the main religious fabric without its social and cultural interlacings. It would be folly, for instance, to assume that the theological controversies among the Norwegian Americans over such questions as human freedom and individual election (or predestination)—controversies that split congregations asunder, set brother against brother, and created competing religious and educational institutions—were essentially the product of philosophical differences. Pastor and farmer alike were caught up helplessly in the whirlwinds that swept over the settlements. The simple truth is that democratic forces long building up in Europe, and to a lesser degree in America, were suddenly released on the frontier, and the immigrant was tossed about in the resulting gales.

After the storms of conflict had subsided, there emerged a church that was peculiarly Norwegian-American. When emotion and partisanship are fully eliminated from the discussion, it can be firmly stated that all the resulting Lutheran churches to which the Norwegians belonged were distinctly American in most of their external and in some of their internal forms, but at the same time they retained the theological essence of the Norwegian state church. One is impressed by the similarities found in these warring synods. Services and meetings were conducted in Norwegian as late as the 1920's, but from then on the move to English was rapid.

So long as it served the interests of the church, the clergymen—those educated in the New World as well as those who came from Norway—effectively exploited and cultivated the ethnic feeling of the immigrants and their offspring. During this period of distinctly Norwegian-American life, they also—if at times grudgingly—led their parishioners from a passive role as members of a state church into the active New World experience of building a church on the foundations of congregational self-government and self-support. When the use of Norwegian became—as increasingly it did after about 1915—both an embarrassment and a hindrance to church work and expansion, the clergy played down the ethnic character of their institution and ceased to be leaders in the conservation and encouragement of things Norwegian. The story is clearly told in the changing name of the church to which a slight majority of the immigrants belonged: Norwegian Lutheran to Evangelical Lutheran to American Lutheran—changes that also reflect mergers with such ethnic elements as Danes and Germans.

The Norwegian-Americans, virtually all of them literate, have been devoted readers of newspapers. In all, well over 500 papers in their own language, perhaps as many as 600, were launched in the New World. In the 1840's and 1850's the immigrants came to feel that they required, in addition to the church, the steadying influence of a newspaper with which they could keep in touch with their countrymen, exchange ideas, become informed of and active in public affairs, and, of course, be entertained. Another factor was the urge to win the respect of native Americans. It is significant that the Norwegian-American papers were not local in nature: they served people widely dispersed and welded them together because of common interests. The press also provided news from the old country, furnished people in the homeland with information about the immigrants, and served as media for the writings of Scandinavian and other authors.

The Norwegian newspapers, like the Swedish, swung toward the Republican party, not only because of its stand on slavery—a vital issue—but also because it was regarded as the exponent of free land to settlers. As indicated earlier, they tended to assume what must be regarded as a liberal stance in the late nineteenth and early twentieth centuries. But their chief purpose from the start was to familiarize their readers with American history, conditions, and issues. Thus they eased the transition process, enabled the immigrants to retain a healthy relationship with the homeland, and prepared them for an active role in American life.

After *Emigranten* (The Emigrant), which began publication in Wisconsin in 1852, the most influential Norwegian-American newspaper was *Skandinaven* (The Scandinavian), launched in 1866 in Chicago. Thereafter came such publications as *Decorah-Posten* (Iowa), *Minneapolis Tidende* (Tidings or Times), *Nordisk Tidende* of Brooklyn, and *Washington Posten* of Seattle, to mention only a few. Today two major newspapers survive—*Western Viking* in Seattle and *Nordisk Tidende,* both in centers of more recent immigration.

The role played by the church and press in the Americanization process made broad allowance for the continued use of Norwegian and an interest in the culture of the homeland. The church did not, until a later day, equate good citizenship with the exclusive use of English, and the press naturally encouraged the retention of the mother tongue. Had these institutions been alone in shaping the psyche of the immigrants, they might have applied the brakes effectively to the speedy cultural impoverishment demanded by the workaday world. If, as some sociologists maintain, the price of attaining economic success was the surrender of the European heritage, then obviously the situation could be saved for the second generation only by a wise and farsighted attitude on the part of the public school.

Unfortunately, no such view prevailed. It is no exaggeration to state that the Yankee "schoolmarm," more than any other person, killed in many immigrant children all interest in their origins and rich inheritance. The books used in the public school have treated American history and life in a manner that excludes virtually any reference to the ancestral country or to the role of the immigrant in the New World. Little wonder that his children sought to erase a close association with their legitimate past. Even worse was the refusal of many teachers to permit any use of a foreign language in the schools or on their playgrounds. It was the unusual child indeed who could resist the implication—he, his language, his ethnic group, and his parents were inferior. Fortunately some children had teachers of immigrant origin who understood the problems of the young minds in their charge—or parents who could guide them to a mature appreciation of two cultures.

Such unintended effects of the American educational system were all the more tragic and ironic when one recalls the enthusiasm with which the Scandinavians welcomed the public school. It had much to offer, and the immigrants knew it. To them it spelled opportunity for their children, and they supported it even in opposition to their pastors in the nineteenth century. Opportunity it did indeed offer for upward mobility—but at the price of an almost unbridgeable gap separating the immigrants from their offspring.

Marcus L. Hansen, a distinguished historian of immigration, maintained that a renewed interest in ethnic backgrounds would come with the third generation of transplanted Europeans. He was overoptimistic. Until the last few years there has been little interest in—but considerable resentment of—things Scandinavian among young and old alike, even among persons of the fourth generation. Very rarely does one find among them more than the most rudimentary knowledge of anything having to do with their European or family past. Until very recently, the young were, in this respect, indistinguishable from their parents.

During the past few years, however, a reaction has set in, partly because of the example given by the blacks, Chicanos, Indians, and others; partly, too, because of a growing disillusionment with the materialistic aspects of the great American Dream, the superficial trappings of our national life. In the search for new values, the Scandinavians—or at least some among them—seem to be reexamining their past and reconsidering its implications. This tendency is notably evident in the present student generation and is in fact a part of its widely publicized revolt. The ease and relatively low cost of transportation have generated considerable travel to the homeland. The consequences of renewed contacts with Norwegian kinsmen overseas may be considerable, and it is possible that many Norwegian-Americans are becoming restive in their status as second-class Anglo-Saxons.

IV

In considering Norwegian immigrant contributions to America's growth and life, one must of necessity begin with farming, as over half of the settlers engaged in agriculture at the turn of the century. It is well, in this connection, to recall that nowhere in the world did farming so nearly resemble that of this country as in Norway. The differences between cotter (*husmann*) and small freeholder (*bonde*)—especially in the southern and western parts of the country—were not great, because of geographical features and the fact that Norway had escaped feudalization. Farms and farm buildings were scattered, as in the New World, where *husmenn* and *bønder* began as equals and remained equals in adjusting to altered circumstances.

It was necessary, of course, to adapt to the use of oxen and, in the early years on the frontier, to find in corn a substitute for the potato as a major food for man and beast alike. Later, many of the Norwegians specialized in raising tobacco in Wisconsin. As the frontier moved westward, they turned to wheat production in Minnesota, the Dakotas, and the Canadian prairie provinces. When they settled in the Pacific Northwest, they returned to a mixed economy closely resembling that of the homeland. In the Rocky Mountain states, California, British Columbia, and eastern Washington and Oregon they learned to irrigate and to raise fruit as well as other products. But the majority in the Midwest became either dairy farmers or producers of such staple crops as wheat, corn, and grasses. In Wisconsin, Minnesota, northern Iowa, North and South Dakota, Saskatchewan, Alberta, and the Puget Sound area, eastern Washington, Idaho, Montana, and part of Texas they became a vital element in American agricultural life.

Many immigrants found it necessary to work in logging camps

and sawmills as a means of getting started as farmers or of supplementing their income. Others, as in the Pacific Northwest, engaged in felling trees during a backbreaking lifetime of clearing the land. Thus the Norwegians—and Swedes—went into the pine woods of northern Wisconsin and Minnesota as lumberjacks and continued this role in cutting and processing the redwoods and firs of California and Washington. The typical lumberjack, in fact, has often been thought of as a Scandinavian in the popular mind and in American folklore. Few Norwegians, however, made great fortunes in the lumber industry, although mention could be made of such exceptions as A. M. Holter in Montana and Simon Benson in Oregon.

It is not at all strange that Norwegian seamen, often sailing under foreign flags, should have visited these shores from colonial times, or that they remained at a later date to benefit from the higher wages, faster advancement, and somewhat better conditions aboard American vessels. Many jumped ship in New World ports; others entered the country legitimately with the expansion of commerce and emigration after the Civil War. These men knew the sea and all phases of the business of sailing; therefore they, with the Swedes, were sought after and preferred by American ship masters.

As the nineteenth century wore on, large numbers of Scandinavian sailors located in the ports of New England and the Middle Atlantic states. They not only sailed before the mast but engaged in wrecking and salvaging operations and worked in shipyards or as longshoremen. They became known, in fact, as persons willing to tackle any maritime task. In winter they frequently went south to enter the trade in lumber, cotton, sugar, and cattle. Similarly, they quickly appeared on the Great Lakes, often preferring the shorter periods away from home and the more humane treatment received aboard the ships that sailed the fresh waters. Inasmuch as such employment was seasonal in character, they usually took work elsewhere during the winter months.

In 1903, 36,761 native Americans and 22,737 naturalized citizens were employed in the U. S. merchant marine; of the latter, 7,615 were Norwegians, 6,268, Swedes, and 1,571, Danes—a total of 15,454 Scandinavians. The figures are similar for the Great

Lakes: on Lake Michigan, Scandinavians accounted for 63 percent of all sailors in 1869–70, and the Norwegians alone constituded 50 percent.

From the days of the gold rush in California, many Scandinavians sailed out of San Francisco in the deep-sea or coasting trades. Later they settled in such cities as Seattle, Portland, and Vancouver. The fleet of lumber schooners plying north from San Francisco was popularly called the "Scandinavian Navy," and the skippers of these craft were known by such names as "Midnight Olson" and "Shake-a-leg Johnson." In the East, perhaps a majority of the yachts and racing vessels have been manned by Norwegian crews.

Because of their skill as navigators, the Scandinavians were commonly given command of their ships. There had been at least 500 Norwegians captains of Great Lakes vessels by 1928. Some, like John North in San Francisco, became builders of ships. After World War I there were 12 Norwegian shipbuilding firms in New York alone. These and other activities attracted large numbers of carpenters, chandlers, ship brokers and the like from among their countrymen. Few Norwegian Americans, however, understood the business opportunities in shipping or cared to take the risks associated with them in the United States.

One Norwegian-American name is likely to remain in the annals of American shipping. It is that of Andrew Furuseth, who devoted the better part of his working years to fighting the poor pay and disgraceful treatment of sailors. An experienced seaman living in San Francisco, he became president of the International Seamen's Union in 1908; in this capacity, he engaged—much of the time as a lobbyist in Washington—in a long struggle for legislation on behalf of the men who went down to the sea in ships. His efforts, greatly aided by Senator Robert M. La Follette, finally resulted in the passage of the Seamen's Act of 1915, often called the sailor's Magna Carta of labor. So great were its benefits that Britain, Norway, and, later, other countries were compelled, in self-defense, to pass similar legislation.

Closely related to sailing is fishing; in this activity, too, the Norwegians transferred their traditions and skills to the New World—and for the same economic reasons. They settled along the Atlantic seaboard, the Great Lakes, the Gulf of Mexico, and the Pacific coast. They played an important role in harvesting mackerel and bluefish in the East, and a minor one in American whaling. They were prominent in working the oyster beds of the Chesapeake and in the seafood industry in the Gulf. It is estimated that a short time ago from 80 to 90 percent of the fishermen on Lake Superior's north shore were Norwegians. On the Pacific coast, they engaged actively in salmon, herring, cod, and tuna fishing and came almost to dominate the fishing of halibut. They were not long in the Puget Sound area before they went north to Alaska waters. As in logging and shipping, they did not become business leaders, although some started canneries and related firms. A prominent figure was Peter T. Buschmann, who sailed to Alaska in 1894 and there entered the fish processing field. The village of Petersburg, largely Norwegian in population, was named for him. If the Norwegian fishermen of the west coast have not profited hugely, they nevertheless own their modern radio-equipped boats. A visit to Ballard, a suburb of Seattle where many of them live, offers ample evidence of economic well-being.

Something like two-thirds of the basic American engineering innovations in the past century were the work of men born and educated in Europe. It was not, of course, solely the technological principles evolved and applied in the Old World that crossed the Atlantic. A considerable number of engineers trained in Europe and sensing the limitless opportunity inherent in the development of America's resources joined the larger body of Europeans who came as immigrants. They provided, after the mid-nineteenth century, a much-needed leadership on the technical frontiers. Men from every country in Europe offering advanced technological education furnished skills which were lacking in America until well into the twentieth century. The flight of engineers to these shores after about 1876 constituted a "brain drain" of proportions comparable to the migration of scientists and artists in our own day.

Not least among these engineers were the graduates of Norway's technical schools at Horten, Trondhjem (Trondheim), Christiania (Oslo), Bergen, and finally the national Institute of Technology, also in Trondheim. In some years as many as 25,

40, even 60 percent of a graduating class boarded ships for America.

Space does not permit anything like an adequate account of the contributions of these engineers. Mention must, however, be made of the work of F. W. Cappelen and K. O. Oustad in constructing concrete arch bridges over the Mississippi in the Twin Cities area of Minnesota, and of Thomas G. Pihlfeldt, for nearly half a century bridge engineer in Chicago, who improved on and perfected the bascule (teeter-totter) bridge that crosses the Chicago River at many points. Similarly, it is necessary to refer to Olaf Hoff's work in solving the practical problems involved in laying units of railroad tunnel in a prepared trench under the Detroit River. He contributed notably to the most revolutionary development in tunnelling since the discovery of the "shield" and the use of compressed air.

Just as Hoff's name is linked with the sunken-tube technique, Ole Singstad's is associated for all time with the special tunnel developed to serve the automobile. The Holland Tunnel in New York City was the first of any size or significance intended to meet the needs of present-day motor vehicles. Singstad made the detailed designs for this project, worked out its unique ventilation system, and completed its construction as chief engineer. In subsequent years he served either as chief engineer or as consultant on the most important vehicular tunnels constructed in all parts of the world.

No less significant have been the contributions of immigrant Norwegian engineers in the design and construction of skyscrapers, in metallurgy, in the development of intricate machinery, in scientific management, in architecture—in fact, in most of the many branches of technology. Yet they constitute only one division in a small army of engineers who came from the schools of Europe. Their story in the New World has been sadly neglected by students of immigration.

Except for small or moderate-sized retail stores and banks, the Norwegians have generally made few important contributions to business and finance. Their experience, both in Europe and in the New World, had not prepared them for such a role and it was not until recent times that they have had adequate reserves of capital. But there have been exceptions. Some engineers, after patenting inventions, moved over into production. Thus Tinius Olsen of Philadelphia, having developed new methods of testing materials of every kind, founded the Olsen Testing Machine Company. Magnus Bjorndal, an electrical engineer, built the Tech Laboratories of New Jersey into a successful manufacturing venture. Familiar to every American is the outboard motor bearing the name of Ole Evinrude. Although not a trained engineer, he had great mechanical skill, which he turned into both a workable product and a large industry in Milwaukee.

Well known to students of American business history is N. O. Nelson of St. Louis, whose large firm, the N. O. Nelson Manufacturing Company, specialized in building and plumbing materials and supplies. Socially progressive, he adopted an enlightened policy toward the welfare of his workers and was a pioneer in introducing profit-sharing with employees and customers alike. In many ways resembling Nelson was John A. Johnson, a producer of farm equipment and one-time president of the Gisholt Manufacturing Company in Madison, Wisconsin. His concern for his employees and his high ethical standards are thoroughly discussed in a recent biography.

The role of the church, both as a conserver of tradition and as a force in Americanization, has been discussed above. It remains to outline its contributions to education. Luther College of Decorah, Iowa, was founded in 1861 as a Norwegian Latin school to prepare young men for the Lutheran ministry; it later grew into a liberal arts college of the American variety. Augsburg College of Minneapolis began as the seminary for another synod of the church in 1869 and in time became another institution of higher learning. St. Olaf College of Northfield, Minnesota, similarly began as a Latin school in 1874, and later became the largest liberal arts college of Norwegian origin. Other colleges enjoying church support are Concordia in Moorhead, Minnesota, Augustana in Sioux Falls, South Dakota, and Pacific Lutheran University in Tacoma, Washington.

This list by no means exhausts the educational ventures of churchmen. Something like fifty institutions of secondary learning—usually called academies—were begun in various centers of Norwegian settlement. Unlike such schools as Luther and St. Olaf, most of them, after a struggle to survive, bowed out before the universal introduction of the American high school. But during their longer or shorter periods of existence they offered opportunities both to the children of immigrants and to the adult newcomers who naturally hesitated to sit with children in the public elementary school. While most of the academies stressed the study of classical languages, they also offered instruction in English, history, and in such practical fields as bookkeeping and arithmetic. Some courses were taught in Norwegian, others in English, and both languages were spoken by the students. The history of Norwegian-American life is replete with accounts of the services rendered by these institutions. Some of their graduates went on to colleges or universities and from there into the professions. The majority perhaps entered business or other occupations immediately following completion of the academy curriculum. The role of such institutions in making possible full participation in American life has been sorely neglected.

Space does not permit a recounting of the activities of the many workingmen's and mutual aid, literary, dramatic, social, and singing societies that sprang up everywhere. And only passing reference can be made to the Norwegian-American hospitals in Chicago, Brooklyn, and Minneapolis, to the seamen's missions in New York and San Francisco, or to the many other organizations that served the immigrants. One mutual aid society, started in Minneapolis in 1895, took the name Sons of Norway; today its many lodges have a membership of about 100,000. In recent years the Sons of Norway have assumed leadership in the promotion of a variety of cultural activities.

Another type of organization, now in its twilight period of life, is the *bygdelag*, whose membership is drawn from persons coming from the same home district in Norway. By the 1930's there were about fifty such societies. The first *lag* was begun in 1902 by immigrants from Valdres; thus the movement came relatively late in the migration story. At their annual or more frequent meetings, they spoke the dialect of the native district and enjoyed its music, dances, and food. They also published yearbooks that constitute a valuable historical source.

Also significant have been the Norwegian male choruses in urban centers. Groups organized as early as 1869 in La Crosse,

Wisconsin, and Decorah, Iowa. Today there are some 50 such choruses, which hold biennial festivals and sing in both Norwegian and English.

The literary tradition of the Norwegians is a strong one, and it was carried to these shores by the immigrants. Many issues of any Norwegian-American newspaper contained poems and stories, and there developed in the New World a number of gifted writers whose audience was limited by the language barrier. Such names as Waldemar Ager, Simon Johnson, and Peer Strømme are unknown to American readers. O. E. Rølvaag also wrote in Norwegian, but his greatest work, the novel *Giants in the Earth,* appeared in English in 1927. It is a story of Norwegian pioneer life in South Dakota, but its theme is the universal one of courageous struggle with nature and the price paid for the resulting victory.

Well known to the general public are such American-born writers as Martha Ostenso, author of *Wild Geese,* and Wallace Stegner, who wrote *The Big Rock Candy Mountain.* In the field of music, F. Melius Christiansen raised congregational singing to near perfection in his famous St. Olaf College Choir.

As might be expected, Norwegians have been active in American skiing. The legendary "Snowshoe Thompson" carried the mails over the Sierra Nevada Mountains from 1856 to 1876 after shaping by hand a pair of skis of the kind he had known in his native Telemark. For the people of California and Nevada there was no name for his skis other than "Norwegian snowshoes." But Thompson was not interested in sports; he merely served as a human link between people east and west of the High Sierras before the coming of the railroad. Elsewhere, in the 1880's, Norwegians started and directed ski clubs and a national ski organization. In other sports, Babe Didrikson Zaharias and Knut Rockne were outstanding.

Among explorers can be found such persons as Bernt Balchen, Admiral Byrd's pilot in the Antarctic and leader in creating Arctic bases for the U. S. Air Force, and Finn Ronne, who mapped and claimed for this country the last uncharted coastline in the Antarctic.

Science has attracted many Norwegian Americans. Ernest O. Lawrence, inventor of the cyclotron, won the Nobel Prize in physics in 1939. Many distinguished names could be given as innovators in chemistry, medicine, history, library science, archeology, linguistics, and biology, but a final appraisal of their careers cannot be made at this time. It is a fact, however, that the support given by the immigrants to education included the encouragement of advanced study. Norwegian-Americans in surprising numbers have earned doctoral degrees and have gone on to make solid additions to knowledge.

In journalism, Victor F. Lawson of Chicago is worthy of special mention. The son of Iver Lawson, one of the founders of *Skandinaven,* he became publisher of the *Chicago Daily News,* president of the Associated Press, and originator of the Postal Savings Bank. From a large number of governors and congressmen, Knute Nelson emerges as of special, if not typical, significance. He served as governor of Minnesota in the early 1890's and was both congressman and senator from that state.

The purpose here, however, is not to attempt a cataloguing of famous names, but to consider individuals from the point of view of the traditions and experiences of the immigrant community. One who emerged from a typical rural Norwegian-American settlement in Minnesota was Thorstein Bunde Veblen, perhaps the most original American social and economic thinker. In such books as *The Theory of the Leisure Class* and *The Theory of Business Enterprise,* he savagely attacked the greed, wastefulness, and general lack of good purpose in American capitalism. What is most significant about his writings is the fact that he judged a profit-mad business world against a background of immigrant values or standards of morality—as did the politicians who were active in progressive movements in the Upper Midwest.

If Veblen attacked the mores of modern capitalism, O. E. Rølvaag, the author, challenged American spiritual wastefulness. Deeply concerned with what happened to people psychologically in the immigration experience, he became a leading exponent of cultural ecology. In everything that he wrote and in his many discussions of the subject, he urged the retention of what is best in the immigrant's tradition. He understood very well the problems presented in the assimilation process, and he warned of the danger of being seduced by the less attractive, materialistic features of American life. When clergymen began to see their ethnic tradition as a stumbling block, he attacked them for their shortsightedness and lack of leadership. One of his books, *Omkring Fædrearven* (Concerning Our Heritage), was written in the heat of journalistic battle and has many shortcomings. But it is perhaps the most effective plea yet penned for a mature attitude toward immigrant culture and for an enriched American spiritual life. It deserves a good translation.

SELECTED BIBLIOGRAPHY

BJORK, KENNETH O. *Saga in Steel and Concrete: Norwegian Engineers in America.* Norwegian-American Historical Association, Northfield, Minnesota, 1947.

————. *West of the Great Divide: Norwegian Migration to the Pacific Coast, 1847–1893.* Norwegian-American Historical Association, Northfield, 1958.

BLEGEN, THEODORE C. (ed.) *Land of Their Choice: The Immigrants Write Home.* Minneapolis, University of Minnesota Press, 1955.

————. *Norwegian Migration to America, 1825–1860.* New York: Arno, 1969.

————. *Norwegian Migration to America: The American Transition.* Norwegian-American Historical Association, Northfield, 1940.

GJERSET, KNUT. *Norwegian Sailors in American Waters: A Study in the History of Maritime Activity on the Eastern Seaboard.* Norwegian-American Historical Association, Northfield, 1933.

————. *Norwegian Sailors on the Great Lakes: A Study in the History of American Inland Transportation.* Norwegian-American Historical Association, Northfield, 1928.

HUSTVEDT, LLOYD. *Rasmus Bjørn Anderson: Pioneer Scholar.* Norwegian-American Historical Association, Northfield, 1966.

LARSON, AGNES M. *John A. Johnson: An Uncommon American.* Norwegian-American Historical Association, Northfield, 1969.

LARSON, LAURENCE M. *The Changing West and Other Essays.* Plainview, N. Y.: Books for Libraries, 1968.

MALMIN, GUNNAR J., ed. and tr. *America in the Forties: The Letters of Ole Munch Ræder.* Norwegian-American Historical Association, Northfield, 1929.

NELSON, E. CLIFFORD, ed. *A Pioneer Churchman: J. W. C. Dietrichson in Wisconsin, 1844–1850.* New York: Twayne, 1973.

Norwegian-American Studies and Records, vol. 1–26. Norwegian-American Historical Association, Northfield.

QUALEY, CARLTON C. *Norwegian Settlement in the United States.* New York: Arno, 1970.

SEMMINGSEN, INGRID. *Veien most Vest,* 2 vols. Aschehoug, Oslo, 1941, 1950.

WEFALD, JON. *A Voice of Protest: Norwegians in American Politics, 1890–1917.* Norwegian-American Historical Association, Northfield, 1971.

IV

From "Paddy" to the Presidency: The Irish in America

By THOMAS J. CURRAN
St. John's University

IRELAND was always an impoverished country, especially during the seventeenth, eighteenth, and nineteenth centuries. It knew the meaning of poverty, hunger, and famine. While some Irishmen emigrated earlier, only in the nineteenth century did millions of Irishmen leave their homeland. Why? What brought the Irish to the United States? How were they received by the native Americans? How successful were the Irish immigrants and their descendants?

Before addressing these questions, however, it might be well to ask whom the Irish blamed for their economic plight. They placed much of the blame on the English. English law restricted them: first, it prevented any industrialization in Ireland. Secondly, it prohibited Catholics—those who refused to recognize the Crown's religious and political dominance—from owning land. Thus these measures reduced the bulk of the Irish population to the status of landless peasants. Furthermore, until the nineteenth century, the Irish had to pay tithes to the Anglican church, a fact which they bitterly resented.

The Irish peasants lived on small land holdings, land which they were forbidden to own; until the 1870's, they could only rent. Those rents tended to increase as the population grew. Between 1740 and 1840, the Irish population tripled. With the increased population came increased demands for land and its concomitant, increased rents. The Irish called them rack rents.

95

Unfortunately, the tremendous increase in population alluded to above brought the Irish peasant to a situation where he depended exclusively on the potato for his food. He also grew, on the more arable land, wheat with which he paid these rack rents. So, the Irish farmer had a rent crop, usually wheat, and a subsistence crop, usually the potato. As the population increased, families found themselves dividing up their limited holdings into smaller and smaller plots. The size of the holdings became so precariously small that even a minimal decline in the output of the soil would have disastrous consequences for large numbers of people.

We know that in 1741 such a disaster did take place. But the potato blight of the 1740's received little publicity, and the horrors of the 1741 blight and famine did not become widely known. It was treated as a local phenomenon. Communication and transportation were not readily available. That is, newspapers were not widely distributed, and the steam press and the telegraph were not yet in existence. The same technological scarcity was apparent in the field of transportation. Railroads were not yet built. Roads and ships were in relatively short supply. Thus, even if the Irish wanted to leave in 1741, they would have found it most difficult.

A century later, however, the situation was different. A number of factors encouraged the Irish to leave. Where Anglo-Irish landlords originally had benefited from the huge increase in the population, there were offsetting problems in the 1830's. In 1838, the British Parliament placed full responsibility for those Irish in the poorhouses on the landlords of Ireland. No longer would these charity cases be supported by English taxes. Thus, even before the famine, some Irish landlords helped their peasants leave Ireland for Scotland, England, or the United States. They hoped thereby to reduce their own poor law taxes.

At about the same time, more and more landlords hoped to make their land more profitable by turning it to sheep grazing and cattle grazing. Thus, throughout, the nineteenth century, as rack rents increased and tenants found it impossible to pay them, the landlords began to evict their tenants and, in many cases, consolidated their holdings. This only intensified the Irish bitterness against the English.

When the great famine of 1845–47 struck, the telegraph and railroad spread the word throughout Ireland and Europe. Disaster faced the Irish people. Not only was emigration a solution for many, but the ships were available to carry the Irish away from their homeland. Because of their poverty, many Irish were accustomed to supplement their incomes by leaving home temporarily and working in Ulster, Scotland, and England. Now that the land had betrayed them, it was easier for them to contemplate a more permanent move.

The potato famine was felt most heavily in the southern part of Ireland. The area of Ulster and Down and the eastern segment of the country were not quite so hard hit by the blight, for these areas did not depend so heavily on the potato. The famine of 1845–47, however, was a disaster of major proportions to the Catholic Irish. Almost half the population was lost either through death or emigration.

Two factors induced a major portion of the Irish emigrants to go to America. Some Irish had already settled in the United States. They wrote home glowing reports of their own progress and the tremendous opportunities available in the States. America became a beacon of hope for the Irish who were forced to flee their homeland. Then, too, more and more American ships were going to England delivering cotton among other things and more English ships traveled back to America. This increased trade provided the vehicles which carried the nineteenth-century Irish from Ireland to America. Tickets, of course, had to be bought. Very often the most impoverished Irish could not leave Ireland for they lacked the means. It was only those who could somehow earn a little money or were given it by friends or relatives in America who could buy tickets and board a ship to the United States.

Generally, passengers had to supply their own food. All too often, an Irishman had only the fifteen or twenty dollars it cost for his passage. For fifteen dollars, you could go on a lumber boat and stop in Canada. Often the Irish boarded these ships with a sack of potatoes as their sole means of sustenance. Not unnaturally, the death rate of these ships was almost as great as the death rate on the slave ships that carried Afro-Americans from their homelands in Africa to the New World. Depending on the ship, the death rate would be somewhere between five and twelve percent—more often closer to the latter than the former.

What kind of men and women left Ireland? The most obvious thing about the nineteenth-century Irish, whether they left in the famine years or thereafter, was a deep and abiding hatred for the English. Secondly, the Irish came as people who were politically alert. Their great leaders, especially Daniel O'Connell, had shown them the advantages of organizing and using their political power, and it had brought them, at least in 1829, the Catholic Emancipation Act, which granted political rights. Thirdly, they recognized the value of vigilante action. That is, the landlords' eviction notices led the Irish to organize into reaction groups; the boycott movement in the last quarter of the nineteenth century was an example. The procedure was to prevent the eviction of tenants. If, nevertheless, tenants were evicted, then the boycotters moved them back into their homes. Any family attempting to rent the home was dealt with harshly by the local neighbors. The result was violence on one side as well as political pressure on the other. Fourthly, there was the realization—a continuing factor even today—that temporary relief from their problems could be found in alcohol. They found in drink a way to forget their harsh living conditions and their difficult circumstances.

Once on the ship, the big concern for the emigrant was what awaited him. Many had read the American letters which led them to believe that things would be better in the New World. They were a group of people with a bitter history that had seen them dominated since the twelfth century by the English, and since the sixteenth century that dominance had become particularly galling because of the religious rivalry between Protestant England and Catholic Ireland. Their poverty was always something they attributed to "the bloody English." Their tendency to go to the bottle as a temporary form of relief for their difficulties was something that was noted time and time again in England as well as in Ireland itself.

But the Irish also brought with them ambition, the wish to create a new life for themselves, and the hope that they would be welcomed. But unfortunately they also brought with them their Catholicism, their bitterness toward the English, their poverty, and their drinking habits. These factors made them less than welcome. Instead of the hoped-for improvements, the Irish encountered rejection.

Most native-born Americans were Protestants. They viewed popery with suspicion. The symbol for the Irish was the name "Paddy." Paddy was a supporter of popery, so Paddy was condemned in an alliterative appellation, Paddy and popery. Then. too, the Paddy stereotype showed him to be rather pig-faced, dirty, stubborn, and, of course, very, very poor.

What kind of people objected to the Irish? Why did they do so? Were there any reasonable grounds for this rejection? In almost every society known to man, and the most recent anthropological studies confirm this view, most people are frightened of newcomers. They distrust that which is strange, that which is foreign. In the United States, particularly when the Irish came in large numbers in the nineteenth century, this distrust became rather formidable. It rested on the poverty and the popery of Paddy and on certain traits that the Irishman brought with him.

In the nineteenth century, the United States was beginning to undergo its basic transformation from an agrarian to an industrialized society. That take-off period was difficult for many Americans because it brought many changes, and change frequently induces suspicion. New values appeared to replace traditional norms.

The criterion of worth became wealth. But the Irish were poor. Their poverty was evident in their shanties and their occupations. By and large the Irish worked in menial jobs. In New York City, for example, three out of every four Irishmen were unskilled laborers.

The consequences of a large unskilled labor pool in the major port cities of the United States—Boston, Philadelphia, New York—was a decline in wages. Whereas in 1830, an unskilled laborer received one dollar or even sometimes $1.25 a day, by 1850, his wage declined to 75¢ a day. To native-born workers, the explanation for the decline was fairly simple: an increase in the labor supply forced a decrease in wages. However, while American labor was hostile to a large influx of workers, to the employer class of the United States, it was a distinct advantage to have these immigrants.

Most American economists of the nineteenth century saw the immigrant as worth approximately $800 to $1,000 to the nation. He came during the most productive period of his life that is, from 15 to 40 and in addition to becoming a producer, he was also a consumer as well as a tenant.

This initial rejection encountered by the nineteenth-century Irish created in the hearts of many of the immigrants a kind of nostalgia for the old country. The hovels, the poverty and the oppression in which they had lived were forgotten. The sketches, songs, and plays of the Irish, and certainly the Irish lament, summarized much of the feeling of neglect and rejection they met with in the United States.

How and why did this rejection become organized? Quite simply, beginning as early as 1835, the Irish, even though they were not as numerous as they became in 1845–55, were already supplying the balance of power in the political contests in New York City. The Irish were considered unprincipled foreigners and corrupters of the American system. Watergate may be a version of native-born corruption of the 1970's, but in the 1840's, 1850's, and 1860's, whenever one heard the word corruption mentioned it would be accompanied by the word "Irish." "Irish" became synonymous not only with Paddy and popery but also with political corruption. It was not unknown, particularly for Democratic politicians, to win an election with the help of Irishmen who had not been in the country more than a day. Tammany Hall politicians would meet a boat at the dock in New York City, take off its human cargo, bring it before a Municipal Court judge and have these men naturalized and then taken to vote. To many Americans, this method was a perversion of democracy. Those who lost political power as a result of this type of electoral behavior were incensed.

Thus the Native American party was formed in 1835 in New York City. The party did not place great stress on keeping the Irish out of New York, nor was it concerned with eliminating all immigration. The basic premise upon which the Native American party rested was simply that America must be ruled by native-born Americans. No foreign-born person should be allowed to vote or to hold public office.

The initial rejection of the Irish in organized form was a rejection of their political power. The Native American party enjoyed a certain amount of success. The party elected a mayor of New York City in 1837. But the success of the movement was relatively short-lived because, again, both the Democratic party and the Whig party, the two major political organizations of the period, were not nominating Irish-born citizens. The fact of the matter was that most native-born Americans, while they might have a hostility and an aversion to the Irish, still hoped that the Irish could be assimilated and become acclimated to their roles as American citizens. In the 1840's, a second organized effort at restricting the political power of the Irish took place with the formation of the American Republican party. This political group also wanted to have America governed by Americans and sought the elimination of the election or selection of foreign-born citizens for any public office. The party's anti-foreignism was clearly aimed at the Irish Catholics. An additional grievance was the Catholic school system.

The Catholic Irish, from the very beginning, set up their own parochial school system essentially for defensive reasons. For example, in New York City the public schools were controlled by Anglo-Protestants. They viewed the Catholics of the nineteenth century in the same way some people viewed the Communists in the twentieth century. This was part of their heritage, and they just accepted the idea that Catholics were somehow dangerous and alien to the American way of life. The schools placed heavy emphasis on Catholic limitations of power, and on the alleged un-Americanism of the Irish because they took orders from a foreign prince in Rome, the Pope. They accused the Church of being opposed to the doctrine of separation of church and state. Thus, the Catholics set up their school system to defend themselves against this kind of hostility in the public schools.

As more and more Irish came, they came without assets which would allow them to pay for their own educational system, the so-called parochial school system. They then made demands for public money. This was a constant irritant in Catholic-Protestant relations in both the nineteenth and twentieth centuries. In 1840, Governor William H. Seward of New York actually called for public aid to parochial education. This was one of the factors which led to the formation of the American Republican party.

The American Republican party was officially organized in 1843 and had very much the same ideas as the Native American party: Americans to govern America and no foreign-born in public office. In addition, they added the stipulation that no public money be used for parochial education and the demand that the Bible must remain in use in the public schools. The Roman Catholics felt that the King James version was heretical. They wanted to use the Douay-Rheims or Catholic version of the Bible, and again this led to problems.

The American Republicans enjoyed a certain amount of success in Philadelphia, Boston, and New York, where they were highly visible, and where rather large numbers of Irish had gathered. The movement failed when it attempted to go national. Many Americans rejected the party because it was termed un-American in attempting to proscribe the Irish because they were Catholic. Party members were also called "church burners" because of the attack by some members on Catholic churches in Philadelphia in the famous Kensington riots of 1844.

In the period from 1845 to 1855 over a million Irish arrived in the United States. In New York State, the foreign-born segment of the population increased to well over twenty percent of the population. One out of every five New Yorkers was foreign-born, and the bulk of them were Irish. This invasion was rather frightening to many Americans. Certainly, one can sympathize with the native-born who looked around and saw in New York City, for example, the budget going from some two million dollars in the 1840's to well over five million dollars in the 1850's. An explanation could be found in the increase in crime and public welfare costs. The Irish were blamed for both. These factors led many to believe that something must be done about the Irish situation.

The failure of the American Republicans coupled with the increased power of the foreign-born led the nativists to form secret societies. The most famous of these was called the Order of the Star Spangled Banner, sometimes referred to as the Sires of '76. Generally they were known as the Know-Nothings. Their platform was very similar to the Native American party of 1835 and the American Republican party of the 1840's, that is, that America must be directed by Americans and that no foreign-born should hold public office. They also called for an extension of the period of naturalization. Though very few foreign-born citizens were elected to public office, still the worry about the Irish immigrants persisted, especially in the East. But the nativists were able to capture only one out of every three American voters. The Know-Nothing party won the statewide election in New York in 1855, and captured the gubernatorial and legislative offices in Massachusetts in 1854–55. They also elected ninety members of the thirty-fourth Congress, but the slavery issue still dominated the period. The threat of the Irish was placed in a secondary category.

The Civil War is sometimes thought as having brought about the acceptance of the Irish. Their participation in the war, it was held, mixed their blood with the native-born in death in defense of the union and terminated the hostility to the Irish in America. Unfortunately, this is not true. The Irish continued to find themselves discriminated against in the 1870's, the 1880's, and even into the 1890's, and the strongest argument against them was their allegiance to the Roman Catholic Church. The dominant factor in rejecting the Irish in post-Civil War America was no longer their poverty or political corruption, although Thomas Nast's brilliant cartoons asserted that the Irish had allied themselves with the Democratic party and corruption. Rejection of the Irish in the '70s and '80s centered on their religion.

The next great xenophobic outburst directed against the Irish was the famous American Protective Association organized in 1887 and reaching the height of its power in 1894–95. Again the Irish were attacked, not so much because they were Irish, but because they were Catholics. Their Catholicism was considered to be totally unacceptable to the bulk of Protestant Americans.

The kinds of people who became involved in these xenophobic outbursts were often sincere Americans. They had grievances that they felt were legitimate. The unease stemming from the persistence of rising welfare costs, crime, and rowdyism is easy to understand. Many agreed with one lawyer's proposed solution in 1883: if you want to get rid of crime in New York City, put all the Irish on board a number of large ships and send them back to Ireland.

In many of the municipalities in this period, the Irish made up to seventy percent of the criminal inhabitants in the jails. In eliminating all the Irish, there would be no criminals, the argument went. At the same time, the country would also be rid of a welfare problem. That solution was unacceptable to most Americans, but even outstanding Americans, the historian and future President Woodrow Wilson, for example, felt that the Irish immigrant was mainly a problem and definitely not an asset.

It was not, of course, until the twentieth century—when the emphasis of the nativists shifted to the so-called newer immigrants, when anti-Catholicism gave way to anti-Semitism, and "anti-Paddy" propaganda gave way to "anti-Pasquale"—that we begin to see the movement of the Irish into the mainstream of American life both political, social, and economic.

Initially, the Irish who came to the United States with the hope of immediately benefiting from the transition, did not win all that they expected. Nevertheless, their compatriots in Ireland continued to emigrate to America. The hostility of many native Americans did not deter them.

Of course, not all the Irish were rejected. Some did become successful. They managed to accommodate themselves to the American establishment and find acceptance. Others found a satisfactory status in politics and the church. By the 1860's certainly, some Irishmen had become Americanized and were accepted by the establishment. Generally, these men came before the outbreak of the famine. Two examples are the Roman Catholic James Shields, who was born in County Tyrone and came to this country in the early 1830's, and John Morrissey, another Roman Catholic who came to America as a child from County Tipperary and settled in Troy, New York with his parents. Both were successful.

In the case of General Shields, he was educated and very well prepared by the time he came to America. His first job was as a school teacher in Kaskasia, Illinois. He studied law and went into partnership with a local German who is discussed in the chapter on the Germans, Gustave Koerner. In 1835, Shields had launched a political career that took him into the Illinois State Legislature where he became a colleague of Abraham Lincoln and Stephen A. Douglas. He then became a Supreme Court Judge in Illinois, the Auditor of Illinois, a General in the Mexican War and then a United States Senator from Illinois in 1849 as a kind of reward for his military service.

Shields' career was rather extraordinary because he was the only man in American political life to represent three states in the United States Senate: Illinois, 1849–55, Minnesota, 1858–59, and finally, in 1879, United States Senator from Missouri. In 1861, he took up the cudgels on behalf of the Union and had a somewhat checkered military career. In his version of it in the 1870's, he presented his accomplishments as a far grander thing than perhaps they were in reality. The point is that Shields did make it, he was accepted by both Catholics and non-Catholics.

He represents the coming of age of the Irish, and in the 1870's, General James Shields went to Irish-American functions relating his experiences as a General in the Mexican War and the Civil War and his supposed friendship with Abraham Lincoln. Almost everyone tried to point to his connection with Lincoln in order to become fully Americanized in the post-Civil War period. In politics, Lincoln was a Whig, and Shields remained essentially a Democrat. They were far from friendly; they almost fought a duel in the 1840's. Still Shields gave to the famine Irish an idol, a man who had made it in the secular world. He was widely hailed and widely respected by them. He was not, however, part of the famine Irish. He was obviously a man who was fairly well trained in his native land. That is, he had a good common school education, and his uncle, who had attended the University of Edinburgh, gave him some additional training. He felt secure enough to become a school teacher shortly after arriving in Illinois in 1831-32. One should also mention that Shields' uncle was a congressman from Ohio: this obviously helped.

John Morrissey's career was equally impressive. He was a Roman Catholic who came to this country in 1833; but he did not remain in New York City. His parents took him to Troy,

New York, then a frontier town. There he had the benefit of a good common school education and only later moved to New York City. He became one of the major saloon keepers and a staunch supporter of the Democratic party. In New York, the Democratic party made effective use of his fist-fighting ability. It used him as the leader of one of its political gangs. One way to capture an election in New York City was to kidnap the opposition party's man who handed out the ballots. Gangs were often used for this purpose.

For John Morrissey, the saloon and fighting were the agencies by which he transformed himself from an immigrant to a successful Irish-American. He became the world champion of boxing in 1858, but his training, if that is the word we can use, was picked up in a variety of saloons, battling other gangs for control of polling stations. In one of his fights in 1855 with an opponent, the famous Butcher Boy Poole, he ran into difficulties. One of his supporters became so incensed that he pulled out a gun and shot the Butcher Boy. Poole, who was the strongman for the opposition Know-Nothing party, died as a result. Morrissey was not implicated. With the money he had acquired in New York City, Morrissey went to Saratoga and purchased the Saratoga Race Track during the American Civil War. This provided an additional base for his financial growth.

After the Civil War, he was elected to congress as a Democrat from Troy for two consecutive terms and decided not to run for reelection in 1870. Subsequently he ran for the New York State Senate and was elected. He continued his ownership of the race track and some gambling casinos and died happily in his bed in his seventieth year. His life indicates that in nineteenth-century America, a man posessing certain kinds of abilities could succeed. Both Shields and Morrissey arrived before the famine. Those who came as a result of the famine had far different problems.

The famine Irish had very little education and they were poor. For them, the Roman Catholic church was a psychic support that was of immeasurable comfort. In the church, they were not abused. Poverty was not condemned. They found a sense of their own worthiness, a sense of their own being.

Very often the Irish were served by Irish-born clergymen.

The most prominent Irish clergyman in the Catholic church in the pre- and post-Civil War period was the Irish-born Archbishop John Hughes who came to Philadelphia as a boy of ten. Hughes was a very aggressive and combative leader. He instilled in his flock a feeling of their own worth, and he insisted that the Irish had nothing to apologize for. In this sense, the church served as a psychic support for the Irish.

It also provided an avenue by which individuals and their families could feel that they had arrived in America. Many of us might find it difficult to think in terms of making it by becoming clergymen. In Ireland, even to this day, to have a brother who is a priest or a son who is a priest is a mark of distinction. While it might be true that many of the famine Irish and their descendants did not appear to prosper financially, they did get a sense of their own worth by the fact that they might have a son or some relative who was a priest. The priesthood in and of itself was an avenue whereby a family could acquire a feeling of its own worthiness.

While many of the Irish did not make substantial sums of money, their children worked. Status might be acquired through the ownership of one's own home. Individually their salaries might not be large, but together they were substantial enough so that some were able to purchase their own homes. In Ireland, as you will recall, in the 1840's and 1850's, the Irish were barred from becoming homeowners. Many of the Irish felt that they had really arrived when they owned their own homes. Many ran these as rooming houses. By 1865, however, the Irish felt more secure. In 1865, a song, "No Irish Need Apply" became popular. That particular phrase, of course, was pejorative, but the Irish turned it into a humorous song:

> I'm a decent boy just landed
> From the town of Ballyfad
> I want a situation, yes
> And I want it very bad
> I've seen employment advertised
> Just the thing says I
> But the dirty spalpin ended with
> No Irish need apply.

I started out to find the house
I got it mighty soon
There I found the old chap seated
He was reading the Tribune
I told him what I came for
When he in a rage did fly
No, he says, you are a Paddy
No Irish need apply.
Well I gets my dander rising
And I'd like to black his eye
To tell an Irish gentleman
No Irish need apply.
Some do think it is misfortune
To be christened Paddy or Dan
To me it is an honor
To be born an Irishman.

Despite this flippancy on the part of the Irish, many native Americans retained their suspicion of the Celts. For example, in 1883, Abraham Lincoln's former secretary, and a future Secretary of State, John Hay, published anonymously a novel dealing with the Irish where they were viewed as a threat to the security and well-being of the American economy, as well as to the American political system. The Irish were still considered synonymous with corruption, with laziness, and with some kind of radical activity. This radical activity label stemmed from the actions of the Molly McGuires, a secret terrorist organization that operated in Pennsylvania. Then, again, the Knights of Labor were led by the Irish-American, Terence Powderly. Nonetheless, it was apparent that despite John Hay and the feeling among some that the Irish were not acceptable, the Irish believed they were good Americans, even though they remained concerned about Ireland.

Certainly, many of the Irish-Americans were very much interested in the Fenian Brotherhood. There was an abortive attempt in 1867 to invade Canada as part of an uprising that was supposed to be coordinated with an uprising in Ireland. Still the Democratic party politicians felt it was incumbent upon them to heap constant condemnation on the British for their failure to do justice to Ireland. Even the Republican party in

1884 adopted this attitude. It was quite obvious that the political power of the Irish was a reality, and both the Democrats and Republicans strove for their support.

By the end of the nineteenth century, with the influx of large numbers of Southern and Eastern Europeans, many native Americans formerly opposed to the Irish now insisted that they had the capacity to assimilate. The appearance of large numbers of Jews, Slavs, and Italians led many Americans to insist that the Irish were an asset; their Americanization was now recognized. Hostility shifted from the Irish to the newer immigrants.

In the twentieth century, the Irish appear assimilated. A man like Harry Golden writing about his experiences in the East side of the New York ghetto in the World War I era, held that to be an American was to be like the Irish policeman. Many of the newly arrived immigrants believed that Irish and American were synonymous terms. For these immigrants, the Irish had arrived. The days of No Irish Need Apply had long since passed. The twentieth century saw two efforts on the part of Irish-Americans to achieve the presidency first in 1928 and again in 1960. In little more than a century, the Irish-Americans' assimilation was a reality.

But do the Kennedys truly represent the Irish? Or, does the Irish-American novelist, James Farrell, in his Studs Lonigan trilogy, represent the actual accomplishments of the Irish-Americans? If one asks how successful were the Irish, one has to raise another query, what did the Irish expect? The Irish who came to America, probably hoped that they could retain their Roman Catholic religion, despite the fears of their Irish prelates, probably hoped for material prosperity, and probably hoped that they could aid in the liberation of Ireland. In some ways the Irish have been successful in all these things. Certainly the Roman Catholic Church is predominantly an Irish-American church, since even today some fifty percent of the Catholic hierarchy is made up of Irish-Americans.

What about material prosperity? Certainly, the Irish have been successful in this regard as well. That is, one can clearly see the distinction between the life-style of today's Irish and the earlier shanty Irish, so-called because many of the Irish when they arrived in the major cities of industrial North America were forced to live in cellars and shanties, primarily because they could not gain access to better living quarters. Not only did they not have the requisite funds; many landlords felt they were a deleterious influence on the building and neighborhood because of their unfamilarity with things like plumbing and running water.

The point is that contrasting the life-style of the nineteenth century, which was accompanied by rejection by various pro-American nativist groups, with the 1970's, where no basic anti-Irish movement exists, indicates tremendous advancement for the Irish-Americans. There has been a change in the native American attitude toward the Irish-Americans. The Irish in the nineteenth century were basically an unskilled labor force, but by the middle of the twentieth century they had begun to move into the professions, particularly into law and politics. They had begun to achieve the same educational levels as their native American colleagues and to play a fairly important role in the life of the nation.

In terms of what is distinctive about the Irish in America, two important factors must be listed: the Roman Catholic Church and secondly, the influence of the Irish on American politics. In terms of the Roman Catholic Church, it is apparent that the Irish-Americans dominated the American Catholic Church. The development, the building, and the expansion of the church was essentially a function of the Irish-born and Irish-American clerics.

In the nineteenth century, the dominant Irish-American cleric was Archbishop John Hughes, whom we have already mentioned. To a large extent, Archbishop Hughes was responsible for the development of the parochial school system, although it is true that the first parochial school was organized long before he came on the scene. But certainly, in the 1840's and 1850's, he became the dominant spokesman for American Catholicism and was recognized as such by other bishops. Bishop Kendrick of Philadelphia constantly turned to Bishop Hughes for advice as to how to proceed in Philadelphia. So too, Bishop Kendrick's brother who was the Bishop in St. Louis was also constantly seeking advice from Bishop Hughes.

Hughes believed that only by militantly defending the

Catholic Church could it survive in America. He was willing to use his energy and influence with the Irish-American constituency, both clerical and lay, to enforce the notion that Irish-American Catholics were one hundred percent Americans because Catholics were God-fearing, moral, law-abiding people. He united the notion of American nationalism with support for the Roman Catholic Church. Therefore, he felt that aid to parochial schools was an essential ingredient of the American creed, and he became the first cleric to insist upon aid to the parochial school system.

That claim was rejected by most of the Protestant community. Protestants felt that public aid was basically a violation of the First Amendment to the Constitution, the notion of separation of church and state, the idea that no religion can be established with the aid of public funds. Hughes introduced the parochial school as a public issue, one that continues to dominate much of Catholic thought and much of the Protestant reaction to the demands on the part of many Catholics for this kind of aid. It was obvious that the Irish-American clergy felt that the parochial school system was essential to the preservation of the Church and most of the Irish-American clergy supported that contention.

Not all Irish-American bishops agreed. Archbishop John Ireland pointed out in a book called *Religion and Education* (1902) that Christ did not establish a parochial school system. He established a church. There was no such thing as Catholic knowledge distinct from knowledge itself. Archbishop Ireland was ignored, and the parochial school system became a major concern of the Irish-American dominated Catholic Church in America.

The Catholic Church in America was in a large part a creation of the Irish and the Irish-American clergy. But many feel that the Catholic faith is no longer as strong in the Irish-American community as it once was. For example, Father Andrew Greeley, the Chicago sociologist, in *That Most Distressful Nation: The Taming of the American Irish* feels that the Irish have been successful but that the faith they brought with them as perhaps their major possession is no longer the dominant influence in their lives as it had been in the nineteenth century.

If we move out of the church into the realm of politics, here again, it is quite apparent that the Irish have had a tremendous influence on American society. Why is that so? In Ireland they had developed a political consciousness, a political awareness primarily because of the great work of Daniel O'Connell. And they had another advantage, they knew the language. For many of the Irish, General Shields and Congressman Morrissey are good examples that politics provided the means for their rise in social status.

In America, political life was not run on the principles of Plato's *Republic* or Aristotle's *Ethics*. The Irish political boss's primary concern was, what do the people want? That was the way the Irish-American began in politics. He tried to find out what the local political community needed and then attempted to provide it. Thus, George Washington Plunkitt, the Tammany political boss at the turn of the twentieth century, was always aware of who had died in his district. If he could not be at the wake, he made certain that one of the club members attended. The family was aware that in their hour of need, the local political machine was at hand. Expenses for burial were provided by these election chieftains. They served as a humane buffer between an alien, industrialized, highly urbanized society and the Irish community. These bosses aspired not only to win the support of their people but also to control elections by this tactic. The process is best summarized by Edwin O'Connor in his *Last Hurrah* and might be considered a particularly Irish contribution to American political life.

There are those who say this is not an achievement. They feel that the whole concept of using the government for social mobility purposes corrupted the American political system, and there is some evidence to support that idea. It becomes a matter of judgment: were the bosses essentially corrupt, or were the bosses essentially valuable buffers, viable people, who had a reasonable function in American political life?

The Irish-American community has provided three candidates for the American presidency. While many people think that Al Smith was the first, in the election of 1928, we must remember that in 1872, the Democratic party nominated for President, Charles O'Connor, a Catholic lawyer from New York. Though most of the Democratic party supported the liberal candidacy of Horace Greeley, the editor of the *New York Tribune*, O'Connor was in fact the first Irish-American Catholic to be nominated for the presidency. In 1960, John F. Kennedy was the first successful Irish-American candidate for President of the United States.

Certainly, the Irish have contributed to a number of other fields as well. One can immediately think in terms of motion pictures and people like James Cagney and Pat O'Brien. Or, one can think in terms of literary figures like Eugene O'Neill, James Farrell, and F. Scott Fitzgerald. In many of the writings of men like O'Neill and Fitzgerald, one has to look very deeply to find the impact of Irish or Irish-American influences on their writings. That, of course, does not apply to men like Edwin O'Connor and James Farrell whose subject matter is the Irish-Americans.

In little more than a century, the Irish-American descendants have moved from the position of the despised, to the point where one of them has occupied the highest office in America, the presidency.

SELECTED BIBLIOGRAPHY

ADAMS, WILLIAM FORKES. *Ireland and the Irish Immigration to the New World from 1815 to Famine.* New York: Russell & Russell, 1967.

ARENSBERG, C. and KIMBALL, S. T. *Family and Community in Ireland*, 2nd ed. Cambridge, Mass.: Harvard University Press, 1968.

BILLINGTON, RAY ALLAN. *The Protestant Crusade, 1800–1860.* New York: Quadrangle, 1964.

BROWN, THOMAS N. *Irish-American Nationalism, 1870–1890.* Philadelphia: J. B. Lippincott Company, 1966.

COLEMAN, TERRY. *Going to America.* New York: Anchor Books, 1973.

CONDON, WILLIAM H. *Life of Major-General James Shields, Hero of Three Wars and Senator from Three States.* Chicago: Press of the Blakely Printing Co., 1900.

CONNELL, K. H. *Irish Peasant Society.* Oxford: Oxford University Press, 1968.

CURRAN, THOMAS J. *Xenophobia and Immigration, 1820–1930.* Boston: Twayne Press, 1975.

CURTIS, L. P. *Anglo-Saxons and Celts*. Connecticut: University of Bridgeport, 1968.

DRAKE, M. "The Irish Demographic Crisis of 1740–41," in Moody, T. W., *Historical Studies*, VI, 1968.

EDWARDS, R. DUDLEY and WILLIAMS, T. DUDLEY, eds. *The Great Famine, Studies in Irish History*. New York: New York University Press, 1957.

HANDLIN, OSCAR. *Boston's Immigrants: A Study in Acculturation*, rev. ed. New York: Atheneum, 1969.

HIGHAM, JOHN. *Strangers in the Land: Patterns of American Nativism, 1860–1925*. New York: Atheneum, 1963.

KINZER, DONALD L. *An Episode in Anti-Catholicism: The American Protective Association*. Seattle: University of Washington Press, 1964.

SCHRIER, ARNOLD. *Ireland and the American Emigration, 1850–1900*. New York: Russell & Russell, 1970.

WOODHAM-SMITH, CECIL. *The Great Hunger, 1845–1849*. New York: Harper & Row, 1963.

V

Those Who Followed Columbus: The Italian Migration to the United States of America

By FRANK J. COPPA
St. John's University

FOREIGNERS have long been fascinated by Italy. They have been lured by the ruins of Greek and Roman civilization, the splendor of the Renaissance, and Rome, the eternal city. Visitors continue to pour into the peninsula, making tourism one of the most important sectors of the Italian economy. This influx has been countered by the millions of Italians who have been constrained to leave home and earn their livelihood in some other European country or across the Atlantic.

There is something of the grand as well as the tragic in the mass migration of Italians. Italy's modern exodus constitutes the largest population movement from Europe in terms of numbers and length of residence abroad. In all not fewer than twenty-six million Italians left the peninsula after the formation of the Kingdom in 1861. In some respects this modern trek to most continents of the world was as heroic as the migration of Italians some two millennia before, which brought the Italic language to France, Spain, Portugal, and Romania and their civilization from one end of the known world to the other. Just as the Romans built bridges, roads, and aqueducts throughout Europe, Asia Minor, and North Africa, the later emigrants built roads, bridges, railways, and subways in Europe and the Americas.

The Italian diaspora is one of the most striking and important features of their recent history. Its impact transcended the home country and stimulated the economic development of those countries which offered refuge to the newcomers. Italians at the turn of the century who could not find employment in the dry and mountainous regions of the South, toiled in the mines of Lorraine, planted coffee in Brazil, and grapes in California. They built roads from Argentina to the Canadian frontier and dug canals and subways in Egypt and New York, flocking to those countries that needed their labor.

This remarkable exodus occurred because the mother country proved unable to utilize the potential of all its sons and daughters. Indeed economic conditions worked to encourage emigration. Since the end of the Renaissance the peninsula was plagued by a series of problems. Trade with the Orient, an important source of wealth, was cut by the spread of Turkish power. Commerce was also curtailed by the geographical discoveries which opened cheaper routes to the East. Paradoxically Italian explorers, cartographers, as well as capital were largely responsible for this Atlantic Revolution which worked to the detriment of their land of origin.

Equally ominous for Italy's future was the evolution of the European political system. She was unprepared for the developments which produced united and strong nation states. The strength of her cities, the prevailing parochialism, the balance of power established among the native dynasties, and the temporal power of the Papacy conspired to keep Italy disunited and at the mercy of the larger, more powerful states. Thus it happened that the country which had dominated the ancient world became the passive prey of France, Spain, and Austria. For several hundred years her economy stagnated under foreign misrule with the connivance of local rulers who thought only of their own narrow interests.

The quiet of the peninsula was disturbed by the Revolutionary and Napoleonic Wars which aroused Italian nationalism, rearranged frontiers, and introduced more efficient methods of business and trade. However, the defeat of Napoleonic France brought restoration and repression. By the time of the Congress of Vienna (1815), Italy was returned to its position of subservience and had to submit to the pretensions of the House of Habsburg. It was divided into eight separate states, each isolated from the other by prohibitive tariffs. Even within the boundaries of any of these states trade was far from free, encumbered by some six to twelve internal duty zones. Italy's largest river the Po could not effectively be used for transportation for between its mouth and Pavia there were some eighty different stations at which the right of search and visit was exercised. Manufacture was almost everywhere hampered by burdensome restrictions inherited from the past and the grinding poverty of most rural regions.

Emigration was not permitted in many parts of the peninsula so that the situation could not easily be improved. For the first two-thirds of the nineteenth century the states of southern and central Italy curtailed the right of departure as part of their mercantilist policy. It was only following the formation of the Italian Kingdom that emigration assumed giant proportions.

Italy at the time of unification was primarily an agricultural country and not a rich one. About one-third of her land was uncultivated mountain or swamp, another third pasture and forest, and less than one-third was actively cultivated. Despite the poverty of its soil its people were fertile and the population reached twenty-seven million in 1871, living at a higher density than either the French or Germans. The standard of living was low, especially in the countryside. Here the home was often a shed without windows or chimney. The furnishings were basic, not to say primitive, and the food was simple and scarce. These accommodations, modest as they were, had to be shared with their chickens, and, if they were fortunate, their pig. While plumbing was poor in Italian cities, it was novel in the provinces.

To make matters worse, the peninsula was afflicted with the scourge of malaria which late in the nineteenth century continued to take a heavy toll of lives and sapped human energy in numerous regions. It was so endemic that in large parts of the peninsula it was considered the norm. As a result the peasant could not live upon the lowlands he cultivated, and a great deal of time had to be squandered in going to and from the fields he worked. The deficiency disease pellagra, which acquired its name in Italy, often made conditions even more difficult. The problems produced by geography and nature were compounded by the evils of an inequitable social system. The greater part of the country's wealth as well as land was in the hands of a small elite who charged high rents and paid miserably low wages. The employment they provided was precarious and they were not always concerned with the condition of the land or the people upon it. Because the overriding preoccupation of a large part of the ruling class was to draw as large an income as possible, they put pitifully little back into the soil.

In addition to the landlords the peasants had to confront other brigands, who still roamed freely over many of the regions of the peninsula. Not only was the peasant physically burdened, he was psychologically stricken. Mobility was rare, and there was little incentive for innovation. In most areas tools tended to be ancient and methods of cultivation antiquated. The poor coped with the problems of life as their ancestors had for centuries before them. Resignation was considered natural, alternatives deemed impossible, patience was essential for survival. Life was viewed as difficult, providing few comforts except for the realization that things could get worse. No one, least of all government, seemed to care for the plight of the peasant.

The manner in which the national government spent its money did not bring relief to the poor but added to their dilemma. Over eighty percent of its income was spent on the national debt, its great power pretensions, and its increasingly large bureaucracy. This left some fifteen percent for all other expenses, and of this less than three percent of the budget was spent on education. Small wonder that the bulk of her people were illiterate. Quintino Sella, the outstanding Minister of Finance of the post-unification period, grimly determined to balance the budget, practiced "economy to the bone" when it came to funding desperately needed services but was generous in imposing a vast array of taxes.

Since the upper classes of Italy, who profited the most from the creation of the Kingdom, were not always prepared to pay their fair share for its preservation, the burden of taxation fell upon others. Enjoying a virtual monopoly of political power—only some two percent of the population voted—the ruling elite found it relatively easy to impose a large share of the tax load upon those least capable of supporting it—the disenfranchised, illiterate masses of rural Italy. Thus while those in power kept the inheritance tax low and opposed an income tax as socialistic, they gladly tolerated a host of burdensome, indirect duties which penalized those who were at the bottom of the economic ladder. Their government forced the poor to pay a price for salt that was forty times its value.

Undeniably unification was a momentous event from the perspective of the national tradition, but from the social point of view it represented the triumph of the middle and upper classes at the expense of the masses. For the poor and underprivileged the unification represented a "missed revolution," a time when real social and economic changes might have occurred but did not. Conditions, in fact, deteriorated following unification. In the period from 1861 to 1880 population growth in Italy outstripped national consumption as population grew by thirteen percent and consumption only by ten percent. Even in the most prosperous parts of the peninsula the per capita income was about half the average found in France. For many, flight appeared the only answer, and for Italy this assumed the role of an increasingly important safety valve.

The history of modern Italian emigration can be divided into five periods. From 1861 to 1881 the government tended to oppose it, while in the next two decades Rome neither encouraged nor discouraged it. At this time emigration was uncontrolled, and those who poured out were not provided with any protection. In the years from 1901 to 1918, the age of Giolitti, the Italian government took the first concrete measures to benefit those who left. This was the period of the greatest outflow, and the most massive migration to the United States, and it is upon these years that the present essay will concentrate. The two decades when the Fascists controlled Italy were years of relatively little emigration. Finally the post-World War II peninsula witnessed a revival of emigration as Italians found their way to the Americas, Australia, with the greatest number going to the other countries of Europe particularly Germany, France, Belgium, and Switzerland.

In the first period from 1861 to 1881 about 120,000 left annually. It was a movement of individuals, most of whom left northern Italy for the other countries of Europe. Proportionately the percentage of males departing in this period was higher than the number of females. In part, this was a reflection of the fact that for many this departure was not considered permanent. Rather the vast majority of those who left to work abroad intended to return home. This is why many did not even tell their neighbors they were leaving the country. In fact, some ninety percent of those who went abroad, returned.

Although we have little precise data of the emigration of these years it is known that substantial Italian colonies were formed across the Atlantic in the United States, Argentina, Brazil, Uruguay, and across the Mediterranean in Algeria, Tunisia, and Egypt. Italian workers helped to build the Alpine tunnels, the Suez Canal, and the railways of North Africa. Given the opportunity as in North Africa and South America, they became farmers and professional men. Indeed in South America they assumed an important political as well as economic role.

Throughout most of the nineteenth century the great mass of Italians who crossed the Atlantic chose to go to South rather than North America. In the Latin countries of the New World their favorite destinations were Brazil and Argentina. During this time they often accounted for half of all the new arrivals in Brazil, and their impact on Argentina was as great. There they affected the national tastes, habits, and even the language. The success of the northern Italians encouraged some southerners to follow in their footsteps.

Southern Italians had even greater incentives to leave than their northern counterparts, for their conditions were more deplorable. "Christ stopped at Eboli" says the Italian proverb, implying that Christian civilization and the amenities of life never penetrated south of Eboli. This adage was used by Carlo Levi for the title of his book which described the frightful conditions, the apathy, and the slow pace of progress in the Lucania where he had been exiled for political dissent during the dark days of Fascism. The same dismal situation prevailed in many parts of the South.

An overwhelming majority of Southern Italians, over ninety percent, depended upon agriculture for their livelihood, but aside from a few extraordinary areas, southern agriculture had to confront severe problems. Mountainous terrain accounted for some eighty percent of the land of the South or *Mezzogiorno.* Ironically much of this terrain was too high to be of much use for agriculture, but not sufficiently high to provide the plains below with a continuous supply of water. Water was only one of the many difficulties of the South. Most of the *Mezzogiorno* did not have sufficient rainfall, and most of that rain fell in winter rather than the growing season. Furthermore, the South was not blessed with navigable rivers and internal waterways, rendering transport difficult and expensive. These economic and geographical liabilities had political and social implications.

At the time of unification the population of the South was divided into three main groups. First a small number of powerful landlords who comprised some one or two percent of the population and owned a good deal of the best land. Secondly, a group of bureaucrats and professional people who were less than ten percent of the population and catered to the needs of the elite classes. Finally the vast majority of the peasants who lived in economic depression and semi-serfdom. Most of the latter owned no land at all and therefore hired themselves out by the day to work the fields of others or leased or owned a very small piece of land which did not produce enough for their subsistence.

The disproportion between the haves and the have-nots could not but engender hostility. Beneath the surface of the southern countryside lay a bitter class hatred because of this sharp division between the poor and the privileged. On the one side there were the landowners and *signori* with their agents and dependents who served them. On the other side there were the peasants who lived in abject poverty. A middle class such as had emerged in France, England, and the low countries was not to be found except in the largest towns of the South, and even there it was far weaker than in Northern Italy. The social and economic problems of the South cried for solution, but its cries fell upon deaf ears.

Initially the national government had little appreciation of the difficulties of the South. The makers of modern Italy had almost all been Northerners. Cavour, the father of the country, had never traveled south of Florence and had intended to create a northern state rather than one embracing the entire peninsula. His successors were as ignorant of the *Mezzogiorno* as he and were prepared to believe the most fantastic stories. Thus it was rumored that the South was the richest part of Italy, perhaps the wealthiest part of all of Europe. This was the myth of the South, *Il mito del Mezzogiorno.* Despite this rhetoric, the reality of the South presented the picture of poverty unknown to other parts of Western Europe. This was explained by another myth, *Il mito del buongoverno,* which claimed that the South had everything but good government. Presumably once it was supplied the region would prosper and all its problems would disappear. A simplistic solution to a very complicated problem.

Understandably it had great appeal to the political elite of the North who were prepared to teach their southern brothers the art of good government. In their minds this meant liberal, parliamentary government. The advantages of this system were not immediately apparent to its supposed beneficiaries. It brought heavy if efficient taxation, which rendered the condition of the poor worse than it had been before unification. Particularly disliked was the *macinato,* the tax on the grinding of cereals, and therefore a tax on the staples of the lower classes. The liberal regime brought conscription in its train, as well as a vulgar anticlerical crusade which struck at one of the few institutions of the South that had provided services for the poor. The free trade commercial policy of the government brought in manufactured goods from abroad and ruined domestic industries, making it impossible for many small farmers to continue living on the land.

A number of factors combined to push the peasants out of Southern Italy. There was the pressure of population upon an infertile land having few industries capable of competing with those of Western Europe. To make matters worse the system of taxation struck at the poor and too often spared the rich, while the laws were not always applied against the *gran signore* but brutally imposed upon the peasants. Finally there was a pervasive discrimination against the poor farmers in large parts of the South where to be a *contadino* was to be less than a person, to be, in fact, considered despicable.

These prevailing problems became particularly acute in the

1880's. In that decade tens of thousand succumbed to the cholera epidemic, and countless others were constrained to move from their villages. Once torn from the protective mooring of their communities, many found it relatively easy to leave the country as well. Others were forced to do so by the shocks which the southern economy experienced. A rapid increase in subtropical fruit production in Florida and California proved detrimental to the exports of Calabria, the Basilicata, and Sicily. Unable to export crops, they found it necessary to export people.

The state of southern agriculture was also affected by the flood of American and Russian grains into Italy and the transportation revolution which drastically cut the cost of shipping produce. Meanwhile the wine growers of Apulia, Calabria, and Sicily suffered when France moved to protect her wine industry and discriminated against Italian imports. The government's solution, agricultural protection, salvaged the economy but not all of its participants.

Elsewhere in the western world, cities were providing opportunities for the unemployed and underemployed of the countryside. However the cities of Southern Italy were essentially preindustrial and had little to offer in the way of employment. Industrial urban centers were developing in the North of the peninsula, especially in the triangle formed by Genoa, Turin, and Milan. However, these cities were attracting the peasants of the region; they had not evolved to the point where they could absorb the southern peasant as well. The difficulties of the South set in motion an increased emigration.

The 1880's witnessed an important turning point in the outflow from Italy. Not only was there an increase in numbers; a larger portion of Southerners now decided to leave for foreign shores. By this time a majority were going overseas rather than to continental countries, and emigration already served as an important means of containing class hatred and disorder in the peninsula. From 1881 to 1890, 188,000 left each year; from 1891 to 1900, 284,000; and from 1901 to 1910, 602,000 left each year.

In the two decades from 1880 to 1900 more Italians chose to go to Argentina and Brazil than the United States, but this soon changed as conditions for emigrants deteriorated in these countries. A yellow fever epidemic in Brazil took a toll of thousands and worked to keep Italians away. Meanwhile political and financial crises in Argentina rendered that country less attractive to emigrants. More and more Italians now looked to North America and particularly the United States. From 1871 to 1880 Italians constituted less than two percent of the immigrants entering the Republic. From 1881 to 1890, six percent, and in the decade from 1891 to 1900 they constituted twenty-four percent of the total. In the twentieth century some four million were to find their way there.

The movement to the United States was encouraged by a number of factors. Agents of steamship companies and labor contractors covered the countryside of Italy in their search for workers. In their recruiting efforts they depicted the United States as a land of plenty, where taxes were negligible, liberty assured, and work plentiful. Brushing aside the language barrier, they told the peasants that the people of America needed their services and would welcome their entry.

Despite the hardship of the Atlantic crossing, Italians were inclined to believe all the good things they had heard about the United States. Those who had settled there earlier sent letters vividly describing the bountiful conditions. These missives tended to be glowing because most immigrants wrote of their successes, not of their failures, in their attempt to convince those they left behind that they had taken the right step. More important, they sent money, more than many of the peasants had ever seen. The practical Southerners decided to go to those areas from which their friends and relatives sent the most—and from this perspective the United States was particularly attractive. Italians continued to venture to the United States because that country was experiencing a rapid industrial expansion and labor, especially of an unskilled variety, was still in great demand.

In toto over five million Italians migrated to the United States in the half century following the acquisition of Rome as capital. The vast majority came from the poor agricultural regions of the South, which accounted for some eighty percent of the total. While it would be an exaggeration to conclude that any large sections of Italy were depopulated by the movement, some towns in Calabria and the Basilicata lost as much as twenty percent of their populations—and this was often the most dynamic element in the community. Prime Minister Giuseppe Zanardelli was told when he visited one town at the turn of the century that he had the good wishes of its 8,000 inhabitants, 3,000 of whom were in America and the other 5,000 who were prepared to follow them. Rome did not seem to be able to provide for the needs of Southern Italians who had no recourse but to emigrate.

Neither the governments of the *Destra*, the right, nor those of the *Sinistra*, the left, were capable of helping the poor of Italy. Divided upon a number of political issues that were of pre-unification vintage, the differences between the two blocs were more apparent than real. Members of both groups were determind to defend the social status quo, considered property sacred, and regarded the bourgeoisie the pillar of political life. In the years from 1861 to 1876 the right, which was northern-oriented, was more concerned with balancing the budget and preserving the Italian state than in uplifting the poor. In 1876 when the party of Agostino Depretis came to power, much was expected. However the rhetoric of his program stood in marked contrast to the performance of the left once in power. Thus the left followed in the footsteps of the right and implemented few reforms that provided immediate relief for the less well-off. More important, the inequitable tax structure of the realm remained unchanged.

Some charged that Depretis was unable or unwilling to help the South because he was a Northerner and so expected more from the Sicilian Francesco Crispi. They were soon to learn that this individual, preoccupied with the great power status of Italy and foreign affairs, was to neglect internal issues, seeking a solution for Italy's problems by acquiring lands in Africa that were more poverty stricken than the home country. Crispi dreamed of an empire in Africa, forgetting the Africa that existed in the Italian South.

At the turn of the century neither the Southerner Di Rudinì nor the Northerner Pelloux did much to aid the South or its people. Like Crispi they tended to support the wealthy landed classes at the expense of the agricultural workers. They were quick to announce extraordinary measures and impose martial law when confronted with worker agitation. Neither was able to cope with the economic stagnation that troubled Italy at the turn of the century.

Only with the accession of the Zanardelli-Giolitti government in 1901 was greater concern shown for the *contadino* and the working class as a whole. Statistics show that the national median of the daily pay of the Italian worker, taking into account the increase in the cost of living, grew in real terms more than 25 percent from 1901 to 1913, despite a shortening of the work day. But it was too little, too late, for by this time a large part of the lower class had concluded that the only escape from the cycle of poverty and deprivation was emigration. As this reached epidemic proportions, the government finally provided help for those who were leaving. In 1901 it created the Commission for Emigration which was entrusted with the task of protecting Italians the world over. It carried on its work by regulating transport and providing those who left with information and legal aid. Considering the hardships confronted by those departing, the Commission was sorely needed.

The decision to emigrate was not always an easy one to make. True, conditions were bad in the old country, but that only accentuated the pessimism of its people. There is a Southern Italian proverb which warns: He who leaves the old behind, knows what he loses, but not what he will find.

Many of the Italians who ventured to the United States remembered that proverb and therefore were reluctant to leave behind all the institutions of their rural background. The most important prop they brought with them was the one that had served them best at home, the family, which included many blood relatives. Before it all other groups paled in importance. Indeed Italians distrusted anyone who had broken with this most important of institutions, considering him rootless and therefore unreliable.

The family of the emigrants was male-dominated with the father at the head. By general consent he was accorded the right, which in many cases became a virtual duty, to discipline his children and his mate. It was said of the wife that:

> Like a good weapon she should be cared for properly
> Like a hat she should be kept straight

Like a mule, she should be given plenty of work
and occasional beatings
Above all, she should be kept in her place as a subordinate

The wife was thus seen as the interpreter of her husband's wishes and assumed the responsibility of serving her family. Nonetheless, she played an important role, taking the initiative in selecting mates for her children, as well as saving the earnings of her husband and unmarried children. It was she who served as the repository of the family funds to which each member contributed according to his ability and means, drawing from it when the need arose.

Organized in this fashion the family provided the newly arrived Italian in the United States with protection and assistance, friendship and associations. As a result few Italians felt the complete impact of being in a new land amidst strange surroundings, for the family cushioned the isolation. It was for this reason as much as any other that far fewer Italians suffered from alcoholism and mental disturbances in comparison to the other large immigrant groups. Likewise proportionately few became public burdens. The myth of the mafia aside, the close family structure of the Italians contributed to their low crime rate. Mario Puzo wrote of his childhood, "I never came home to an empty house; there was always the smell of supper cooking. My mother was always there to greet me, sometimes with a policeman's club in her hand. But—she was always there, or her authorized deputy, my older sister."

The reliance upon the family for support and comfort was strengthened by the hostile atmosphere the Italian found outside in the American society at large. The difficulties encountered by an immigrant group to the United States varied in proportion to its size, the rapidity of its arrival, the resources it brought to the new country, its visibility, and finally its leadership. On almost all of these counts the Southern Italians who flocked to the east coast at the turn of the century were destined for serious trouble. The very size of this migration did not portend well for their acceptance. Their presence was all the more conspicuous because the Italian flow to the United States had been light between 1860 and 1880. In sharp contrast, some four million Italians flocked here between 1890 and 1920.

To make matters worse, a good part of the press did not assume a responsible position toward these new arrivals. American newspapers had very little to say about the great economic, social, and political progress being made in Italy under the astute leadership of Giovanni Giolitti. Stories of Italy's great industrial spurt forward did not sell copies as did lurid and all too often imaginary tales of brigands, the black hand, and the mafia. Given this type of coverage small wonder that some visualized Italians as criminals of the most cruel and bloodthirsty variety. For too many the words Italians and stiletto became inseparable, largely because the press almost always chose to accentuate the vices of the minority to the neglect of the virtues of the majority.

This campaign was unfair and inaccurate because the Italian government made it difficult, if not impossible, for nationals with criminal records and connections to emigrate. Hence when the prefect of Reggio informed the Minister of the Interior Giolitti in 1901 that the notorious brigand Musolino, who could not be apprehended, was disposed to emigrate to America, Giolitti responded that to favor the flight of an assassin to America was absolutely inadmissible.

Not only were Italians unjustly maligned as criminals, they were often depicted as beggars and the charge frequently levied on them was that the large Italian families entering threatened to become a drain on the national charity. Statistics, however, told another story. Riis found that the Germans contributed 8 percent of the street beggars in New York City, the native Americans 12 percent, the Irish 15 percent, while the Italians accounted for less than 2 percent. The figures for the various national groups in the country's houses of charity confirm the New York findings, for the Irish constituted 30 percent, the Germans 19 percent, the English 8.5 percent, and the Italians 8.1 percent.

Confronted with the facts some journalists admitted that the Italians were industrious and had close family ties; they did not deny that they fabricated stories to sell newspapers. There was a rationale for their behavior, for when they circulated unfavorable accounts about other groups they found themselves inundated with protests. The Italians, on the other hand, did not seem to mind, for generally they did not respond. In part this failure to react energetically was due to the fact that they lacked the organization and education enjoyed by the more vocal and respected minorities.

The mass emigration of Italians to the United States began a mere decade after the acquisition of Rome and reached its climax when the first generation of citizens had reached maturity. Hence those who had left did so not as Italians but as Venetians, Lombards, Neapolitans, Calabrians, and Sicilians. Contributing to this provincialism was the spirit of *campanalismo*, a distrust of all social, cultural, and political contacts beyond the point where the *campanile* or parish bell tower could be heard. Small wonder that Italians in the United States moved within very narrow circles and found it difficult to cooperate with their fellow countrymen who did not share their own particular dialect, customs, and food.

The differences between Northern and Southern Italians were especially marked, with the Northerners enjoying most of the advantages. Having a continuous contact with the peoples of Western Europe, they possessed many of the cultural and physical features of the older American stock. Native Americans found them less foreign and therefore more acceptable than their Southern brothers. The fact that their region had brought about unification and initially dominated the new state gave them a pride which Southerners did not share. The Northerners also had more money and schooling than their Southern counterparts. Their adjustment was quicker and easier because they were relatively few in number and better dispersed throughout the country.

Southern Italians arrived in much larger numbers and were all the more visible because of their overwhelming presence in urban areas. A number of interrelated factors contributed to their concentration in the cities of the Northeast. The finances of the Southerner played an important role. According to one study at the turn of the century, Scandinavians brought $16.25 per capita when they came; Germans $16.65, and Southern Italians $8.84. The Southern Italians did not have the funds to travel to the hinterland, let alone to purchase land. It must also be remembered that most of these people did not have fond memories of agriculture in the old country and were not motivated to return to the land. Furthermore, many of the migrants did not originally intend to remain permanently in this country and therefore hesitated making such a lasting commitment as the acquisition of a farm.

When one adds to these considerations that most opportunities in America at the turn of the century were to be found in urban areas, it is not surprising that the bulk of Italians remained in the cities. In New York they replaced the Irish and Poles on the work gangs, repairing streets, building skyscrapers, and digging subways. The Italian wife, like her Jewish counterpart, entered the garment industry. In Chicago Italians were employed in the stockyards, while in Pennsylvania and West Virginia they worked underground in the mines. They stayed in the cities because their relatives and friends were there. As late as 1920 the Italian-American population was 85 percent urban and only 15 percent rural.

The teeming conditions of the Italian communities disturbed native Americans and older immigrants who did not understand or appreciate the reasons for such overcrowding. The density of population in these quarters was high because of the large number of families which took in boarders. Contributing to, if not creating, the congestion, was the attitude of the older American population. They declared many sections of the city off limits for the Italians, creating a ghetto situation. The little Italies seemed even more crowded than they were, because the poor had little incentive to stay indoors and because they were accustomed to carrying on all sorts of activities in the streets, as they had in the old country. The presence of pushcarts and peddlers contributed to the confusion.

While these communities may in retrospect appear picturesque, overcrowding played a part in promoting the high tuberculosis rate among Italians in America. This was only one of the problems they confronted. Since they lodged in slum housing, they were associated with these slums, indeed accused of creating them. Their sociability and street life also frightened natives, while the use of their own language generated the fear that America was being inundated by a foreign wave. The abuse of Italians was both verbal and physical. Irish toughs often waited for them as they returned from work and assaulted the smaller Italians. When the latter resorted to the knife to protect themselves, they were branded cowardly and dangerous.

Although Italians in the United States generally found employment, their lives were hard. The pay they received was low, and the work day long. There was no unemployment insurance, and they were often the first to be fired. The Italians had also to cope with an unsympathetic and suspicious police and the scheming *padroni* who were supposed to be their friends.

The *padrone* played an important role in bringing Italian workers to the United States and directing them while here. Originally the system was similar to that of contract labor with the *padrone* going to Italy to recruit peasants, providing them with the fare for the passage to the jobs he had acquired for them. Since the *padrone* was more or less free to handle the worker as he wished, the prospect of exploitation was great. This was facilitated by the fact that the poor were illiterate and usually unfamiliar with American labor conditions. Thus many *padroni* overcharged the worker for the passage across the Atlantic as well as for finding the immigrant a job. This was called *bossatura* and might range from one to ten dollars. By one means or another the *padrone* obtained a profit from the immigrant he served and showed little concern for the conditions these Italians faced, so long as he himself fared well.

Since the *padrone* often used his workers as strike breakers, this earned for them the hatred of the other workers who accused the Italians of driving down the price of labor. Furthermore initially few of them found their way into the unions. Southern Italians did not at first know if they would remain permanently in the United States and did not see the point of joining such an organization. Nor were they welcomed into these labor groups. The other workers did not understand the Italian immigrant's position and were quick to criticize and slow to appreciate the difficulties he confronted.

Of the various groups with whom the Italians came into conflict, the Irish were the most important. For one thing the Italians assumed many of the jobs unskilled Irish immigrants had formerly filled. The neighborhoods into which they poured had been Irish before their massive migration, and finally the Italians like the Irish were Catholics and therefore found themselves worshipping in the same church.

Some Irishmen in the church were intensely prejudiced against the Italians. In part this stemmed from the role that Italy had played in depriving the Pope of his temporal power. A number of American clerics continued to see Italy and the Italians as the despoilers of the Papacy and the Church. So widespread was this prejudice that some Catholic schools in the United States did not teach the Italian language until 1929, when a concordat was signed between Church and State in Italy.

In addition the Irish-American clergy often felt that Italo-Americans were not sufficiently orthodox and manifested too casual an attitude toward religion. They were shocked by what they termed the remnant of paganism in their practice—especially their love of Church processions with the parade of statues of various saints. To an Irish-American community not quite secure and seeking acceptance from the native population, such practices, as well as the religious feasts in honor of a pantheon of saints from San Gennaro to St. Anthony, were taboo. Thus they came out with a vengeance against the Italian emphasis on statues and condemned the "superstitious" basis of many of their beliefs.

The Italians, in turn, found much that was wanting in the Irish dominated American Church. They felt it lacked warmth and considered it tinged with puritanism. At the same time they found the laity far too submissive to the clergy. Accustomed to having the state support the Church, they were upset by what seemed to be the obsession of the American Church with raising money. Unwilling or unable to support their own Church, they were nonetheless chagrined that oftentimes the only place they could hear an Italian mass was in the basement of an "Irish" Church.

Not always accepted in the Church on their own terms, the Italians, as we have seen, were also burdened with the stereotype of being a violent, crime-ridden group. Everytime an Italian defended his honor, the press made a point of stressing his nationality so that even minor mishaps were characterized as vendettas and crimes of passion. In addition to the distorted picture of individual Italians, Americans were warned that there existed an Italian organized crime group known as the Black Hand.

In the early 1880's the police in Andalusia, Spain, announced that they had discovered a secret society, the Black Hand, whose members had sworn to destroy the landowners of the district. Although arrests followed swiftly, there were those who doubted that such an organization existed, including Bernaldo de Quirós, sent by the government to investigate the phenomenon. The scanty evidence produced in court seemed to show that it was a police invention that enabled them to condemn the leading anarchists of the area, without regard for innocence or guilt.

Given the fact that Southern Italians and Spaniards had similar sounding names and looked alike to the natives—as the epithets wop and dago indicate—and that some Italians were involved in the anarchist movement, it was not difficult to transform an alleged Spanish anarchist group into a supposed Italian crime syndicate. There were those who were convinced that the Black Hand in America was as mythical as it had been in Spain. The writer Gaetano D'Amato argued that the myth became notorious because of the sensational stories in the newspapers. The police and law enforcement agencies chose to believe the most lurid tales to justify their own incompetence. By elevating the status and power of their enemy their ineptitude was explained away by the alleged skill and power of the organization they claim they confronted.

A similar situation was to develop in regard to the Mafia. The Sicilian word Mafia is not found in Italian writing before the nineteenth century. Giuseppe Pitre believed that it came from a district of Palermo and it expressed at once beauty and excellence. The word first appeared in the criminal sense with a capital M in the title of the dialect play, *I Mafiusi della Vicaria* which dealt with life in Palermo's jail. The word is used by Sicilians in two different though related senses. On the one hand it is used to denote an attitude which until recently was fairly widespread in Southern Italy. This notion of mafia leads the individual to distrust most people outside of the family unit and to disregard them as relatively unimportant. On the

other hand Mafia is also used to describe small criminal bands
or *cosca* found in the western provinces of Sicily.

The attitude of mafia was in no small measure due to the
oppression endured by the Sicilians who were ruled by one
foreign people after another. Because the laws were not admin-
istered honestly, the government totally discredited, and the
courts impotent and corrupt, those who rebelled against this
oppressive system were considered heroes. Unable to trust the
constituted authorities, they constructed their own code of law
and justice based on the feudal code of chivalry introduced by
the Normans in the eleventh century. Within this system a wrong
had to be avenged by personal action, as the work of friends or
relatives. This method of justice was enforced by the law of
silence, the code of *omertà*, which forbade one from providing
the police with information.

In a land where the distances were great and the law alien,
there was a certain logic to this system. The criminal Mafia was
also conditioned by the environment of Sicily, where men found
it necessary to band together to protect their families and property against invaders. To enforce their justice they gathered
money from those who sought their protection, and later demanded protection money even when there was no danger
present. In this manner the Mafia moved from protection to a
protection racket.

As a criminal group the various bands—which have collectively
been termed Mafia—were not a vast association of malefactors
grouped into a well defined organization with branches throughout the island of Sicily, but rather were to be found only in the
northwestern part of the island where they engaged in extortion,
kidnaping, and cattle rustling. It was the romanticists who wove
the colorful stories of a mafia organization and created the legend
of elaborate hierarchies, secret ritual, and far-reaching influence.
It was not difficult to hoodwink the people in a land where illiter-
acy, poverty, and superstition were endemic.

The reality of Mafia in Sicily differs substantially from the
American notion. For one thing the Sicilian Mafia not only lacks
central organization, it is almost confined to rural areas. In
America organized crime is essentially an urban phenomenon.
Furthermore, sociologists and historians have traced many of

the problems of Italy to extreme individualism and the inability of her people to cooperate. Ironically they are nonetheless presented as capable of organizing and running the most efficient crime cartel in the world.

The American sociologist Daniel Bell has suggested that in a certain sense the Americans themselves are the creators of the Mafia. It is their mania for organization and classification that has defined the eastern establishment, the Wall street elite, the brain trust and the power brokers. It is only natural that the criminals have their own organization and leadership, their own power elite—the Mafia. This preoccupation with the Mafia has brought success to those who capitalized upon this fascination by their alleged exposés, mafia novels and movies, television series, and even telecast interviews with mobster chiefs. Recently even some Italians have gotten into the act. Thus the dust-ridden town of Corleone, south of Palermo, which Mario Puzo used for the name of the "Godfather family" has sought to capitalize on this publicity by claiming to be the Mafia's hometown. Although this self proclaimed dubious distinction has brought several hundred naive, and generally English-speaking tourists a month to Corleone, the able-bodied men of the community continue to run abroad to escape the cycle of poverty and despair. In fact the population has been cut in half during the past two decades, despite its new tourist trade.

Likewise this Mafia madness has not been very profitable for the vast majority of Italian-Americans. As a result of this attitude, police in some localities in the United States almost always sought an Italian suspect when a gangland crime was committed. First in novels and newspapers, later in the theater, movies, and television, the criminal was all too often provided with an Italian-sounding name. Small wonder that from time to time innocent Italians were the victims of mass hysteria as occurred in New Orleans in 1891, following the murder of David Hennesy, the police chief. Reportedly before dying he had blurted out that the dagoes did it, and this was sufficient to issue orders to arrest all the Italians the police encountered. At the beginning of 1891 the state brought nine Italians to trial for the crime. Although not one was convicted by the courts, an outburst of anti-Italian sentiment stimulated by the press provoked the shooting of nine imprisoned and defenseless Italians, while two others were lynched.

The New Orleans massacre horrified sane Americans as well as Europeans, but it was not the only occasion in which Italians were the victims of mob action. As late as 1920–21, the arrest, trial, and subsequent execution of Nicola Sacco and Bartolomeo Vanzetti was colored by a strong hatred of Italians. The foreman of the jury which passed upon the fate of the men referred to Italians as dagoes. Furthermore during the trial the testimony of some sixteen Italians, who swore that the men were miles away from the scene of the crime, was discounted. Vanzetti said after his sentencing, "I am suffering because I am a radical and indeed I am a radical; I have suffered because I was an Italian and indeed I am Italian."

This discrimination, coupled with the other problems the immigrants confronted, played a part in the decision of large numbers of Italians to return home. In the eyes of some, too many remained and they wished to prevent more from coming. In 1916 Madison Grant issued an ominous warning in his *Passing of the Great Race*. He asserted that Nordics were a superior race, while the people of the Mediterranean basin were inferior and had vulgarized America's social, cultural, and political life. In line with many of his arguments the American Congress in 1917 passed legislation requiring immigrants to be literate, thus discriminating against the poor of Southern Italy. This was not considered sufficient by the restrictionists, for additional legislation was passed in the postwar period, 1921–24, establishing a quota system which franky discriminated against newer immigrant groups such as the Italians. Their quota was established at some 6000, and it remained at this level until the system was abolished in 1965.

Despite the discrimination, Italians not only assimilated but achieved considerable success. Some assumed that the ethnic communities that mushroomed in the cities of the Northeast reproduced homeland conditions exactly and worked against Americanization. In reality the so-called little Italies represented an important step from the old world patterns. Neither fully Italian nor fully American, such communities were instrumental in helping immigrants from a rural society adjust to an urban, competitive one. In these neighborhoods, called ghettos by some, an important evolution occurred among Italians. For one thing men who in the old country never considered the possibility of cooperation or even contact with co-nationals from other towns and provinces were now constrained to work with their fellow countrymen. At the same time they developed a number of institutions to help them adjust to their new life-style. Among these were banks, a press, real estate firms, employment and travel agencies, and most important of all, mutual aid societies.

It is true that the last institution mentioned existed in Italy and played an important role there, but the societies created by the Italians in America tended to differ from those found in the Kingdom. There the societies were almost always confined to the middle classes and were strongest in the urbanized areas of the North and center of the peninsula. They were labor-oriented and in many respects the predecessors of the trade union. In the United States they were rather different, concentrating upon insurance and social assistance. Those who joined paid small monthly sums in the expectation that the group would provide for them and their families in case of illness or death. At the same time they served to educate their members in the ways of the larger society.

The Americanization of the Italians like that of other immigrant groups has been a three-generation process. The person who emigrates usually does not become fully acclimated because he possesses too many ties to the old country. Those born in the United States of immigrant parents, members of the second generation, face the greatest difficulties because they are caught between two cultures, that of their parents and that in which they must live. Torn between the two they are sometimes not fully accepted by either. Finally the third generation, the grandchildren of the immigrants, are by and large American.

The Italian family which provided invaluable services for the Italian immigrant, while protecting its children, shielded them from certain positive aspects of American life as well. Thus it discouraged mobility if that meant movement away from the home. This was especially true for daughters of a family who were closely watched even after marriage.

Likewise the Italian family did not always have a healthy

attitude toward education. The first generation of Italians tended to be suspicious of the public schools which created problems between parents and children. Furthermore coming from a rural and peasant background, they did not always appreciate the value of education. Then, too, the school removed the children from the job market, preventing them from fully contributing to the family income. Philosophically the public schools, which looked upon children as individuals with lives of their own to lead, upset the traditional notion of subordination for the good of the family. Some parents complained that the school made of their children people of leisure, which they felt was inappropriate for their class and position. The immigrants were most concerned with the need to earn a living and to send as much as possible to Italy to repay their debts. More often than not they found no time for cultural or educational pursuits. Thus the school system could only influence the first generation through the second, and often it produced conflict rather than accommodation.

The first and second generations were also divided in their attitude toward the Church. If the old-timers felt that the Church in America was not sufficiently Italian, even after some concessions had been made to their sentiments, the second generation considered these concessions old fashioned and out of place in the new land. Not dependent upon religious ceremonies and church holidays for their entertainment, the young found American practices more to their liking. In the conflict between the generations the Church largely sided with the new against the old, considering them the wave of the future.

The second generation rejected other life patterns which their parents brought with them from Italy. They quickly cast away most of their superstitions, styles of dress and grooming, as well as many of their recreational activities. Also eliminated were a number of rural traditions which were not seen to be relevant in an urban environment. Quite often they were hostile to Italy as well as to their parents. Furthermore their relatives were in the habit of telling them how difficult life was in Italy, so they would better appreciate their current situation. What they often accomplished instead was to teach their children to dislike Italy so intensely that they wanted nothing to do with it.

For a number of reasons the Italian culture brought by the immigrants to America was not strongly maintained by the second generation whose overall culture was more American than Italian. Yet the Italian element was not completely absorbed either in the second or indeed the third generation. Although the children of the immigrants were anxious to Americanize and identify with their peers, they did not overturn the family-centered social structure. This, in turn, assured that certain Italian practices would survive, and almost always food habits were preserved. The generation gap notwithstanding, children had a need to communicate with their parents, so most members of the second generation could speak some Italian or regional dialect. Finally some energetic members of the first and second generation made some heroic, if not always successful efforts, to preserve the Italian traditions and to stress the Italian contribution to American life.

Many of the early studies of the Italian impact on the United States suffered from defensiveness and filio-pietism. Reacting against the real discrimination and lack of information about their past, a number of first and second-generation Italian-Americans sought to set the record straight. Lacking proper training they often resorted to compiling the names of prominent figures in the little Italies throughout the country. Concentrating on outstanding personalities and particular events they neglected the social organizations, cultural traditions, and everyday life of the vast majority of Italians who had come to America. Money, too, was spent in such a manner as to reveal a lack of concern with the community's immediate needs in order to improve their image. Thus at a time when Italian-Americans required all sorts of services, various groups were collecting money to erect statues and monuments to Columbus, Verrazzano, and Garibaldi. These went up in rapid succession while many social needs were ignored.

These efforts were not in vain because they helped to educate Americans to the fact that Italians played a crucial role in the opening of America. The New World was after all discovered by one Italian and named after another. If Columbus laid the foundation for the great trans-Atlantic empire of Spain it was the Caboti—the Cabots—who gave the English their claims in

America and Giovanni da Verrazzano who provided the French with theirs. Italians not only commanded the crews that undertook the voyages of exploration, they provided much of the naval expertise and manpower as well. Thus fully one-third of the men who circumnavigated the globe with Magellan hailed from Italy. As missionaries of the Church they played an important role not only in America but in Africa and Asia as well. When the Chinese, confident that they were the only civilized people, came into contact with the Italian Jesuits, they added the Italians to their list of civilized people.

Despite the recognition of the important role of the Italians in the age of discovery, the initial impact of the Italians in the new world was to be limited. In large part this was due to the fact that the Italians worked under the flag of other nations or were employed in the service of the Church—there being no united Italy at the time. Certainly individual Americans such as Thomas Jefferson appreciated the contributions of Latin Europe and considered the Renaissance an Italian development. However due to the patterns of settlement, Anglo-Saxon practices rather than Italian culture shaped early America.

Still there was an Italian influence in the early Republic. Some maintain that the principles expressed in the Declaration of Independence were first enunciated by the Italian Cardinal and Saint, Roberto Bellarmine. They insist that this defender of the Catholic Church in the sixteenth century influenced Locke who in turn influenced Jefferson. A more immediate Italian influence upon Jefferson was the Tuscan Filippo Mazzei. It was at the suggestion of Benjamin Franklin that Mazzei drew up plans for the cultivation of vines, olive trees, and silk in Virginia. With the help of Jefferson, who offered him a large tract of land, this Tuscan carried out his agricultural experiments. Eventually he became involved in American politics.

Mazzei, who had absorbed democratic and republican ideals, found no prejudices against the British constitution when he arrived in the colonies in 1773. He knew that if the Americans were to be incited against the mother country they would have to abandon their admiration for English political practices. When he brought this opinion to Jefferson's notice, the latter encouraged him to produce a series of papers to influence public opinion. The newspaper articles he published under the pseudonym of Furioso helped to prepare colonial opinion for the impending break. His influence was far-reaching. Some of the words in the Declaration of Independence are found in an article which Mazzei had written in Italian and which Jefferson translated into English.

Another figure who provided the colonists with inspiration was Pasquale Paoli whose struggle for freedom first against the Genoese, then against the French, served as a model for the colonists. Paoli was well known in New England and the Central Atlantic states, and among his admirers were the Sons of Liberty who played an important role in the struggle for liberty. General Clark must share with Giuseppe Vigo, who provided the military intelligence and material needed to make the victory at Vincennes (1799) possible, the credit for winning the Northwest Territory. In addition, many believe that William Paca of Maryland, one of the signers of the Declaration of Independence, was of Italian origin.

After independence the Italian immigrants who left records were in the categories of political exiles, musicians, priests and missionaries, and painters. Jefferson was responsible for recruiting a group of Italian musicians who were to constitute the real basis of the band of the United States Marine Corps. Although excerpts from various Italian operas had been heard in the United States, it was not until 1825 that such an opera was performed in its entirety in Italian. Soon thereafter Italian opera houses were established, and they looked to the famous La Scala of Milan and San Carlo of Naples for inspiration.

In 1859 Costantino Brumidi, the Michelangelo of the capitol building, settled in Washington. A refugee of the revolutionary upheaval of 1848 and the restoration of 1849, he was employed by the federal government to decorate the rotonda and other parts of the capitol to which his name is rightfully linked.

Despite the great contribution of talented individuals, the overall impact of Italians in America before the Civil War was slight. In large measure this was due to the small size of the Italian community. The 1880's were to be the turning point; within the next three decades millions of Italians were to pour into the United States. The vast majority of these new immigrants came from the poor agricultural regions of the South and were by and large drawn from the lower classes of that burnt-out and depressed region. Preoccupied with earning a living and saving a sufficient sum to pay off their debts, they did not always appreciate the value of a liberal education.

The unfortunate attitude of many Italian families to education was a major factor in limiting the progress and influence of the second generation. All too many Southern Italians regarded the schools as institutions for their social superiors and not suited for their own children. Nor was there always a healthy attitude toward change among the Southerners. "Do not make your children better than you are" warns one Southern Italian proverb which was carried to the new land. Many peasants believed that the road to security was paved by hard work—that is by physical work, the kind of toil they had experienced since time immemorial.

While not always rewarding to the individual Italian-American, the backbreaking labor they contributed helped to build America. Providing their children with positions in the construction industry and appreciating vocational instruction and craft training, they did not generally see the need for higher education. As late as 1960 only six percent of the graduates of the City College in New York had Italian names, in a city with a very large Italian-American population. Perhaps this is why the history of the Italians in America remains to be told in a scholarly and comprehensive fashion.

In the area of business the Italian-Americans showed greater initiative, establishing thousands of small contracting and construction concerns, dry cleaning establishments, garment factories, produce handling firms, wholesale food companies, grocery stores, and restaurants. In the production, processing, and sale of food in the United States the Italians played a key role.

No less important was the impact of their cuisine which unlike some others is of a popular rather than upper-class origin. It was a gift which almost every Italian brought with him from the old country. Its influence has been far-reaching; it has been estimated that there are no less than 40,000 Italian restaurants in the United States. So popular has this cuisine become that American food concerns vie with one another in the preparation and sale of Italian specialties such as minestrone soup and various types of macaroni. Edibles such as broccoli, artichokes, oregano, eggplants, and zucchini, which at one time could only be found in Italian groceries and specialty shops, can be bought in supermarkets throughout the country. A number of foods such as lemon ice, pizza, and spaghetti have become so common as to render them as much American as Italian. Pizza in fact has almost replaced the "hot dog" as the nation's fun food, and Italian ices provide severe competition for the ice cream industry.

The Italian-American's frequent use of tomatoes, fresh vegetables, and fruit not only changed national tastes but altered American patterns of agriculture. In the Northeast a number of Italians turned to truck farming, supplying vegetables and fruits to the large urban centers. In New Jersey they developed berry farms, pepper fields, and vineyards, helping to make it the garden state. In New York they reclaimed swampy soils and played an important role in its fruit and wine production. An enduring farming achievement occurred in the west with the founding of the Italian Swiss Colony. Their good luck was shared by the Di Giorgio family, the largest shippers of fresh fruit in the world, the Gallo vineyards, which found a national and international market, and Marco Fontana, who established the Del Monte Company. In the financial sphere no name in California is as important as Amadeo Giannini who founded the Bank of America, the largest bank in the United States and the world. Another Amadeo, this one's family name was Obici, moved from a fruit stand specializing in the sale of roasted nuts to form the Planter Peanut Corporation.

In religious matters the Italian achievement in the United States was not as great. The Italian influence was not able to rival the Irish predominance in the American Catholic Church. Indeed it was not until 1954 that the first Italian-American bishop was appointed in the United States, though it must not be forgotten that Francesca Cabrini who was canonized in 1946 was the first declared saint in the United States. Furthermore, if Italians in America largely adopted Irish religious practices, they were not completely absorbed. They popularized the practice of having masses, prayers, and novenas as well as feasts in honor of patron saints. At the same time they contributed to the cult of the Virgin Mary or as she is known in Italian, the Madonna, the Mother of all. And in some neighborhoods the procession persists while there is revival of interest in the religious feast.

In politics, too, the impact of the Italian-Americans has not been spectacular because of the lateness of their arrival, the stigma of crime, and a failure to produce educated men who were politically motivated. Most important of all, Italian-Americans have seldom been sufficiently organized to be bloc voters. Despite these drawbacks some Italian-Americans achieved success. Perhaps the best known was the colorful mayor of New York City, Fiorello La Guardia. In 1946 John Pastore became the first American of Italian extraction to be elected governor of any state, and in 1950 Rhode Island made him the first Italian-American to sit in the Senate. Only in 1962 did an Italian-American receive a post in the presidential cabinet.

What the future holds for the political aspirations of Americans of Italian descent is difficult to say—but given the craze for Americanization it does seem that whatever success is attained will be an individual rather than a group achievement. Estimates of the size of the Italian-American population vary widely. According to one study there are some five million who might be classified as first generation, another five million in the second generation category, and some ten to twelve million in the third and fourth generations. Those in the last groups are thoroughly American. However, the Italian economic miracle after World War II, the influence of Italy on fashion and culture, the growing tourist trade to Italy, and the great popularity of Italian products have made them less fearful of revealing their background. It is paradoxical that many Italo-Americans of the third and fourth generations have had to be induced by the respect shown to things Italian by their Anglo-saxon, middle-class peers to appreciate Italy. Could this be assimilation carried to its logical conclusion?

SELECTED BIBLIOGRAPHY

This selected bibliography is not intended for the scholar, the specialist, or those acquainted with foreign languages, particularly Italian. Rather it is designed for those general readers who would like to delve more deeply into some of the topics examined in the essay. It is for this reason that I have included only those works that are widely available and written or translated into English.

AMFITHEATROF, ERIK. *The Children of Columbus: An Informal History of the Italians in the New World.* Boston: Little Brown and Co., 1973. A readable though very general work.

CLOUGH, SHEPARD B. *The Economic History of Modern Italy.* New York: Columbia University Press, 1964. This is a useful survey of the economic conditions which contributed to the massive Italian emigration.

DE CONDE, ALEXANDER. *Half Bitter, Half Sweet: An Excursion into Italian-American History.* New York: C. Scribner's Sons, 1971. It is valuable not so much because of its presentation of new material—it has very little that is new—nor because of the originality of its interpretation, but rather because of the breadth of its coverage and the author's bringing together of issues and matters scattered elsewhere. Particularly useful is the long and informative bibliographical essay which will be appreciated both by the scholar and the interested amateur.

FERMI, LAURA. *Illustrious Immigrants: The Intellectual Migration from Europe.* Chicago: University of Chicago Press, 1968. This volume concentrates upon the later European immigrants and especially the intellectual elite.

FOERSTER, ROBERT F. *The Italian Emigration of our Times.* New York: Russell and Russell, 1968. The standard and still the best work on the modern Italian migration and the influx of Italians into the United States. The scores of volumes which followed it lacked its breadth, objectivity, and scholarship.

GANS, HERBERT J. *The Urban Villagers: Group and Class in the Life of Italian-Americans.* New York: Free Press of Glencoe, 1962. An important sociological study of part of the Italian-American community.

IORIZZO, LUCIANO and SALVATORE MONDELLO. *The Italian-Americans.* New York: Twayne Publishers, 1971. This first volume in the "Immigrant Heritage of America Series" concentrates upon the Italian-American experience in New York State.

LUZZATTO, G. "The Italian Economy in the First Decade after Unification," in *Essays in European History, 1789–1914*. Edited by F. Crouzet and others. New York: St. Martin, 1970. This essay provides a good picture of the economic and fiscal conditions in Italy under the various governments of the *Destra* during the first years after unification.

MARIANO, J. H. *The Italian Contribution to American Democracy*. Boston: Christopher Publishing House, 1925.

NELLI, HERBERT S. *Italians in Chicago, 1880–1930*. New York: Oxford University Press, 1973. A detailed study of Italian-Americans in this midwestern city.

ROLLE, ANDREW. *The Immigrant Upraised: Italian Adventures and Colonists in an expanding America*. Norman: University of Oklahoma Press, 1968. Looks at those Italo-Americans who settled beyond the eastern seaboard and the major cities of the United States.

SCHIAVO, GIOVANNI. *Four Centuries of Italian-American History*. New York: Vigo Press, 1952. A broad survey of the contributions and experiences of Italians in America.

————. *Italians in America before the Civil War*. New York: Vigo Press, 1934.

TOMASI, LYDIO (ed.). *The Italian in America: The Progressive View, 1894–1914*. New York: Center for Migration Studies of New York, Inc., 1972. The thirty-nine articles collected in this book originally appeared in *The Charities Review: A Journal of Political Sociology* from 1891 to 1914. This magazine concerned itself with the major issues of the day and consequently devoted considerable attention to the New immigration and the Italian influx into the United States. The editor has reprinted here most of what appeared in the magazine on immigration in general, with a concentration on what contemporaries had to say about the massive Italian immigration of the Giolittian decade. The scope of the articles is very broad and covers such diverse topics as health, poverty, education, labor, crime, and assimilation and achievement.

TOMASI, SILVANO M. and MADELINE H. ENGEL (editors). *The Italian Experience in the United States*. New York: Center for Migration Studies, 1970. This collection of essays treats such topics as recent Italian emigration, the distribution of Italians in America, the Italians in urban areas, the Italians and the Church, and the Italians and labor.

VI

The Jews: From the Ghettos of Europe to the Suburbs of the United States

By MORTON ROSENSTOCK
Bronx Community College, New York

ON July 4, 1776, the total Jewish population of the newly established nation was probably not over 2,000 people. As we celebrate the bicentennial of American independence, the Jewish population of the United States is estimated at 6,000,000. The overwhelming bulk of this growth took place in the forty years from 1880 to 1920, when the Jewish community grew from 250,000 to 3,500,000, primarily as a result of a massive wave of immigration from Eastern Europe. The process of immigration and its concomitant effects have profoundly influenced the nature of the American Jewish community and, indeed, helped shape the course of world Jewish history. It is perhaps symbolic that the famous poem inscribed on the base of the Statue of Liberty as a welcome to all new immigrants was written by an American Jewish poet, Emma Lazarus:

> Give me your tired, your poor
> Your huddled masses yearning to breathe free
> The wretched refuse of your teeming shore.
> Send these, the homeless, tempest tossed to me.
> I lift my lamp beside the golden door.

Who were these Jewish immigrants, where did they come from, and why did they come? Immigration to the United States, in general, was a result of the interplay of forces of attraction

147

and expulsion. That is, it depended largely on the intensity of the negative forces in the country of origin and the attractiveness of the United States during any given period. Jewish emigration was part of the general European movement to this country, but it also displayed distinctive origins, characteristics, and results. Jewish immigration has been divided into three broad waves, the Sephardic during the colonial period, German from 1830 to 1880, and East European thereafter. Although this categorization is not completely accurate historically, it may be used cautiously for the sake of convenience in describing Jewish emigration.

The first wave, numerically very tiny, consisted of Jews whose origin was directly or indirectly the Iberian peninsula, Spain, and Portugal. These Sephardim, to use the Hebrew term, were joined later in the colonial period by a substantial group of Ashkenazim (Jews originating in Central and Eastern Europe). They set the pattern and tone of American Jewish life, just as colonial America laid the basis for present-day America. The twenty-three Jews who landed on Manhattan Island in what was then New Amsterdam, in September 1654, were the pioneers of Jewish settlement on mainland North America. Their arrival at this particular destination was somewhat accidental, but their motivation was clear. They had been expelled from Brazil after the reconquest of that area by the Portuguese and were thus, in effect, refugees fleeing religious persecution. In future decades, other Jews arrived in the colonies, most of them seeking economic opportunities, some fleeing from Portugal, where they had been forced to live as Marranos, or secret Jews. The major colonial Jewish settlements were along the eastern seaboard, in New York, Newport, Philadelphia, Charleston, and Savannah. By the American Revolution, the small Jewish communities had achieved economic success and enjoyed religious freedom and most, though not all, civil rights. Nevertheless, immigration remained at a trickle, and by 1830 the community numbered no more than 5,000 in a total population of 10,000,000.

From 1830 to 1880, the Jewish population in the United States grew fifty-fold. This was a result of the so-called second wave of immigration, that of the Ashkenazic German and Central European Jews. German Jews generally emigrated to the United

States for the same reasons that caused a massive outpouring
of non-Jewish Germans during the same era. That is, an economic
depression set in during the 1830's and 1840's, especially in rural
areas of Germany, as a result of shifting conditions in agriculture
and changes wrought by emerging industrial capitalism. Added
to the economic motivation was the severe political repression,
particularly in such reactionary German states as Bavaria which,
for example, imposed limitations on Jewish marriages and residence in its towns.

The sea voyage to America, in the pre-Civil War period, was
uncomfortable and sometimes hazardous. "The food is so bad,"
wrote one immigrant, "that, in comparison, the pigs in Bohemia
are fed with delicacies." The German-Jewish immigrant was
almost universally poverty-stricken upon his arrival in the United
States, but he came during an age of dazzling geographic expansion and economic growth, both in agriculture and industry.
Although the Jewish community in New York City (which had
become the main port of entry) grew to 40,000 by the Civil
War, most German-Jewish immigrants were attracted to the
interior by economic opportunities on the advancing western
frontier. Unlike the later Russian-Jewish immigration, the German Jews moved along the Erie Canal, the Ohio, and the Mississippi Rivers and founded new Jewish settlements in such cities
as Cincinnati, St. Louis, Chicago, and dozens of smaller towns.

The third wave of Jewish immigration was the most massive.
More than 2,000,000 East European Jewish immigrants entered
this country during the years from 1880 to the effective closure
of the gates in 1925 by the quota system. As a consequence, the
Jewish population of the country rose dramatically:

Number of Jews in United States

	Total Population	*Jews*	*Percent*
1877	43,661,968	250,000	0.52
1897	72,106,120	937,000	1.31
1907	88,787,058	1,776,885	2.00
1917	103,690,473	3,388,951	3.27

The new Jewish immigration was part of a tremendous upsurge
of general immigration from Southern and Eastern Europe but,

again, had distinctive characteristics. The majority of East European Jews came from the small towns (*shtetl*) of Russia or Galicia where the Jews had developed a unique culture whose elements included Orthodox Jewish practices, the Yiddish language, and a value system which placed great emphasis on learning.

Why did so many abandon this for the unknown New World? Certainly a basic factor was the overwhelming growth of Jewish population which tripled on the European continent in the nineteenth century, creating economic pressures which could not be resolved in the relatively backward countries of Eastern Europe. Changes in agriculture and the beginning of the factory system added to the economic dislocation of Jewish petty traders and artisans. In the Russian Empire (where Jews were restricted to the so-called Pale of Settlement) and Romania, political repression was an important catalytic factor. In Russia, government-sponsored, violent anti-Semitic attacks (*pogroms*) took place with increasing frequency after 1881. The Russian May Laws of 1882 added further restrictions on Jewish economic and educational horizons. By the 1880's, the improved physical basis for immigration, that is, railroads and steamship lines, simplified the process of movement. Further, the winds of Western enlightenment had reached Eastern Europe, loosening communal bonds. New secular ideologies, including socialism and Zionism, were making inroads into the traditional culture.

At the same time, the attraction of America, the Golden Land, was considerable. Impoverished Jews learned of neighbors or relatives who had emigrated and who had made a niche for themselves, and, in many instances, these new Americans assisted in bringing them across the Atlantic. Thus, the movement fed upon itself, in a snowball effect. Finally, it should be noted that political repression alone was insufficient to cause such a massive emigration. Galician Jews, who were politically equal in the Austro-Hungarian Empire, but who were more poverty-stricken than Russian Jews, emigrated at a higher rate than any other East European Jewish group.

From 1881 to the outbreak of World War I Jewish immigration increased dramatically:

Jewish Immigration, 1881–1914

1881–90	193,021
1891–1900	393,516
1901–10	976,263
1911–14	411,199

Almost all these immigrants made the United States their permanent home. Thus, they had an extremely low re-emigration rates as against other immigrants:

Re-emigration Rate, 1908–1914

Jews	7.14%
Irish	9.36%
Poles	29.10%
Southern Italians	44.71%

Jewish immigration was largely a family affair, with a high proportion of women and children. Occupationally, Jews differed from other immigrants of this era, in that most other ethnic groups were mainly agricultural workers and unskilled laborers, whereas very few Jews were in those categories, most classifying themselves as skilled workers.

The ocean voyage, for most of the immigrants, was initiated in Bremen, Hamburg, or Liverpool, most often in steerage class accommodations. Arrival in the United States was typically through New York where they were processed, first at Castle Garden and after 1892 at Ellis Island. Despite difficulties, the initial impression of the new land was usually favorable. Abraham Cahan wrote: "The magnificent verdure of Staten Island, the tender blue of sea and sky, the dignified bustle of passing craft.... It was all so utterly unlike anything I had ever seen or dreamed of before. It unfolded itself like a divine revelation." Most immigrants, arriving with minimal funds, if any,' were assisted by relatives or neighbors from the old country. Others were aided by philanthropic agencies established by the already existing Jewish community, such as the United Hebrew Charities of New York and the Hebrew Sheltering and Immigrant Aid Society (HIAS).

Negligible during World War I, Jewish immigration resumed in the 1920–24 period, but slowed again after the passage of restrictive legislation. From 1925–33, fewer than 100,000 Jews entered the country. From 1933 to the end of World War II, about 150,000 Jews, mostly refugees from German Nazism, managed to arrive, bringing with them considerable intellectual and managerial skills. Since 1946, approximately 250,000 Jews have emigrated to the United States, ranging from displaced persons and Hungarian refugees to Cubans and Egyptians.

Jewish immigrants after 1880 tended to concentrate in urban areas along the East coast rather than to scatter to the interior as had earlier German Jewish immigrants. Efforts by Jewish organizations and philanthropists to disperse immigrant Jews, such as Jacob Schiff's Galveston project, and the work of the Industrial Removal Office from 1901–12, although not altogether failures, had little significant impact on this basic pattern of Eastern-urban settlement. There were many reasons for this, but fundamental was a change in the American economic structure. The country had moved rapidly from a rural-agricultural base to an urban-industrial base. The old American frontier was gone, and the new frontier was in the cities. Jews landing in New York, Boston, Philadelphia, and Baltimore found relatives and philanthropic institutions awaiting them. They also found easy entrance into light industrial employment. Although many Jewish agricultural settlements were started in various parts of the country, most proved economically unsound. Consequently, Jews, who had lacked agricultural experience in Europe, tended to become urban workers and businessmen. By the 1970's, two-thirds of the American Jews lived in four metropolitan centers with about half in the Greater New York region.

The contemporary American Jewish community consists largely of the children and grandchildren of the East European post-1880 immigrants. The descendants of the earlier German Jewish immigrants, while no longer numerically significant, continue to play important roles. Actually, it is becoming increasingly difficult to separate the two groups. Over the past half century, there has been a coming together based on common problems, domestic and overseas, participation in joint social and philanthropic groups, and, finally, intermarriage. American Jewry, although its rate of growth has slowed considerably, is still the largest in the world; in fact, it is the largest in Jewish history.

Upon arrival in America, Jewish immigrants of the late nineteenth and early twentieth centuries tended to settle in densely populated sections of the great cities—Boston's North End, Chicago's West Side, Philadelphia's downtown, and, above all, New York's Lower East Side. Life in these areas of primary settlement was, as one writer put it, "a panorama of hardship, misery, poverty, crowding, filth, uncertainty, alienation, joy, love, and devotion." New York's East Side was symbolic. In 1917, 500,000 Jews were crowded into a few square miles. As early as 1893, the Tenth Ward had 70,000 Jews, or 700 per acre. Up to the age of twelve, Alfred Kazin recalls, a Brownsville child scarcely encountered non-Jews, except for policemen and teachers.

Housing in the Jewish quarter of New York consisted primarily of five-story walk-up tenements, most often squalid, unsanitary firetraps. Rents were not excessive, but wages were so low that families were frequently forced to keep lodgers in order to be able to pay the rent. The result was extreme congestion. Fortunately, disease was not a serious problem, although the tuberculosis rate was considerable at one time.

The majority of Jewish immigrants in the urban centers were wage earners, at least at first. A substantial number, however, were peddlers, small businessmen, skilled craftsmen (printers, carpenters, painters), clerks, and a few were professionals. Hester Street, known as the *Chazermark*, or Pig Market, and other streets on the Lower East Side were jammed with pushcart peddlers loudly advertising their assorted wares.

Very few Jews went into heavy industry; for the most part, Jewish workers tended toward the garment industry in its various branches. There were many reasons for this concentration. Some Jews had been needle-trades workers in Eastern Europe, although the majority were so-called "Columbus tailors," that is, they learned their trade in America. At the end of the nineteenth and the beginning of the twentieth century, the ready-made clothing industry grew spectacularly, at first in men's clothing and later in women's clothing. In New York, many of the clothing manufacturers at first were German Jews who combined philanthrophy with a desire to use cheap immigrant labor. To one employer, immigrants were "people who obey the law, are

God-fearing, patient, industrious, and satisfied with little." Characterized by fragmentation, seasonal changes and dog-eat-dog competition, the garment trade was not a pleasant one, but it offered advantages to the newcomer. Because it did not require heavy capital investment, the worker of today could fairly easily become the entrepreneur of tomorrow. In addition, the minute breakdown of tasks in clothing production made it relatively simple for the new immigrant to acquire a skill in a short time. At its height, a million Jews depended on the needle trades for their economic existence. It quickly became a Jewish industry, with the newer East European Jews rapidly rising to ownership.

Working conditions in the garment industry were generally poor, especially where the worker did not work in the main factory but was employed by a "contractor" in a "sweatshop." Jacob Riis reported a ride on the Second Avenue Elevated: "Every open window of the big tenements . . . gives you a glimpse of one of those shops as the train speeds by. Men and women, bending over their machines or ironing boards at the windows, half-naked. . . . The road is like a big gangway through an endless workroom where vast multitudes are forever laboring. Morning, noon and night, it makes no difference; the scene is always the same." Long hours, low wages and constant toil were the lot of the garment worker. Morris Rosenfeld, pessimistic poet of the sweatshops, described them bitterly:

> The sweatshop at midday—I will draw you a picture:
> A battlefield bloody; the conflict at rest;
> Around and about me the corpses are lying;
> The blood cries aloud from the earth's gory breast.
> A moment . . . and hark! The loud signal is sounded,
> The dead rise again and renewed is the fight. . . .
> They struggle, these corpses; for strangers, for strangers!
> They struggle, they fall, and they sink into night.

In 1911, the Triangle Waist Company factory was consumed by fire, killing 146.

The greenhorn, or newcomer, was often hired by employers who had come from the same town in Europe (a *landsman*). The employer obtained a cheap laborer, the immigrant obtained a small livelihood and experience. Yet, despite all the poverty, overcrowding, and overwork, the standard of living for most Jewish immigrants was higher than it had been in Europe. Jobs were available, food was plentiful, there was always the hope of saving money and even of sending the children to college.

An East Side peddler, interviewed by the *New York Evening Post* in 1903, said: "It is enough that I am a merchant. What is such a life? What can I do for my people or myself? My boy shall be a lawyer, learned and respected of men. And it is for this that I stand here, sometimes when my feet ache so that I would gladly go and rest. My boy shall have knowledge. He shall go to College."

The basic instrument for the Americanization of the immigrant family was the American public school system. Jewish children, imbued with the traditional European Jewish emphasis on intellectual achievement, did remarkably well in the public schools and, before long, were enrolling in New York's municipal colleges and others throughout the country. One non-Jewish writer remembered of Boston's Jews that:

Every Jewish junk-dealer from Chelsea, every shopkeeper or delicatessen proprietor in Dorchester, every tailor or fur-worker in Mattapan, above all else wanted his son to become a professional man. And because nearby Harvard was America's oldest and most illustrious university, he wanted him to go there and to no lesser place. For this, any and every sacrifice was worthwhile, for this the first generation Jew would grub away his working hours.

Closely allied with the public schools in the process of Americanization were the settlement houses and the public libraries. In New York, for example, the Educational Alliance, Henry Street Settlement, and University Settlement provided a variety of services and educational activities for adults as well as for the younger generation. The Yiddish press, the most characteristic example of the richly varied cultural life in the immigrant Jewish ghetto, also aided the immigrant in adjusting to the New World. The *Bintel Brief*, a famous feature introduced by the *Jewish Daily Forward*, mirrored the manifold problems of the immigrant at work, marriage, child-parent relations, religion, and politics, through letters to the editor and their sensible, pragmatic responses.

The immigrant generation, and especially its children, acculturated rapidly in language, dress, and habits. Often, this caused sharp clashes between the generations as the young abandoned family traditions and discipline. Hundreds of orthodox congregations founded synagogues but the old-style religion, fostered by old-fashioned religious education, lost its attractiveness for many. In an attempt to Americanize the orthodox faith of the immigrant and salvage the younger generation, leading Reform Jews financed the Jewish Theological Seminary to train Conservative rabbis. Orthodoxy itself felt the impact of America and attempted adjustment through such means as the Young Israel movement. In the meantime, the older generation was adjusting also through the medium of fraternal orders, such as the Workman's Circle, and thousands of small *landsmanshaften* (groups based on town or origin) which provided social, health, and death benefits.

The older established Jewish community at the turn of the century, consisting mostly of Reform Jews of German background who were by then thoroughly Americanized, initially viewed the new East European Jewish immigrants with shock and horror. Nevertheless, the "uptowners" saw it as a necessity for their own status, as well as a moral obligation, to aid and uplift the "downtowners." Men such as Jacob Schiff and Louis Marshall gave unstintingly of their funds and energies for this purpose, and although their efforts were often regarded as patronizing by the new immigrants, much was accomplished. The settlement houses, hospitals, asylums, vocational schools, and myriad other projects cushioned the process of Americanization, and the existence of the established Jews provided role models for the new immigrants. Eventually, a process of communal consolidation took place, both within the East European group and later between "downtown" and "uptown."

Today, the American Jewish community can be characterized in sociological terms as behaviorally acculturated but not structurally assimilated. It continues to display social cohesion and, to some extent, isolation. A recent study of Detroit, for example, showed that 77% of its Jews report all or nearly all of their close friends as Jewish. It is a middle-class, suburban, child-oriented community. With the exception of a few enclaves of ultra-orthodox Hasidim, acculturation is almost total, and 80% of the community is now native-born.

The American Jewish population, about 6,000,000, is somewhat less than 3% of the total, but their significance is much greater if measured by the conspicuousness of individual Jews and the general contribution of Jews to American culture. In fertility rates, Jews have been consistently lower than Catholics and Protestants and, except for some Orthodox Jews, overwhelmingly accept birth control and the right of abortion. In combination with a decline in immigration, the low fertility rate seems to indicate a continuing proportional decline in the Jewish population ratio to that of Christians.

Geographically, American Jews are highly concentrated, with 60% in the Middle Atlantic states alone. Ten population centers hold 80%: New York, Los Angeles, Philadelphia, Chicago, Boston, Miami, Washington, Baltimore, Cleveland and Detroit. Ninety-five percent live in urban centers. Jewish concentration has slowed the impact of assimilation and has also magnified the Jewish role in American society.

Within a half century after the arrival of the mass of Jewish immigrants, their children and grandchildren have made American Jewry equal or above any other ethnic group in educational progress. Recent statistics indicate that well over four out of five Jews of college age are in college, and although the gap between Jewish and non-Jewish college attendance rates is narrowing, Jews are still quite prominent in American higher education. In recent years, there has been a shift of interest as many Jews have moved into new educational fields in science, engineering, business, and college teaching. Rapid secular education has led .to the not inconsiderable problem of Jewish cultural survival, and attempted solutions have included the establishment of Hillel foundations and Jewish Studies programs on many college campuses.

Economically, Jews epitomize America's affluent society. Their upward economic mobility has been greater than that of any other immigrant group, and their income level is now comparable to that of the oldest established American groups, such as Episcopalians and Presbyterians. American Jewish occupation distribution has foreshadowed that of American society at large.

In 1900, 57% of East European Jewish male immigrants were blue-collar workers; today, it is less than half that figure in New York, and even lower elsewhere. The largest occupational group today is that of manager-proprietor, with many self-employed, and the number of professionals has increased dramatically. In the United States at large, the proportion of doctors is 1:700; among Jews, it is 1:140. Still underrepresented in banking, public utilities, insurance, and heavy industry, Jews are highly visible in the entertainment world, electronics, real estate, and in the computer business.

Socially, American Jews have moved from the grimy ghettos of primary settlement to secondary urban areas and are now increasingly concentrated in suburban "gilded ghettos." In relation to the general population, Jews display a lower divorce rate, lower infant mortality rate, and lower alcoholism rate, but a higher marriage age and a higher rate of neuroses. Although the traditional rejection of intermarriage with non-Jews is still high, there is mounting evidence of a shifting pattern among the younger generation. Estimates of intermarriage rates vary widely and may be inaccurate, but recent studies indicate that as many as 40% of new marriages, especially among native-born college graduates, are with non-Jews. Simultaneously, there has been a substantial growth in conversions to Judaism, especially among those who have married Jews.

In religion, World War II was followed by a widely advertised religious revival which, although usually marked by absence of personal faith and traditional practice, has led to substantial institutional achievements. Basic to present-day American Judaism is a sense of group loyalty and survivalism, in large measure associated with the impact of the Nazi Holocaust and the rise of the state of Israel. Recently, new pockets of belief have emerged — neo-orthodoxy, Hasidism, the day school movement.

Israel plays an increasingly crucial unifying role in American Jewish life, both in terms of philanthropy and ideology. The poet, Karl Shapiro, caught the symbolic significance of Israel to many American Jews:

When I see the name of Israel high in print
The fences crumble in my flesh; I sink
Deep in a Western chair and rest my soul.
I look the stranger clear to the blue depths
Of his unclouded eye. I say my name
Aloud for the first time unconsciously.

Israel is seen as an anchor protecting American Jewry from the destruction of Jewish values and from newly emerging social problems in America, as well as a source of pride and a substitute for traditional faith. The response of American Jews to Israel's crises in the Six Days War of 1967 and the Yom Kippur War of 1973 clearly indicated Israel's crucial role in American Jewish life.

In 1811, Gershom Mendes Seixas, minister of the oldest Jewish congregation in the country, wrote that "The United States is, perhaps, the only place where the Jews have not suffered persecution, but have, on the contrary, been encouraged and indulged in every right of citizens." To Seixas and to most American Jews thereafter, anti-Jewish prejudice, legal restrictions and discrimination of the type so common in the Old World were almost nonexistent in the New World. Full civil rights and equality before the law, with relatively minor exceptions, have been in existence ever since the early nineteenth century. Nevertheless, anti-Jewish stereotypes, social discrimination against Jews, and nativist anti-Semitism have not been totally absent, and, in fact, were major factors in certain periods.

Anti-Semitism today is a combination of the belief that Jews are distinguishable from non-Jews, a fear of Jews, the desire to keep them at a distance, and a willingness to discriminate against them. It is based upon a stereotype which often combines contradictory elements: the Jews are clannish, but at the same time pushy; they are international financiers and international communists; they are materialistic, and greedy and cheaters, yet too bookish; too aggressive, yet too withdrawn and introverted. The roots of the stereotype stem from various religious, psychological, economic, political, and sociological factors, and, in all likelihood, combine these characteristics in various proportions at different times.

During the eighteenth century and for a good part of the nineteenth, anti-Semitism in the United States was relatively absent. The number of Jews was quite small, they were widely dispersed, and most of them were rapidly acculturated. The country was undergoing economic growth, and the frontier acted as a safety valve for social discontent. The slavery issue diverted attention from the Jews, and nativist prejudice, when manifested, for example, in the Know-Nothing movement, was directed primarily at Catholics. Still, the old European image of the Jew as the mysterious outsider, heretic and despoiler, had been brought over to this country. Jacob Henry was refused his seat in the North Carolina legislature in 1809, Mordecai M. Noah was recalled from his consulship in Tunis in 1815 and Uriah P. Levy underwent a succession of courts-martial in the United States Navy. Nevertheless, the country's religious and ethnic diversity tempered the impact of anti-Jewish feelings, and there were no really serious incidents. Jewish immigrants rapidly achieved economic success and social integration.

The first substantial, open anti-Semitic agitation in the United States appeared during the Civil War, a period of severe economic dislocations, political unrest, and frayed tempers. Both in the North and in the Confederacy, Jews were accused of smuggling, profiteering and draft-dodging. The Confederate leader, Judah P. Benjamin, was a favorite target. On December 17, 1862, General Ulysses S. Grant issued Order #11, expelling all Jews from the military area under his control on grounds of economic subversion. Although Grant's order was quickly countermanded at Lincoln's direction, this was a clear instance in American history of official anti-Semitism.

In 1877, a wealthy Jewish banker, Joseph Seligman, was refused admission to the Grand Union Hotel in Saratoga Springs, New York. This event symbolized a new trend in the country, a growing tendency to exclude Jews from social contacts. The increase in social discrimination against Jews—in resorts, social clubs, private schools—was part of an effort by the older, socially dominant elite groups not to compromise their status in the changing Gilded Age. Jews were regarded as having advanced too quickly and were to be kept in their "place."

The rise of social discrimination coincided with the great mass

Jewish immigration at the end of the nineteenth century and, to a great extent, was based on social conflict as well as irrational prejudice. More threatening, potentially, was the development of racist ideologies and the rampant nationalism of the 1890's and early 1900's. Eastern patrician intellectuals, such as Henry Adams, and Western agrarian radicals, such as Ignatius Donnelly, both saw Jews as a symbol and cause of their discontent. The image of the Jew, fairly benign up to this point, changed to that of the arch-conspirator in the hated, feared city who was attempting to impose the gold standard on the suffering workers and farmers. Respectable voices increasingly clamored for restriction of immigration. Prescott Hall, Boston Brahmin head of the Immigration Restriction League, exploded: "To hell with Jews, Jesuits, and steamships!" Senator Henry Cabot Lodge, distinguished academicians such as John R. Commons, Henry Pratt Fairchild, and Edward A. Ross all contributed to the anti-immigrant crusade. Madison Grant, in his 1916 book, *The Passing of the Great Race*, explicitly condemned the impact of Jewish immigrants on America.

The immigration restriction movement met with some success before 1917, but the impact of wartime nationalism and xenophobia made restriction inevitable at the close of World War I. Racist propaganda, such as Burton J. Hendrick's *Jews in America* (1923), continued labor union pressure, and the fear of a renewed immigrant flood resulted in the Immigration Acts of 1921 and 1924. Under these laws, a limited quota system was established favoring Northern and Western Europeans as against Southern and Eastern European immigrants. Partially motivated by a desire to keep East European Jews out, these laws subtly enshrined anti-Semitism in American legislation for more than forty years until the quota system was finally eliminated.

Jewish leaders, responding to the need to deal in a more unified manner with anti-Jewish manifestations at home and abroad, established important defense agencies at the beginning of the twentieth century. Among them were the Anti-Defamation League of the B'nai B'rith (1913) and the American Jewish Congress (1920), but the most influential in the early decades of the century was the American Jewish Committee (1906). Led by outstanding figures in the Jewish community (Jacob Schiff,

Louis Marshall, Mayer Sulzberger, Cyrus Adler, and others), it consistently battled anti-Jewish discrimination, usually with quiet, behind-the-scenes influence. One of its earliest victories was the abrogation of the Russo-American commercial treaty of 1832, under whose terms the Czarist Empire had been discriminating against American Jews.

In 1913, a rare instance of violent anti-Semitism occurred. This was the lynching of Leo Frank in Georgia following his mob-inspired conviction for the murder of a little girl. Behind it was the frustration of lower-class Georgians, urged on by the vicious propaganda of Tom Watson, the Southern populist leader. More significant than the isolated Frank case was the wave of nativist nationalism and religious fundamentalism which swept the country in the post-World War I decade. During the 1919–20 Red Scare, the notion of a Jewish-Bolshevik nexus was firmly implanted in the popular mind. The charges of the forged *Protocols of the Elders of Zion,* that international Jewry was engaged in a conspiracy to dominate and rule the Christian world, received wide dissemination in a seven-year campaign sponsored by Henry Ford's magazine, the *Dearborn Independent.* The pressure of lawsuits and boycotts eventually brought an apology from Ford to American Jews in 1927, but the damage had been done. The banker-Bolshevik, international Jew stereotype had been grafted on the older anti-Christ, Shylock image.

The Ku Klux Klan of the 1920's, which had at its height 4,000,000 adherents, included an anti-Semitic component in its ideology, but its chief targets were Negroes and Catholics. Aside from sporadic anti-Jewish boycotts, it was unable to achieve any political success against Jews. In the same years, social discrimination reached new heights. In higher education, quota systems limited the number of Jews who could enter the more prestigious colleges and universities. President A. Lawrence Lowell publicly announced in 1922 that Harvard was considering a quota on Jewish students. Lowell's scheme was turned down after public protest, but anti-Jewish quotas survived, often in disguised form, well into the 1940's and were particularly disquieting in medical education.

During the 1930's, economic depression, resentment against Roosevelt's New Deal, and the influence of German Nazism produced an upsurge of ideological anti-Semitism. Scores of anti-Semitic groups, often led by religious fundamentalists, propagated anti-Jewish feelings. These were the years of Gerald L. K. Smith, Gerald Winrod, William Pelley's Silver Shirts, the German-American Bund, and most important, Father Charles E. Coughlin. Isolationist leaders Charles Lindbergh, Burton Wheeler, and Gerald Nye, in the years just before American entrance into World War II, pointed to the Jews as pushing the country into war. After Pearl Harbor, wartime tensions stirred anti-Semitic sentiments. In 1944, a public opinion poll showed 24% regarded the Jews as a menace to America.

In the decades since World War II, isolated tiny fringe groups, such as the American Nazi Party and the National Renaissance Party, continued to inveigh against Jews. More threatening have been ultraconservative movements, McCarthyism in the 1950's, and the John Birch Society in the 1960's. Interestingly, these movements never expressed anti-Jewish programs, although they did attract anti-Semites. The postwar era also saw a decline in social discrimination. In 1945, the President of Dartmouth College admitted and publicly defended his college's use of a quota on Jews; in 1970, the President of Dartmouth College was Jewish himself, and currently, 25% of the student body at Ivy League colleges is Jewish. Jewish faculty members at senior colleges nationally are about 10%; medical school quotas on Jews have gone, club and resort discrimination has decreased. There has been a simultaneous decline in anti-Semitic attitudes. Those who subscribed to the old Shylock image declined from 50% in 1939 to 20% in 1960. Only 6% reject Jews as fellow workers and only 3% as neighbors.

The reasons for the post-World War II changes include the acculturation of the Jewish community and its stabilization following the end of unrestricted immigration; widespread acceptance of the concept of cultural pluralism, popularized in the 1930's and 1940's; the continued availability of other targets such as Communists and blacks; and favorable governmental attitudes reinforced by voting power. We have, it has been claimed, entered upon an age of transtolerance, in which open bigotry has become disreputable. Still, some forms of social discrimination persist, particularly in the higher levels of major corporations. Whereas Jews are 8% of the college-trained population, they are only ½% of the executives in large companies. Recent studies have shown that there still exists a substantial segment of the American population which accepts a religion-based anti-Jewish stereotype. Since the late 1960's, friction between blacks and Jews in urban areas has increased over such matters as housing, schools, crime, and the affirmative action program. During recent years, also, anti-Israel propaganda from the New Left and its allies has perhaps displayed disguised anti-Jewish feelings.

Anti-Semitism in the United States is not entirely extinct but is normally not expressed in public. The viability of the American political system, economic stability, the interfaith and ecumenical movements have all aided in this development. Yet, latent prejudices exist, and history has demonstrated that prejudice may be translated into open discrimination when social conflicts and tensions become severe.

In 1790, George Washington wrote a famous letter to the Jewish congregation of Newport, Rhode Island which included a succinct statement of his view of Jewish status in the newly born United States:

All possess alike liberty of conscience and immunities of citizenship. It is now no more that toleration is spoken of as if it was by the indulgence of one class of people that another enjoyed the exercise of their inherent natural rights. For happily the Government of the United States, which gives to bigotry no sanction, to persecution no assistance, requires only that they who live under its protection should demean themselves as good citizens in giving it on all occasions their effectual support.

In essence, this commitment summarized what might be called the American Jewish social contract: Jews would provide accommodation to the culture and loyalty to the government; America would provide freedom of opportunity and public neutrality to Jewishness.

Has this contract worked over the past two centuries and what have the Jews achieved under it? One can identify at least three major areas of Jewish achievement: the strengthening of social justice and civic progress, business and industry, and culture. Most Jews over the years have been content to work and earn a living for their families, but if there has been a predominant motif in Jewish participation in American public life, it has been the pursuit of social justice. This has been true especially in the twentieth century, and one of the prime factors was the contribution of the Jewish labor movement.

The first Jewish unions in the garment industry were established in the 1880's but were relatively unsuccessful for many years in achieving their aims. Rent by ideological quarrels and factionalism, the Jewish socialists concentrated too much attention on the secular messianic age they envisioned rather than the immediate problems of their constituents. After the turn of the century, Jewish unionism turned from ideological objectives to a more pragmatic approach, partly due to the influence of Abraham Cahan and the *Jewish Daily Forward.* The general labor movement, under the leadership of Samuel Gompers, an immigrant Jew who had risen to head the American Federation of Labor, had shown the way to success—concentrate on skilled workers and aim for practical, bread-and-butter objectives. Following this shift to the Gompers approach, a series of strikes in the needle trades, from 1909 to 1914, resulted in remarkable victories. The famous Protocol of Peace (1910), for example, whose chief architect was Louis D. Brandeis, granted union recognition, a preferential shop, abolished subcontracting evils, and established a sanitary board and a board of arbitration.

Two major unions emerged from the Jewish garment trades, the International Ladies Garment Workers Union (ILGWU), later led by David Dubinsky, a Jewish immigrant who had spent time in a Czarist Siberian prison, and the Amalgamated Clothing Workers of America (ACWA), led by Sidney Hillman, a Jewish immigrant who had studied at the yeshiva in Kovno. Both men were outstanding leaders of the progressive wing of the American labor movement. Under their guidance, Jewish unions were trail blazers in providing auxiliary services to members (pensions, housing, education, health, recreation) and in promoting efficiency and stability in their industry by cooperative efforts with employers in management engineering. At the same time, they stood in the forefront of politically liberal causes, with Dubinsky helping to found New York's American Labor Party and later, its Liberal Party, and Hillman emerging as a powerful influence on Roosevelt's New Deal. In recent decades, Jewish membership in the garment unions has declined substantially as Jews moved to other occupations. Jewish labor leaders, however, are still prominent, especially in newer unions of government workers and professionals and are again serving as pioneers in these areas of union activity.

Jews have held elective political office in the United States for more than a hundred years, including senators and governors in states where there were very few other Jews. Oscar S. Straus, the first Jew to serve in the Cabinet, was appointed Secretary of Commerce and Labor by Theodore Roosevelt in 1906. At the other end of the political spectrum, the first socialist congressmen were Jews, Victor Berger and Meyer London. After the Russian Revolution, Communism proved attractive to some Jewish workers and intellectuals in the 1920's and 1930's but declined precipitously after the success of the New Deal and the revelations of Stalinist repression and anti-Semitism. Jews, imbued with a liberal political tradition, switched their political loyalties overwhelmingly to the Democratic Party when it became the standard-bearer of progressive politics under Alfred E. Smith and Franklin D. Roosevelt.

The intellectual foundations and practical accomplishments of the New Deal owed much to Jews. Louis D. Brandeis, the first Jewish Supreme Court justice (appointed in 1916), was referred to by FDR as "Isaiah." Herbert H. Lehman, the first Jewish governor of New York State, was an innovative New Dealer, and Felix Frankfurter, appointed to the Supreme Court in 1939, was one of Roosevelt's chief consultants. Other prominent Jewish New Dealers included Henry Morgenthau, Jr., Secretary of the Treasury, Samuel Rosenman, Isidor Lubin, Mordecai Ezekiel, David K. Niles, Ben Cohen, Robert Nathan, Anna Rosenberg, and David Lilienthal. In recent decades, Jewish liberalism has persisted, despite the middle-class affluence of the majority of the Jewish community. Jews, for example, voted more heavily for John F. Kennedy than did Irish Catholics, and such national leaders as Jacob Javits and Abraham Ribicoff continue the liberal tradition. American Jews have been leaders in a variety of public movements and causes, ranging from general civil rights defense (ACLU), to Negro civil rights (NAACP), to such recent phenomena as the New Left (Mark Rudd), women's liberation (Betty Friedan, Gloria Steinem), consumerism (Bess Myerson), and ecology (Barry Commoner).

Jews have played a prominent role in the American economy, especially in certain branches of business and industry. In the late nineteenth and early twentieth centuries, Jewish bankers achieved an important place in the highest reaches of American finance—the Seligmans, Jacob Schiff, the Warburgs, Lehman Brothers, and others. Although still active, many of these older Jewish firms are now run by non-Jews. More significant was the achievement of Jews in retail trade, particularly the creation and development of department stores. Macy's (owned by the Straus family), Sears Roebuck (brought to fame by Julius Rosenwald), Bloomingdale's, Bamberger's, Altman's, Gimbels, the Lazarus family, are some of the leaders in the department store business. Recently, Jews have been actively pioneering the newest branch of retailing, the discount chains.

The garment industry, of course, has been a major area of Jewish achievement. Samuel Eliot Morison, in his *Oxford History of the United States,* states: "Human dignity owes much to the Hebrew organizers of the garment trades who wiped out class distinctions in dress. Jews may take credit for the fact that American women are the best dressed in the world and can do so on a slender purse." With the exception of the Guggenheim family's interest in mining, Jews have played a relatively small role in heavy industry but have made important contributions to newer industrial achievements in such areas as computers, electronics, radio-television (David Sarnoff of RCA, William Paley of CBS), Xerox, and Polaroid. Jews figure importantly in the real estate and building industries, with such leaders as Levitt, Uris, Lefrak, Tishman, Zeckendorf, Minskoff, and others.

The contribution of Jews to American culture has been disproportionately large. In medicine and science, the names are a virtual who's who: Simon Flexner (bacteriology), Abraham Flexner (medical education), Joseph Goldberger (pellagra), Casimir Funk (vitamins), Bela Schick (diphtheria), Selman Waksman (antibiotics), Jonas Salk and Alfred Sabin (polio), Albert Michelson (optics), Albert Einstein (relativity), Isidor

Rabi (physics), J. Robert Oppenheimer (atomic bomb), Edward Teller (hydrogen bomb), Hyman Rickover (nuclear submarine), Norbert Wiener (cybernetics). Psychiatry and psychoanalysis have a high percentage of Jewish practitioners.

In law, education, and the social sciences, contributions are equally impressive. Among judges, such figures as Louis D. Brandeis, Felix Frankfurter, Benjamin Cardozo, Arthur Goldberg, and Abe Fortas have reached the Supreme Court bench, and other Jews—Irving Lehman and Simon Sobeloff—have presided over state supreme courts. E. R. A. Seligman, Leon Keyserling, Arthur Burns, Paul Samuelson in economics, Franz Boas, Melville Herskovits in anthropology, Morris R. Cohen in philosophy, Richard Hofstadter and Oscar Handlin in history, illustrate the variety of Jewish academic contributions. The first Jew to serve as president of a general American college was Paul Klapper in the 1930's. Today, Jews are presidents of such universities as Chicago, Pennsylvania, Rutgers, and Dartmouth.

Jews in American literature, music, and art are numerous and have made major contributions. Among the novelists have been Saul Bellow, Bernard Malamud, Irwin Shaw, Norman Mailer, Philip Roth, Herman Wouk, Meyer Levin, J. D. Salinger, Leon Uris, Irving Wallace, Howard Fast, and I. B. Singer. Poets and playwrights include Arthur Miller, Delmore Schwartz, Karl Shapiro, Allen Ginsburg. Jews have been leaders in literary criticism and linguistics: Lionel Trilling, Alfred Kazin, Leslie Fiedler, Irving Howe, Noam Chomsky. Journals published or edited by Jews, such as *Commentary, Partisan Review, New York Review of Books* have had a major influence on the American literary scene.

In music, there have been George Gershwin, Aaron Copland, Ernest Bloch, Kurt Weill, and Arnold Schoenberg among the composers, and such names as Heifetz, Menuhin, Stern, Milstein, Goodman, Horowitz, Ormandy, Bernstein, Walter, and Koussevitzky among performers and conductors. Opera singers include many Jews, among them Peerce, Tucker, Resnick, Peters and Sills. Jewish painters and sculptors have included Jo Davidson, Chaim Gross, Moses and Raphael Soyer, Ben Shahn, Jack Levine, Adolf Gottlieb, Max Weber, Larry Rivers, Mark Rothko. Jewish patrons of the arts have had major and lasting impact upon such institutions as the Metropolitan Opera, Guggenheim Museum, Hirshorn Collection, and Lincoln Center.

Jews have been active in journalism (Joseph Pulitzer, Adolph S. Ochs, Arthur Sulzberger, Eugene Meyer, Dorothy Schiff, Walter Annenberg) and have been associated with leading publishing firms (Simon and Schuster, Random House, Alfred Knopf, Book-of-the-Month Club). The motion picture field, especially in its earlier days, was heavily Jewish (Goldwyn, Mayer, Selznick, Loew, Brandt, Warner). The Broadway theater also owes much to Jews (Belasco, Shubert, Merrick, Hellman, Odets, Kaufman, Simon). Popular entertainment (Cantor, Jolson, Jessel, Tucker, Benny, Berle, Levinson, Bruce, Marx, Kaye), Tin Pan Alley (Kern, Romberg, Berlin, Rodgers), folk music (Dylan, Simon and Garfunkel), and even sports (Baer, Leonard, Greenberg, Koufax, Luckman, Holman, Spitz, Reshevsky, Fischer) have had major Jewish contributors.

Jewish philanthropy has been a pacesetter for the country in its professional organization and highly efficient services. The art of giving has been reduced (or raised) to a science in the American Jewish community, and vast sums have been collected for domestic and overseas projects sponsored by local welfare federations, the United Jewish Appeal, and other agencies.

If the United States is indeed cultural pluralism's orchestra of many ethnic groups, then the internal achievements of the Jewish community have added considerably to the richness of orchestral sound. The multitude of synagogues, schools, organizations, seminaries, cultural institutions, and publications have created a remarkably rich and varied American Jewish life. All indications point to the continued strengthening of the Jewish cultural scene, as well as an undiminished outpouring of talented contributors to general American culture.

SELECTED BIBLIOGRAPHY

CAHAN, ABRAHAM. *The Rise of David Levinsky*. New York: Harper & Row, 1974. Written by the editor of the *Jewish Daily Forward*, this novel graphically presents the saga of Jewish immigration in fictional terms.

DINNERSTEIN, LEONARD, ed. *Anti-Semitism in the United States*. New York: Holt, 1971. A useful collection of articles and excerpts from books dealing with anti-Semitism.

FEINGOLD, HENRY. *Zion in America*. New York: Hippocrene, 1974. Well-written survey of American Jewish history, incorporating much of recent scholarship in the field.

FISHMAN, PRISCILLA, ed. *The Jews of the United States*. Philadelphia: Quadrangle, 1974. Based on the *Encyclopedia Judaica*, this offers much useful information.

GLAZER, NATHAN. *American Judaism*. rev. ed. Chicago: University of Chicago Press, 1972. Brief but excellent analysis, written with perception and understanding.

HANDLIN, OSCAR. *Adventure in Freedom*. Port Washington, N. Y.: Kennikat, 1971. Good survey of American Jewish history.

"A Century of Jewish Immigration to the United States," in *American Jewish Year Book*, 50 (1948–49), 1–84. Valuable article drawing together important data.

HIGHAM, JOHN. *Strangers in the Land: Patterns of American Nativism, 1860–1925*. New York: Atheneum, 1963. Outstanding historical work on American prejudice, this provides essential background for understanding American anti-Semitism.

HOWE, IRVING. *World of our Fathers*. Philadelphia. Jewish Publication Society, 1976. Vivid portrait of the East European immigrant generation, with emphasis on Yiddish culture.

KARP, ABRAHAM, ed., *The Jewish Experience in America*. 5 vols. New York: Ktav, 1969. A compendium of major articles from the journal of the American Jewish Historical Society.

LEARSI, RUFUS. *The Jews in America*. rev. ed., New York: Ktav, 1972. Useful survey of American Jewish history.

MARCUS, JACOB R. *The Colonial American Jew, 1492–1776*. 3 vols. Detroit: Wayne State University Press, 1970. A major scholarly work on all aspects of colonial American Jewish history.

METZKER, ISAAC, ed. *A Bintel Brief*. New York: Ballantine, 1972. A collection of readers' letters to the *Jewish Daily Forward*, a Yiddish newspaper, illuminating the everyday problems of Jewish immigrant life.

RISCHIN, MOSES. *The Promised City: New York's Jews 1870–1914*.

New York: Harper & Row, 1970. Fine monographic study of a crucial period in the history of the most important American Jewish community.

ROSENSTOCK, MORTON. *Louis Marshall, Defender of Jewish Rights.* Detroit: Wayne State University Press, 1966. Study of intergroup problems and the defense activities of American Jewish leadership during the first three decades of this century.

SCHAPPES, MORRIS U., ed. *A Documentary History of the Jews in the United States, 1654–1875.* 3rd ed., New York: Schocken, 1971. Excellent collection of documents with useful introductions.

SKLARE, MARSHALL. *America's Jews.* New York: Random House, 1971. Clear and comprehensive sociological summary of American Jewry's status and problems.

STEMBER, CHARLES, ed. *Jews in the Mind of America.* New York: Basic Books, 1966. Anthology containing many perceptive studies of the Jewish image in twentieth century America.

TELLER, JUDD L. *Strangers and Natives: The Evolution of the American Jew from 1921 to the Present.* New York: Delacorte, 1968. Informative survey of recent decades.

VII

Black Americans:
Immigrants Against Their Will

By JOHN HENRIK CLARKE
Hunter College

AMERICANS who came from Africa were not immigrants in the usual sense. If they were immigrants at all, they were immigrants against their will. Therefore, in looking at the black Americans and their impact on the English colonies that became the United States, a different vantage point and frame of reference must be used. First, there is a need to locate the Africans on the maps of human geography, history, and culture and then explain how and why the slave trade started.

The Africans are a very old people, and they have played many roles in history from saints to buffoons. They have been both the makers and destroyers of great nations. The Africans have met the Europeans many times on the crossroads of history. In the closing years of the fourteenth century, Europeans began to recover from the confusion of the Middle Ages and once again pushed outward.

During the latter half of the fifteenth century, European nationalism was reflected in the expansion of trade in both slaves and manufactured goods. The marriage of Queen Isabella and King Ferdinand gave Spain the unity to drive out the Moors. Portugal, likewise, was becoming a powerful Mediterranean and Atlantic nation.

European skill in shipbuilding had improved, and, in search of new worlds to conquer and souls to convert, Europeans began to venture beyond their shores. There are many reasons why the

172

Europeans had not embarked upon worldwide exploration before this time; their ships were small and unsafe for long sea journeys; while oars were sometimes used to propel these ships, the outcome of all voyages depended largely on the wind; there were few good maps or instruments to guide sailors through unknown waters. Furthermore, at that time most Europeans were ignorant of the shape of the world; indeed, some of them thought it was flat. The Portuguese sought to disprove this, and, about the middle of the fifteenth century, they began trading with the people along the west coast of Africa, to which they gave the name "guinea" after the Sudanic Empire of Ghana.

In 1488, Bartholomew Diaz had sailed around the southern tip of Africa. About ten years later, another Portuguese sailor, Vasco da Gama, sailed past the point reached by Diaz. With the help of an Arab pilot, Vasco da Gama reached India in 1498. For Europe, the door to the vast worlds of Asia and Africa was open.

Initially, the Europeans did not come to Africa to find slaves. For years they had heard stories of the great riches of Africa. At the Battle of Ceuta against the Moslems in 1416, Prince Henry the Navigator of Portugal heard about the prosperity of Timbuktu and the wealth of the great states along the west coast of Africa. He also heard stories about a great African Christian king named Prester John.

Before the end of the fifteenth century, the Portuguese sailors had come to know the general shape of the continent of Africa. They traded regularly with African countries from 1471 on. Forts were built along the coast of West Africa. The most famous of these forts, still in existence, is Elmina Castle in what is now Ghana. This fort was started in 1482 by a Portuguese captain, Don Diego d'Azambuja. Because of the large profits gained by the Portuguese in their trading in this country, they called it the Gold Coast.

Social and political unrest began to develop among some of the nations of Africa at the time Europe was regaining its strength and a degree of unity. The first Europeans to visit the west coast of Africa did not have to fight their way—they came as guests and were treated as such. Later they decided to stay as conquerors and slave traders. In order to gain a position strong enough to attain these ambitions, they began to take sides in tribal disputes. They used racist as well as religious arguments to justify their subjugation of the Africans.

During the latter half of the fifteenth century Spanish ships began to interfere with and challenge the dominant position of the Portuguese in the slave trade. This caused the Portuguese to build a cluster of forts along the West Coast of Africa to protect their interests. They landed in Elmina early in the year 1482. The leader of the expedition, Diego de Azambuja, wasted no time in asking to see the country's reigning king, Nana Kwamena Ansa. The Portuguese offered friendship, but Ansa was slow in accepting their promises. Unfortunately, he did not gain enough time to rally the support of his people and allies. He did not want the Portuguese to settle in his country, and he did not believe their promises. After the king refused the offer of "friendship," Azambuja ordered the small army waiting in ships off shore to land. With this expeditionary force he occupied the area without permission. This act of violence is typical of the Europeans of the fifteenth century. They had no respect for the customs and cultures of the Africans with whom they were coming into contact.

King Nana Ansa's antipathy to imperialism is exemplified by the speech he made to the Portuguese on this occasion. He could foresee that the Africans were going to be called upon to prey upon one another and would be left helpless, disorganized, and demoralized. The Ghanian writer, K. Budu-Acquah, has observed that the speech, "shows equally well the development of the Akan language, its poetry which is 'as perfect and musical as any Latin or Roman language' and 'if the richness of language be an index to the mental development of a people,' one can say that the natural eloquence of the Akan people is a sure indication of a balanced and highly developed mental equipment."

The king's speech is worth quoting to show that all African heads of state were not naive about the intentions of the Europeans, on the eve of the slave trade.

The king said:

I am not insensible to the high honour which your great master the Chief of Portugal has this day conferred upon me. His friendship

I have always endeavoured to merit by the strictness of my dealings with the Portuguese and by my constant exertions to procure an immediate landing for the vessels. But never until this day did I observe such a difference in the appearance of his subjects; they have hitherto been meanly attired; were easily contented with the commodity they received; and so far from wishing to continue in this country, were never happy until they could complete their landing and return. Now I remark a strange difference. A great number, richly dressed, are anxious to be allowed to build houses, and to continue among us. Men of such eminence, conducted by a commander who from his own account seems to have descended from the God who made day and night, can never bring themselves to endure the hardships of this climate; or would they be able to procure any of the luxuries that abound in their own country. The passions that are common to all men will therefore inevitably bring on disputes; and it is far preferable that both our nations should continue on the same footing as they have hitherto done, allowing our ships to come and go as usual; the desire of seeing each other occasionally will preserve peace between us. The sea and the land being always neighbors are continually at variance, and contending who shall give way; the sea with great violence attempting to subdue the land, and the land with equal obstinacy resolving to oppose the sea.

This was the beginning of European colonization, the beginning of the hunting ground for procuring slave labor, and the disruption of the African religion, culture, and social systems. As the Spanish began seriously to compete with the Portuguese in the slave trade, the Pope intervened and attempted to define their respective spheres of influence.

Europe's Reformation and the subsequent conversion of England and Holland to Protestantism in the sixteenth century also had repercussions in Africa. Protestant kings no longer felt bound to obey the authority of the Pope and to recognize his division of the world. Owners of ships in these countries felt free to enter the slave trade in areas that the Pope had assigned to the Portuguese and the Spanish in 1493. Francis I of France voiced his celebrated protest:

The sun shines for me as for others. I should very much like to see the clause in Adam's will that excludes me from a share of the world.

The King of Denmark refused to accept the Pope's ruling as far as the East Indies was concerned. Sir William Cecil, the famous Elizabethan statesman, denied the Pope's right to "give and take kingdoms to whomsoever he pleased."

England, France, and the Dutch began to challenge Spain and Portugal, the Iberian axis. They insisted that they too had a right to colonies in South America and the Caribbean Islands. They also insisted that they had a right to the slave labor that was needed in order to develop the sugar, tobacco, and cotton plantations of the New World.

The discovery of the Americas and the Caribbean Islands was to bring about the intensification of the inhuman trade. The French, Dutch, Danes, and English also built trading posts along the West Coast of Africa.

The fact that a form of domestic slavery existed in West Africa prior to contact with Europeans is often used to excuse the European slave trade. The two systems had few similarities. The tragic and distinguishing feature of the slave trade that was introduced by the Europeans was that it totally dehumanized the slave and denied his basic personality. This crucial act was supported by a rationale that was created, in part, by the Christian Church and later extended by the writers and pseudo-scientific racists of the seventeenth and eighteenth centuries. The myth of a people with no history and culture emerged from this period.

The slave trade prospered, and Africans continued to be poured into the New World. Figures on the subject vary, but it has been estimated that during the years of the African slave trade, Africa lost millions of her sons and daughters. This was one of the most tragic acts of protracted genocide.

Contrary to popular belief, the first Africans who came to the New World were not in bondage. Africans participated in some of the early expeditions mainly with Spanish explorers. The best known of these African explorers was Estevanico, sometimes known as Little Steven, who accompanied the de Vaca expedition during six years of wandering from Florida to Mexico. The remarkable thing about Estevanico, who came to America in 1527, is that he was an extraordinary linguist. He learned the language of the local Indians in a matter of weeks.

Because of his knowledge of herbs and medicines, he was accepted as a deity by some Indian tribes. In 1539, Estevanico set out from Mexico in party with Fray Marcos de Niza in search of the fabulous Seven Cities of Cibola. When most of the expedition, including Fray Marco, became ill, Estevanico went on alone and opened up what is now known as New Mexico and Arizona.

A number of historians have stated that Pedro Mino, one of the pilots of the command ship of Christopher Columbus, was an African. In the discovery of the Pacific in 1513, Balboa carried thirty Africans who helped to clear the road across the isthmus between the two oceans. In the conquest of Mexico, Cortez was accompanied by a number of Africans. Incidentally, one was a pioneer of wheat farming in the New World.

In the exploration of Guatemala, Chile, Peru, and Venezuela, Africans arrived nearly a hundred years before they reappeared as slaves in Jamestown, Virginia, in 1619. Thus, Africans were major contributors to the making of the New World, and they did not come culturally emptyhanded. Many of the Africans brought to the New World such skills as ironworking, leatherworking, and carpentry.

Before the breaking up of the social structure of the West African states such as Ghana and Songhai and the internal strife that made the slave trade possible, many Africans, especially West Africans, lived in a society in which university life was fairly common and scholars were held in reverence. In that period in West African history, the university of Sankore at Timbuktu was flourishing, and its great chancellor, the last of the monumental scholars of West Africa, Ahmed Baba, presided over the university. A great African scholar, he wrote 47 books, each on a separate subject. He received all his education within Africa; in fact, he did not leave the Western Sudan until he was exiled to Morocco during the invasion in 1594.

It is quite clear that there existed in Africa prior to the beginning of the slave trade a cultural way of life that in many ways was equal, if not superior, to many of the civilizations then existing in Europe. And the slave trade destroyed these cultures and created a dilemma that the African has not been able to extract himself from to this day.

There were, in the Africans' past, rulers who extended kingdoms into empires, great armies that subdued entire nations, generals who advanced the technique of military science, scholars with wisdom and foresight, and priests who told of gods that were kind and strong. During and after the forced migration of Africans to the New World, every effort was made to destroy their memory of having ever been part of a free and intelligent people.

The greatest destroyer of African culture, the greatest exploiter of the African, was the plantation system of the New World. The African was transformed into something called a "Negro." He was demeaned. Of all the slave systems in the world, no other dehumanized the slave more than that started by the Europeans in the fifteenth century. They created myths that nearly always read the African out of human history, beginning with the classification of the African as a lesser being. The Church's justification for slavery was that the African was being brought under the guidance of Christendom and that he would eventually receive its blessings.

There were several competing slave systems involving black Africans. Each must be looked at separately. In Cuba and Haiti, the Africans were often a majority of the population. This is also true of certain portions of Brazil. Therefore, the system operated differently in these areas, and although it was still slavery, the Africans in it had some cultural mobility.

In South America and in the West Indies, the slave master did not outlaw the African drum, African ornamentations, African religion, or other things dear to the African, remembered from his former way of life. This permitted a form of cultural continuity among the slaves in the West Indies, Cuba, and South America that did not exist in the United States.

In the Portuguese area, in the West Indies, and often in South America, the plantation owner would buy a shipload or half a shipload of slaves. These slaves usually came from the same areas in Africa, and they naturally spoke the same language and had the same basic culture. Families, in the main, were kept together. If a slave on an island was sold to a plantation owner at the other end of the island, he could still walk to see his relatives. This made for a form of cultural continuity among

the slaves in South America, Cuba, and Haiti, that later made
their revolts more successful than revolts in the United States.

In the United States, an attempt was made to destroy every
element of culture of the slaves. No other system did so much
to deny the personality of the slaves or to ruthlessly sell family
members away from each other. The American slave system
operated almost like the American brokerage system. If a person
bought twenty slaves at the beginning of the week, and found
himself short of cash at the end of the week, he might, if the
price was right, sell ten. These ten might be resold within a
few days. The family, the most meaningful entity in African life,
was systematically destroyed. In spite of these drastic drawbacks,
the Africans in the United States made a meaningful contribution to the preservation of the country in which they were slaves.

Another neglected aspect of the African in the New World
is the role of the African women. Many families of the New
World originated from cohabitation between the white slave
master and the African woman. Later, these same slave masters,
especially in the United States, made and supported laws for-
bidding their own offspring to acquire an education or sit beside
them on public transportation. In Haiti, the African woman
sometimes had a kind of semi-legal status. In South America,
especially in Brazil, sometimes the white slave master married
the African woman and she became a free person. This condition
did not prevail in the United States.

The mentality, the rationale, and the various ways of justify-
ing the slave trade had already started in Europe with the
attempt to justify the enslavement of other Europeans. It is
rarely recalled that at first there was a concerted effort to obtain
European labor to open up the vast regions of the New World.
Also forgotten is the fact that, in what became the United States,
white enslavement started before black enslavement.

In an article, "White Servitude in the United States," *Ebony
Magazine*, November, 1969, the Afro-American historian Lerone
Bennett, Jr., provides the following information about this period:

When someone removes the cataracts of whiteness from our eyes,
and when we look with unclouded vision on the bloody shadows of
the American past, we recognize for the first time that the Afro-

American, who was so often second in freedom, was also second in slavery.

Indeed, it will be revealed that the Afro-American was third in slavery. For he inherited his chains, in a manner of speaking, from the pioneer bondsmen, who were red and white.

The enslavement of both red and white men in the early American colonies was a contradiction of English law. It contained no provision for slave labor. Yet, forced labor was widely used in England. This system was transferred to the colonies and used to justify a form of slavery that was imposed upon red and white men.

It was decreed that the apprentice must serve from four to seven years and take floggings as his master saw fit; the hired servant must carry out his contract for his term of service; convicts of the state, often including political offenders, were slaves of the state and sometimes sold to private owners overseas. The colonists claimed those rights over some of their white fellow countrymen. A large class of "redemptioners" had agreed that their service should be sold for a brief term of years to pay their passage money. There was also a class of "indentured" servants bought by their masters under legal obligation to serve for a term of ten years and subject to the same penalties of branding, whipping, and mutilation as African slaves. These forms of servitude were supposed to be limited in duration and transmitted no claim to the servant's children. In spite of this servitude, the presumption, in law, was that a white man was born free.

The English settlers, had, at once, begun to enslave their Indian neighbors, soothing their conscience with the argument that it was right to make slaves of pagans. In large numbers, the Indians fled or died in captivity, leaving few of their descendants in bondage. The virgin soil of the new English settlements continued to require more labor. This led to a fierce search for white labor that subsequently led to a search for black labor.

By the end of the seventeenth century Europeans saw in African manpower the means to secure labor for the building of the Americas. The Africans, upon entering into the slave system of the Americas, became exposed to a diabolical and consistent application of mental and physical torture. As the Africans reflected on their miserable state, and the strange and brutal conditions surrounding them, they became creatures of conflicting emotions caught in the throes of nostalgia. Very often the Africans would recklessly gamble their lives away in suicidal attempts to destroy the entire slave system. These attempts only had limited success—but enough to drive fear into the hearts of the slave-owning hierarchy. The prime targets of the Africans during these attacks were the slave masters and their families.

As a consequence of these spasmodic attacks, the slave owners soon realized that they were in danger of losing face and money, and sometimes their lives. They decided that a full course of action, spiritual, physical, and psychological, had to be implemented if the Africans were to be transformed from proud rebellious men to docile servants. The plans of the slave owners entailed some of the most extreme forms of torture. Despite the atrocities inflicted on the Africans as a means of breaking their spirit, the slave masters soon realized that this alone would be useless as long as the Africans retained their proud spirit. The Christian Church contributed to the submission of the Africans to the desired slave code of conduct demanded by the plantation economy.

The Reverend Kyle Haselden, editor of the magazine *Christian Century,* made the following comment (New York Times, August 2, 1964) on the role of the church in the planting of racism in the United States:

The religious community in American society produced and sustained—sometimes on Biblical grounds—the anti-Negro bias which has permeated the American mind from the beginning of the nation until the present day. Out of the nation's religious community come Biblically and doctrinally supported theories of racial inferiority, and from this same source came immoral ethical codes which justified the exploitation of the Negro and demanded that the white man hold himself in sanctifying aloofness from the Negro.

Blacks did not submit without a fight. As early as 1663, a group of slaves joined white indentured servants to plan a rebellion.

Later too, some slaves took the Christian version of the Bible literally and believed that God meant all men to be free. Such a slave was Gabriel Prosser, of Virginia, who felt in 1800 that he was divinely inspired to lead his people out of bondage. Over 40,000 slaves were involved in his revolt before it was betrayed.

While different manifestations of resistance to slavery and colonialism existed throughout the seventeenth and eighteenth centuries, the best organized resistance came in the nineteenth century. The nineteenth century freedom movements in Africa, the West Indies and in the United States made the present-day, twentieth-century movement possible. In fact, the whole of the nineteenth century for us can justifiably be called "The Century of Resistance." Concurrent with the slave revolts in the United States there were anticolonial revolts in Africa. The new Western capitalist class was demanding more profits from the slave system, while the British were actually changing from one form of slavery to another. In the United States there was no such pretending.

In his essay "A Brief History of the Negro in the United States" John Hope Franklin gives us this picture of the half century before the Civil War:

By the beginning of the nineteenth century there were unmistakable signs of profound economic and social change taking place in the United States. The commercial activities of the new nation were expanding; and there were those who already were beginning to think in terms of promoting industrial development similar to that which was occurring in England and on the Continent. Beyond the areas of settlement, rich new land was beckoning settlers who could plant staple crops and enjoy the freedom offered on the frontier. In 1803, the United States purchased the vast Louisiana territory, and although it would be many years before the entire area would be settled, Americans and European immigrants were rapidly moving beyond the mountains. The greater portion of the people who moved from the Atlantic seaboard were committed to the institution of slavery, and if they had any slaves they took them along. Not even the War of 1812, in which several thousand Negroes fought, halted the march of Americans and slavery into the new West.

There were two distinct freedom movements among Afro-Americans during the first part of the nineteenth century. One represented by continuous slave revolts and the other by "free" black men and women who were engaged in a concerted effort to free their enslaved brothers and sisters. The movement, led by "free" black petitioners for freedom, was started during the latter part of the eighteenth century by men like Prince Hall. He was ably abetted by others in the nineteenth century.

When Hall arrived in Boston, that city was the center of the American slave trade. Most of the major leaders of the revolutionary movement of that day were, in fact, slaveholders or investors in slave supported businesses. Hall, like many other Americans, wondered: What did these men mean by freedom? The condition of the free black men, as Prince Hall found them, was not an enviable one. They were free in name only. Discriminatory practices severely circumscribed their freedom of movement.

By 1765, he saw little change in the conditions of the blacks, and though freemen at least in theory, he considered them debased as though they were still in bondage. In 1788, he petitioned the Massachusetts Legislature, protesting the kidnaping of "free" Negroes. This was a time when American patriots were engaged in a constitutional struggle for freedom. They had proclaimed the inherent rights of all mankind to life, liberty, and the pursuit of happiness. Hall dared to remind them that the black men in the United States were human beings and as such were entitled to freedom and respect.

Many other blacks aided the cause of abolition. Frederick Douglass was the noblest of all American black men of the nineteenth century and one of the noblest of all Americans. This great abolitionist's civil rights views are as valid today as they were a century ago. Samuel E. Cornish and John B. Russwurm started a newspaper in order to tell the black man's story from his point of view. Russwurm, talented editor and politician, is generally credited with being the first black graduate of an American college (Bowdoin, 1826). Henry Highland Garnet, a fiery Presbyterian minister, was a leader of the militant abolitionist wing. Sojourner Truth, the first black woman to become an antislavery lecturer, was also a strong leader in the feminist movements of the nineteenth century. Harriet Tubman was a pioneer rebel and slave activist who later served as a nurse, scout, and spy in the Civil War. John Brown, called "God's Angry Man," was the first white martyr to die for black freedom. Among other white men who helped to create the first freedom movement, Wendell Phillips and William Lloyd Garrison were outstanding.

In 1857, the famous Dred Scott Decision theoretically opened all territories to slavery. But before any considerable number of slaves could be taken to them, the Civil War began, and Congress, in 1862, prohibited slavery in the territories. After four years of conflict, Northern victory in the Civil War resulted in the emancipation of the slaves. The slaves had played an important part in the achievement of their freedom. Some 186,000 black troops took part in 198 battles and skirmishes and suffered 68,000 casualties. The total number of blacks, including servants, laborers, and spies, amounted to more than 300,000. President Lincoln acknowledged that the war could not have been won without the help of black troops.

In the opening chapter of his book, *Black Reconstruction,* Dr. W. E. B. DuBois has stated: "Easily the most dramatic episode in American history was the sudden move to free four million black slaves in an effort to stop a great Civil War and forty years of bitter controversy, and to appease the moral sense of civilization."

The appeasement, if it was an appeasement at all, was shortlived. For eleven years following the end of the Civil War black Americans participated in the political life of the nation on both state and national levels. For the first time in the nation's existence it seemed as if its democratic promise was going to be kept. By 1875, the tide turned against the blacks in the South and in the rest of the country. The Republican party bargained away the political rights of black Americans in order to pacify the brooding white South. Some black politicians held on for a few more years, but their heyday in American politics was over.

The period in Afro-American history from 1877 to 1901 is the nadir—the lowest point—the time of the greatest depression. This is the period when blacks lost the right to participate in the government of this country. During this period lynching became common and most of the Jim Crow laws also came into being.

By the early part of the twentieth century, the Afro-American people had produced an intellectual class in revolt against the second-class citizenship that had been fastened upon their people. This revolt, led by the great scholar W. E. B. DuBois, did not stop the solidification of disenfranchisement and segregation in the South. Southern politicians and Northern philanthropists had already anointed Booker T. Washington, of Tuskegee Institute, and declared that he was the leader of the Negro people. The people themselves were never consulted in this matter.

The Afro-American journalist, Loren Miller, in a speech, "The Call for Leadership," delivered at Stanford University in California, 1962, makes the following appraisal of Dr. DuBois for this period:

When W. E. B. DuBois won the battle for the minds of Negroes in his historic conflict with Booker T. Washington, his victory signalized the triumph of his concept of the talented tenth as the leaders of, and the spokesmen for American Negroes. We believed that members of this Talented Tenth—educators, ministers, lawyers, editors, doctors and dentists, political leaders—would, in the very process of securing an education to fit them for their professions, furnish pragmatic proof of the invalidity of the then current doctrine of racial inferiority. He was confident that this educated and select minority would lead the masses in a sustained and purposeful assault on the restrictions that doomed the Negro to poverty and degradation; it was an essential aspect of the DuBois credo that the talented tenth would accept its role as servants of the other 90 percent, just as he believed he had done. . . . DuBois and his contemporaries fashioned the NAACP as the chosen instrument of the elite to whom he believed the masses should look for guidance and salvation.

The concept of the Talented Tenth failed because the black elite did not assume the responsibility expected of them. They were too busy imitating the white middle class and retreating from their own people. DuBois, without their assistance, embarked upon a more radical course of action. During the early part of this century he became the intellectual father of his people. After the death of Booker T. Washington in 1915, his leadership was unchallenged until the emergence of Marcus Garvey in the early twenties. Dr. DuBois, more than any other person, sowed the seeds of what is now called "The Black Revolution."

Near the end of the nineteenth century this intellectual giant took up the fight and ably carried it to the middle of the twentieth century. He is the father of the present struggle against racism and for African redemption. Men like Marcus Garvey, though they differed with DuBois, would draw in part from his intellectual conclusions.

There is now an international struggle on the part of people of African descent against racism and for a more honest look at their history. On university campuses and in international conferences they are demanding that their history be studied from a black perspective or from an Afrocentric point of view. This has taken the struggle against racism ito the world's campuses, where the theoretical basis of racism started. It has helped to create new battle lines. Some still do not recognize that removing this racism is the healthiest thing that present-day black scholars can contribute to the world; that in the cry for black power and black history, black people are saying a very powerful, complex, yet simple thing: "I am a man." The struggle against racism all along has been a struggle to regain the essential manhood lost after the European expansion into the broader world and the attempt to justify the slave trade.

The struggle within the black educational institutions has centered, in most cases, on how to remove the stigma of slavery and make black Americans, the immigrants against their will, think better of themselves and prepare to demand full citizenship status. Black Americans came into the twentieth century with some of the unresolved educational problems of the nineteenth century. Carter G. Woodson called attention to this in two near-classic, though still neglected books, *The Education of the Negro Prior to 1861* (1919) and *The Mis-Education of the Negro* (1938). Dr. Woodson tells us:

It required little argument to convince intelligent masters that slaves, who had some conception of modern civilization and understood the language of their owners would be more valuable than rude men with whom one could not communicate. The question, however, as to exactly what kind of training these Negroes should have and how far it should go, were to the white race then as much a matter of perplexity as they are now.

Often the motive of the slave owners who agreed on some education for their slaves, was to make them more productive workers on the plantation. From the beginning the black Americans were educated to serve others and not themselves. In *The Education of the Negro Prior to 1861*, Woodson outlines the beginning of black education in this country.

The history of the education of the ante-bellum Negroes, therefore, falls into two periods. The first extends from the time of the introduction of slavery to the climax of the insurrectionary movement about 1835, when the majority of the people in this country answered in the affirmative the question whether or not it was prudent to educate their slaves. Then followed the second period, when the industrial revolution changed slavery from a patriarchal to an economic institution, and when intelligent Negroes, encouraged by abolitionists, made so many attempts to organize insurrections that the pendulum began to swing the other way.

The early advocates of the education of Negroes were of three classes; First, masters who desired to increase the economic efficiency of their labor supply; Second, sympathetic persons who wished to help the oppressed; and Third, zealous missionaries who, believing that the message of divine love came equally to all, taught slaves the English language that they might learn the principles of the Christian religion. Through the kindness of the first class, slaves had their best chance for mental improvement. Each slaveholder dealt with the situation to suit himself, regardless of public opinion. Later when measures were passed to prohibit the education of slaves, some masters, always a law unto themselves, continued to teach their Negroes in defiance of the hostile legislation. Sympathetic persons were not able to accomplish much because they were usually reformers, who not only did not own slaves, but dwelt in practically free settlements far from the plantation on which the bondsmen lived.

The Spanish and French missionaries had a different approach to the education of the slaves. Some of them were anxious to see the Africans enlightened and brought into the church. This was a change from their previous position when they had originally advocated the enslavement of the Africans rather than of the Indians.

The position of these Catholic missionaries forced the English into a more positive stance in matters relating to the education of Africans. Dr. Woodson tells us that, "the English were put to shame by the noble example of the Catholics. They had to find a way to overcome the objections of these who, granting that the enlightenment of the slaves might not lead to servile insurrection, nevertheless feared that their conversion might work manumission." This situation forced the English to deal with a contradiction within the Christian church that still exists. Can a Christian hold another Christian as a slave and still be a Christian? In order to deal with the urgency of this matter the colonists secured, through legislation by their assemblies and formal declaration of the Bishop of London, the abrogation of the law that a Christian could not be held as a slave. Missionaries were sent out by the Society for the Propagation of the Gospel among "Heathen" in the Foreign Parts, and they undertook to educate the slaves so that they could obtain converts.

Reaction to this plan was not slow in coming. During the first quarter of the nineteenth century, especially in the South, reactionaries forced public opinion to gradually prohibit the education of Africans, except in some urban communities where progressive blacks were able to provide their own schools. The massive slave revolts that came during this period convinced a large number of whites, some of them former allies of the blacks, that the educating of blacks was a dangerous thing. This opinion continued until after the Civil War when blacks began to build new institutions, mainly schools. Most of these new schools soon began to fall into old traps. They were imitations of white schools, whose teachings were offensive to black people. Now the education of Afro-Americans began to move on several levels. Education in churches, community centers, and homes began to supplement the education in the schools. In these independent institutions, lay historians began the formal search for the African heritage.

In what can still be referred to as "The Booker T. Washington Era" (1895–1915), new men and movements were emerging. The Niagara Movement, under the leadership of W. E. B. DuBois and Monroe Trotter, was born in 1905. Some of the ideas of the Niagara Movement went into the making of the NAACP in 1909.

During the years leading to the eve of the First World War and those that immediately followed, the flight from the South continued. Over a half million blacks migrated northward in search of better paying wartime jobs, better schools for their children, and better housing. For a short while they entertained the illusion that they had improved and had escaped from the oppression of the South. The illusion was short-lived. Race riots in wartime (East St. Louis, 1917) and in the postwar period (Chicago, 1919) awakened the new urban settlers to reality. In Washington, D. C., President Woodrow Wilson and the southern Democrats who had come to power with him had introduced segregation in federal facilities that had long been integrated.

Booker T. Washington died in 1915. An investigation into his last years revealed that he had privately battled against disenfranchisement and had secretly financed law suits against segregation, but publicly he maintained his submissive stance. With Washington gone, and the influence of the "Tuskegee Machine" in decline, a new class of black radicals came forward. For a few years DuBois was at the center stage of leadership. As the founder-editor of the NAACP's *Crisis* magazine, DuBois urged in 1918, "Let us, while this war lasts, forget our special grievances and close ranks shoulder to shoulder with our fellow citizens. . . ." The continued discrimination against black Americans, both soldiers and civilians, soon made W. E. B. DuBois regret having made this statement. The end of the war brought no improvement to the lives of black Americans. The then prevailing conditions made a large number of them ripe for the militant program of Marcus Garvey. This was the beginning of the heroic and troubled years of the black urban ghetto.

More recently, and especially in the past two decades, discrimination has abated though it has not been eliminated; job possibilities for blacks have been broadened and educational opportunities expanded. Most important of all, black Americans are finally freeing themselves of the negative stereotype which burdened them for so many years.

Black people, in America and in the rest of the world, now stand at the crossroads of history, seeking new definitions of themselves and new directions. In the book *Tom-Tom,* the writer John W. Vandercook has said, "A race is like a man, and until it uses its own talents, takes pride in its history, and loves its memories, it can never fulfill itself completely."

Today Afro-Americans are beginning to use their talents more creatively in their struggle for total liberation and nationhood. This is why they are taking pride in their own history. They are searching for a way to better relate to Africans in Africa and in other parts of the world. There are clear indications that they will move beyond Pan-Africanism and help to build a world union of African people. This will not make us relate less to America, but more, though in a different way.

Now that we are becoming more aware of our history and how to use it as an instrument of our liberation, we know that we are the only immigrant group which was invited here. Those who invited us waited anxiously for our arrival. They sent large ships to transport us, manned by well-armed thugs. We faced no unemployment problem. There were plenty of jobs waiting for us. The jobs that we did helped to make America.

SELECTED BIBLIOGRAPHY

Budu-Acquah, K. *Ghana, The Morning After*. London: Goodwin Press, 1965, pp. 13–17.

Clarke, John Henrik. "The Impact of the African on the New World: A Reappraisal." *The Black Scholar* (February, 1973), pp. 32–39.

––––. "The Influence of African Cultural Continuity on the Slave Revolts in South America and in the Caribbean Islands," Conference paper for the Third International Congress of Africanists, Addis Ababa, Ethiopia, December 9–19, 1973.

––––. "Race: An Evolving Issue in Western Social Thought," Paper for The Graduate School of International Studies, University of Denver, Denver, Colorado. Presented at Aspen, Colorado, June 7–9, 1970.

––––. "The Nineteenth Century Roots of the African and Afro-American Freedom Struggle," Paper prepared for presentation at the Second International Congress of Africanists, Dakar, Senegal, December 11–21, 1967.

Davis, John P. *The American Negro Reference Book*. New York: Prentice-Hall, 1966.

DuBois, W. E. B. *Black Reconstruction in America 1860–1880*.

Cleveland and New York: Meridian Books, The World Publishing Company, 1965, pp. 3–16.

FRANKLIN, JOHN HOPE. *Reconstruction After the Civil War.* Chicago: University of Chicago Press, 1961, pp. 152–73.

WILLIAMS, ERIC. *Capitalist and Slavery.* New York: Capricorn Books, 1966, p. 3.

VIII

The Asian Experience in the United States

By FRANK CHING

Staff Member, *New York Times*

ASIANS ventured to the United States for the same reasons as the first settlers from Europe; they were looking for a better life. They came in waves, mainly from China, Japan, and the Philippines. The first to arrive were the Chinese who came to the United States in the nineteenth century. News of the discovery of gold in California in January, 1848, served as a tremendous incentive for the poorer classes. Most thought that, with a few years of hard work, they would be able to return to their villages and live in comfort. Stories of the discovery of gold were so widespread that California became known to the Chinese as the "Mountain of Gold."

Most of the Chinese who left the old country for America came from farming villages in the southern coastal province of Kwangtung. After generations of toiling on the land, they were accustomed to hardship. By 1851, there were 25,000 Chinese in California. From 1851 to 1860, 41,000 Chinese emigrated to the United States, while an additional 64,000 arrived in the 1860's. These Chinese brought with them traditional values, such as reverence for one's ancestors, filial piety, hard work, and thrift.

The journey from Kwangtung was expensive as well as long and arduous, with the average trip taking at least a month, and sometimes as much as two months. For this reason and because they expected to return home some day, most men left their wives behind, and few women joined the men on their journey. As a result, the Chinese community in the United States from the earliest days was sexually imbalanced, with the men vastly outnumbering the women.

The Chinese engaged in a variety of activities. Some of the early immigrants worked in the gold fields, others opened stores or served as mechanics. In 1863, the United States began construction of the Trans-Continental Railroad. Because there were not enough white workers, the railroad hired Chinese. Eventually, the railroad was completed with the help of thousands of Chinese laborers. When work on the railroad ceased, the Chinese sought work in the mines, on the farms, in land reclamation, and in domestic service. By 1870 the Chinese made up one-tenth of the farm labor supply in California. This rose to a third in 1880 and, by 1884, it was up to fifty percent.

The high tide of Chinese emigration to the United States was reached in the 1870's, when more than 100,000 crossed the Pacific. Although these new arrivals came with high hopes, they were quickly disillusioned. Their influx coincided with an economic depression in the United States, and the Chinese were made the scapegoats for many of the nation's difficulties. They were accused of taking jobs away from white men and of lowering the standard of living because they were willing to work for less.

The Chinese were made to bear the blame for the country's woes because they looked different. The men at times wore their hair in a queue, which subjected them to scorn and ridicule. Partly by their own choice and partly because of rejection by American society in general, they lived in Chinatowns. And, because most were single men, or had come without their wives, they lived in bachelor quarters, several men sharing a room.

Dennis Kearney, an immigrant from Ireland, was the demagogue who did the most to fan the anti-Chinese flames. His followers formed the Workingmen's party. Kearney ended each harangue with the words: "The Chinese must go!" These words became imprinted on the nation's consciousness. In 1879, for example, *Harper's Weekly,* which described itself as a "journal of civilization," printed on its front cover a picture of a Negro and a Chinese, with the words "The Nigger Must Go" and "The Chinese Must Go" under the pictures. The caption said: "The poor barbarians can't understand our civilized republican form of government."

Small wonder that during this period the Chinese were victims of individual and collective violence. They were stoned and assaulted, robbed, and sometimes murdered. When attacks were made against Chinese camps, the Chinese had no legal recourse, for they were not allowed to testify against white men. It was at this time that the phrase "having a Chinaman's chance" came into vogue.

After the mid-1870's, outbreaks of violence became increasingly common: Chinese farmers were killed, laundries and homes were burned and their occupants shot as they tried to flee the flames. In some places entire communities were massacred or driven out of town. One Chinese who survived recounted the indignities that he and others suffered:

Every Saturday night, we never knew whether we would live to see the light of day. We operated a laundry near a mining camp. Saturday was the night for the miners to get drunk. They would force their way into our shop, wrest the clean white bundles from the shelves and trample the shirts, which we so laboriously finished. If the shirts were torn, we were forced to pay for the damage. One night, one of the miners hit his face against the flat side of an iron. He went away and came back with a mob. We knew that our lives were in danger, so we fled, leaving all of our possessions and money behind. We were lucky to escape with our lives, so we came east.

In this atmosphere, anti-Chinese legislation was passed, both by the states and the federal government. In 1882, Congress approved the Chinese Exclusion Act, which made Chinese immigration to the United States illegal. The Chinese thus gained the distinction of being the first people declared undesirable by the United States Congress. The Chinese Exclusion Act was meant to last for ten years, but was extended repeatedly until 1943. Those already here were not allowed to bring their wives into the country. Men who returned to China to seek a bride were not permitted to re-enter.

Thus, while immigrants were pouring in from Europe, the Chinese were kept out. In 1882, the year the Exclusion Act was passed, more than 100,000 immigrants entered the country from Britain, while a quarter of a million came from Germany.

As a result of the increasing discrimination against the Chinese on the West Coast, they began to disperse eastward. There they mainly operated laundries and restaurants—occupations in which they were not in competition with white men.

During the second half of the nineteenth century, Hawaii, which was still a kingdom and not part of the United States, needed field hands for its sugar plantations. The Chinese, one of the first immigrant groups to arrive, played a key role in the development of the island's economy. In the 1860's and 1870's, thousands of Chinese were transported to Hawaii to work on sugar plantations. By 1896, the Hawaiian population had reached 109,000, with close to 8,000 being Chinese.

The Hawaiian authorities, fearing a flood of immigrants, ordered restrictions on the number of Chinese who could enter the kingdom. In spite of these restrictions, Chinese in Hawaii did not suffer the oppression and exploitation of those on the United States mainland. This factor helps to account for the professional success of many Chinese-Americans in that state today. With the exclusion of Chinese laborers in the 1880's, another source of unskilled labor had to be found. The Hawaiian sugar plantations and Californians turned to the Japanese.

On February 8, 1885, 943 Japanese—676 men, 159 women, and 108 children—emigrated to Honolulu. Before leaving Japan, the men signed a three-year contract with the Hawaiian government. The Japanese thus arrived on the Hawaiian and American scene a full generation after the first Chinese immigrants landed. The Japanese came with wives and children and thus were able to lead more normal lives.

China, divided by the various colonial powers into spheres of influence, could do little for its nationals abroad. Japan, on the other hand, was gaining strength under the Meiji restoration, and the government showed great concern about the welfare of its citizens.

Japan officially sanctioned emigration in 1886, and from that year until 1890, about 200 Japanese arrived in the United States a year. The 1890 census shows only 2,039 Japanese in the country, compared to about 100,000 Chinese.

In the 1890's the number of Japanese immigrants averaged about 1,500 a year. But after the turn of the century, the number increased dramatically. In the first decade of the twentieth century, 129,000 immigrants arrived from Japan.

The first Japanese settlers to reach the United States were greeted by a not unfriendly newspaper comment:

These groups of Japanese are of the better class, talk English, and are very anxious to find a permanent home in this state. It is in the interest of California to welcome and encourage these immigrants. There is probably much knowledge in the possession of these Asiatics that we could profit from, to compensate us in some measure from the very enlightened prejudice against their coppery color. They will at all events teach us how to produce teas and silk, some useful lessons in frugality, industry, and possibly politeness.

Before long, however, the welcome for the Japanese was withdrawn. The lesson in politeness had not been learned. In May, 1900, eighteen years after the Chinese Exclusion Act was passed, a mass labor meeting was held in San Francisco to urge Congress to extend the exclusion law to include the Japanese.

In 1905, the California state legislature passed a resolution asking Congress to "limit and diminish the further immigration of Japanese." This started the cycle of anti-Japanese legislation, which paralleled the legal discrimination against the Chinese. Fear and hatred of the Japanese were fanned by the press. In 1905 the *San Francisco Chronicle* printed anti-Japanese articles under such inflammatory headlines as "Japanese invasion the problem of the hour: more than 100,000 of the little brown men are now in the United States." Other headlines declared that "crime and poverty go hand in hand with Asiatic labor;" "Japanese sweatshops are a blot on the city;" "Japanese a menace to American women;" and "Brown men an evil in the public schools."

Anti-Japanese feeling was not localized in California. Although President Theodore Roosevelt, in his 1905 annual message, called for a nondiscriminatory immigration policy, he wrote in May, 1905, that he thought the California legislature was right in its protest against Japanese immigration "for their very frugality, abstemiousness and clannishness make them formidable to our laboring class." However, Roosevelt made it clear that California's actions were an affront to Japan and could plunge the United States into war.

On October 11, 1906, the San Francisco Board of Education precipitated a crisis by issuing an order to exclude all Chinese, Japanese, and Korean children from neighborhood schools and to segregate them in an "Oriental" school. The Japanese Government launched an official protest against this treatment of its nationals.

President Roosevelt, apprehensive of Japan's military strength, openly supported the Japanese position against the California school law. The respect that he accorded Japan was largely due to Japan's easy victory over China in 1894 and over Russia in 1905. His secretary of state, in a secret memo, disclosed the fears of the Federal Government:

The Japanese are a proud and sensitive warlike people. They are particularly sensitive about anything which questions that equality. One-tenth of the insults which have been visited upon China by the United States would lead to immediate war.

Japan is ready for war. It probably has the most effective equipment and personnel now existing in the world.

We are not ready for war, and we could not be ready to meet Japan on anything like equal terms for a long period. The loss of the Philippines, Hawaii and probably the Pacific coast with the complete destruction of our commerce in the Pacific would occur before we were ready for a real fight.

In any controversy that arises, we shall not only be in an attitude absolutely without justification as between us and Japan, but without justification in the eyes of the world because of the things done in San Francisco. The exclusion of the children and the boycotting of the restaurants—this constitutes a clear violation of our treaty with Japan. We will then be in a controversy in which Japan is justified. Even if there were no violation of the treaty, the attitude taken toward the Japanese is intrinsically unfair and indefensible. The Japanese are far superior to a very large part of the immigrants who are coming into our Atlantic ports from Eastern Europe. They rank high among people of the world in civilization and the qualities of good citizenship. They associate and always will associate upon equal terms with the best and most highly cultivated and the ablest of mankind.

These words reflect the esteem in which Japan was held. President Roosevelt was able to persuade the San Francisco school officials to give up their discriminatory rules so that no Japanese child attended the "Oriental" school. In order to prevent further aggravation of the situation in California, the United States in 1907 and 1908 urged that the Japanese Government itself set up a program to limit emigration. The result was a so-called Gentlemen's Agreement, under which the Japanese Government agreed to screen and limit the number of its nationals who would be issued passports for the United States.

Because of the Gentlemen's Agreement, under which Japan agreed not to issue passports to laborers except to those "who already have been in America and to the parents, wives, and children of laborers already resident there," there was a sharp decline in the number of Japanese immigrants. While 30,000 came in 1907, before the agreement, the number was halved the next year. This was further cut in 1909, when only 3,000 came.

In spite of the furor it aroused, the number of Japanese who came to the United States was relatively small, even in the peak year of 1907. From 1890 to 1940, about 200,000 Japanese came to the United States. In the same period, 25 million immigrants, mostly from Europe, entered the United States.

In 1922, the United States Supreme Court confirmed the special status of Japanese and other Asians as aliens ineligible for citizenship, in contrast to European and African immigrants, who could be naturalized. In 1924, Congress cut off all immigration from Japan—and other Asian countries—by prohibiting entry of all persons ineligible for citizenship. Thus, by 1924, the United States Congress acted to keep out all Asians.

Unlike the Chinese, however, Japanese men were able to find wives in Japan through the picure bride system. Under it, the family of a male immigrant would find a suitable young woman to be his wife, and the two would exchange photographs. If both parties were satisfied, the woman would come to the United States as the wife of the Japanese immigrant. Sometimes a whole group of these picture brides came aboard the same ship. They were met by the men, who identified them by means of the photographs.

In spite of the Gentlemen's Agreement, Japanese in the United

States continued to encounter discrimination, which sometimes took violent forms. In 1909, a variety of anti-Japanese bills were offered by state legislators, not only in California but in Nevada and Oregon as well. These measures were supported by both Republicans and Democrats.

One bill in California called for the exclusion of Japanese children from schools attended by white children; another would prevent aliens from becoming members of boards of directors of corporations; and one would permit municipalities to segregate into specified areas "those aliens whose presence may be inimical to health and public morals." Other measures proposed restrictions of land ownership by aliens.

In 1910, the Democratic state platform in California advocated the exclusion of all Asian labor and the adoption of a measure "preventing Asiatics, who were not eligible for citizenship in America, from owning or leasing land in California." The climax of California's legal discrimination came in 1913 with the passage of the anti-alien land law.

But while Californian legislators could pass discriminatory laws against Japanese immigrants, they could not legally discriminate against the American-born children of these Japanese immigrants. The issue of the entry of Japanese women into the United States therefore, became highly charged. The *San Francisco Chronicle,* in an editorial, said that for every picture bride who came there would eventually be a number of "citizens who become landowners, leading the dual life of American citizens and Japanese subjects."

Because of the picture bride controversy, the United States Department of State asked the Japanese Government to do something to alleviate the situation. That Government, in response, announced that passports would not be issued to picture brides after February 29, 1920 and that all such passports would expire on September 1, 1920. As world tensions rose in the 1930's and fear of a possible war with Japan increased, Japanese in the United States became victims of an increasingly hostile atmosphere.

After the United States declared war on Japan as a result of the attack on Pearl Harbor, President Franklin Delano Roosevelt issued Executive Order 9066, which ordered the internment of all Japanese on the West Coast, including those who were American citizens by birth. The total Japanese population in the United States at the time was about 130,000, and 90 percent of them were put in concentration camps as "enemy aliens." About two-thirds of these were American-born citizens.

The Government claimed that the abrogation of citizenship rights was necessary because of wartime conditions. No attempt, however, was made to intern Americans of German or Italian ancestry. In May, 1942, the assistant chief of the Army's Western Defense Command's Civil Affairs Division said:

In the case of the Japanese, their Oriental habits of life, their and our inability to assimilate biologically, and what is more important, our inability to distinguish the subverts and saboteurs from the rest of the mass made necessary their class evacuation on a horizontal basis. In the case of the Germans and the Italians, such mass evacuation is neither necessary nor desirable.

Posters were put up giving instructions to all persons of Japanese ancestry to go to the nearest civil control station so that they could be incarcerated in concentration camps—or, in the euphemism of those days, evacuated. They were only allowed baggage they could carry. Because of the forcible evacuation, the Japanese had to sell their property at a fraction of its market value. Property losses amounted to hundreds of millions of dollars, and a generation of Japanese-American children emerged scarred by their wartime experience.

While World War II meant hate and suspicion, even incarceration for years in concentration camps as "enemy aliens," for Japanese Americans, it signaled a turn for the better for Chinese Americans. Because China was an ally of the United States in its war against Japan, the United States Government, after sixty-one years, finally repealed the Chinese Exclusion Act and permitted Chinese to emigrate and be naturalized as United States citizens. But the number of Chinese who could emigrate each year was strictly limited to one hundred five, an insignificant number. European countries with much smaller populations were assigned quotas hundreds of times larger. This meant that, if 5,000 Chinese had wanted to enter the country, they would have had to wait for 50 years, while 5,000 Europeans could enter the country in a few months. The law was racially discriminatory; it stipulated that any person who had more than 50 percent Chinese blood was considered Chinese, no matter what his citizenship or country of residence was.

The war split the Asian communities in the United States along Japanese and Chinese lines. Because of the violent anti-Japanese atmosphere, some Chinese, for self-protection, wore buttons that proclaimed themselves Chinese, or that read "I hate Japs too." Chinese communities, caught up in the war atmosphere, raised funds for the war against Japan, and visiting Chinese officials and generals were welcomed with parades in Chinatowns.

The United States War Department recognized the difficulty of telling Chinese and Japanese apart and issued a guide on how to spot a Japanese. According to this publication, the Japanese are shorter than the Chinese and "looks as if his legs are joined directly to his chest." The guide, reflecting the prevailing anti-Japanese, pro-Chinese sentiment, also said that Chinese eyes are set like those of Americans and Europeans, whereas Japanese eyes are slanted toward the nose. The description given would be laughable if it were not so damaging, not only to Japanese but to all Asian Americans.

The stereotypes of Asians accepted by Americans differed from one generation to the next, and conflicting images often existed side by side. On the one hand, for example, China—and The East in general—is thought to be the repository of ancient wisdom, whose sages may provide solutions even to present-day problems. On the other hand, Asians are thought of as being ignorant and superstitious. They are alternately regarded as passive and gentle or cruel and barbaric.

The most vicious stereotypes of Asians were perpetuated in the films of the 1920's and 1930's.

In the films of this period, China—and Chinatown, U. S. A.—was invariably pictured as a place of mystery and intrigue, where evil lurked behind closed doors and where anything was likely to happen—and often did. Films of this period were based almost entirely upon published short stories, novels, and plays current at that time.

The Fu Manchu films of the period were the best—or worst—examples of this genre of films.

Studio publicity described the Chinese villain in such terms as these: "Menace in every twitch of his finger; a threat in every twitch of his eyebrow; terror in each split-second of his slanted eyes." In posters, the hero and heroine were seen shrinking in terror from the huge shadow of Fu Manchu's figure.

Perhaps the best known Chinese film character of the period was the detective Charlie Chan. He was depicted as a wise and inscrutable man who spoke in fortune cookie aphorisms. Though his presentation was defended as that of a positive characterization, portraying a Chinese as wiser than a Caucasian on the regular police force, Charlie Chan films have also been found objectionable for a variety of reasons. The primary one is that in presenting a stereotyped Chinese, albeit one who is wise, Charlie Chan is shown as being, not inhuman like Fu Manchu, but nonhuman. In a society where assertiveness is valued as a manifestation of manliness, Charlie Chan is always humble, non-threatening, non-aggressive. He keeps his arms folded and walks in shuffling steps. Moreover, the Charlie Chan role has always been played by white actors made up with slanted eyes. His bumbling sons, however, are played by real Chinese.

The casting of Caucasian actors as Asian characters in films and plays is a problem that still remains unresolved. The charge of stereotyping will continue to be made as long as Asian actors are considered unqualified to portray Asians. When only Caucasian actors can be found to act the way directors believe Asians should act, something is wrong somewhere.

Aside from the Fu Manchu and Charlie Chan series—both of which continue to be shown on television—many other films are deemed objectionable to Asians. The Japanese American Citizens League has designated as objectionable such films as "Air Force" with John Garfield, "Across the Pacific" with Humphrey Bogart, "Purple Heart," "Little Tokyo, U.S.A.," "Black Dragon," "Behind the Rising Sun," and "Betrayal From the East."

The majority of these films are not classics and have little artistic merit. Their continued appearance on television adds fuel to racial bigotry, hatred, and suspicion. It should be possible for the industry to make films of high quality and entertainment value without doing so by maligning Asians or any other minority group.

Another source of stereotype-building—and one that attacks young minds before they are able to distinguish fact from fiction—are the comic books. These are often much more harmful than the "rots of ruck" or "no tickee, no washee" variety. They show diabolical Asians plotting to take over the world and drooling over white women.

When Asians are not depicted as plotting the end of the white-dominated world, they are portrayed as uttering Eastern clichés, such as Charlie Chan. But though Charlie Chan and Fu Manchu were worlds apart, one benign and the other evil, both linked Chinese and Asians with mystery, reinforcing the image of the "mysterious East" and the "inscrutable Oriental."

The image of cruel, inhuman Asians has been fostered within the context of the cold war of the last few decades. The United States Government, after the establishment of the People's Republic of China in 1949, withheld diplomatic recognition from the Communist Government and tried to isolate and contain its influence. This policy of unremitting hostility was not moderated until recently when the Kissinger and Nixon initiatives brought about a reversal in United States policy.

The United States has always maintained a position of superiority in dealings with Asians. It gave independence to the Philippines only a generation ago. After World War II, it maintained an occupation army in Japan. The Chinese Nationalist Government in Taiwan was almost totally dependent on Washington for its survival. And China—the largest country in Asia and the most populous in the world—was regarded as a deadly enemy. In this atmosphere, it is small wonder that Asians were depicted in the American media as inferior and barbarous. The immense influence that the United States Government wields was forcefully illustrated when a Gallup Poll survey after President Nixon's trip to China found a dramatic turnabout in the opinions that average Americans held of the Chinese people. Predominantly negative images, such as "warlike," "cunning," "untrustworthy," etc., were no longer stressed, whereas positive qualities, such as "thrifty," "hardworking," and "honest" came to the fore.

It should be clear, then, that the fortunes of Asian Americans seem inextricably tied to the foreign relations of the United States. This was illustrated also during World War II, when Japanese Americans were interned, but the total exclusion of Chinese immigration was lifted, because China was a wartime ally. Also during World War II, the United States finally permitted the naturalization of Asians, as it has previously permitted the naturalization of all other races and nationalities. By this step, the United States acknowledged that Asians were here to stay, that they were not temporary visitors, but prospective citizens of a country that boasted that it was a nation of immigrants. And with the official acceptance of the government, Asian communities also found it easier to think of themselves not as foreigners but as Americans, as settlers who had come from Asia, as other Americans had come from Europe and Africa.

The immigration law was fundamentally revised in 1965, during the Johnson Administration, and the discriminatory national-origins quota system abolished. The present immigration law emphasizes re-uniting families, regardless of country of origin.

As a result large numbers of Asians have been able to enter the country in the 1960's and 1970's. The great majority have been Chinese and Filipinos, though there have also been significant numbers of Japanese, Koreans, and other Asians.

Many of the new Chinese immigrants gravitate to the major urban centers of San Francisco or New York. Unlike Chinese immigrants of the last century, these Chinese often arrive as family units. Also, these new immigrants consciously come here to stay, to build a new home in a new country.

This new immigration has helped to bring the number of Chinese in the country to the 500,000 mark. Even so, the Chinese are outnumbered by some 600,000 Japanese-Americans.

Many of these new immigrants arrive with little aside from their personal belongings. Because most do not speak adequate English, they are unable to find jobs that are commensurate with their training. Many others do not have special training to begin with. Most gravitate to the local Chinatown, where they can find others who speak their language, and where they can obtain food to which they are accustomed. They pay exorbitant fees to live in dilapidated, roach-infested housing. They are unable to get proper medical care, because hospitals do not have adequate bilingual personnel. They have little occupation choice. Many of the men work in restaurants, as cooks or waiters, while the women work in garment factories, where they are paid, not by the hour but by the piece, and often it is only a few pennies per piece.

Because in most cases both father and mother work, the children lack parental supervision. Students who had performed reasonably well in Hong Kong found themselves unable to cope in the new, unfamiliar environment, in a language they do not speak. As a result, some drop out of school, and youth gangs are formed. The number of shootings and knifings and street fights is increasing, and drug addiction is looming as a major problem in America's Chinatowns.

The plight of these Asian Americans is insufficiently understood by the public at large, which still views Chinese and Japanese as model minorities, who have made it in the American system, and who have little or no crime or juvenile delinquency. The supposed success of Chinese and Japanese is used as a reproach to other nonwhite minorities, who are told that, if the Asians could do it by dint of hard work, so can they.

But the sad fact is that many Asian Americans have not made it. The United States Government, which has for decades kept out Asians, is now permitting immigration, but it is not providing the services necessary for the adjustment that new immigrants have to make. Bilingual and bicultural personnel are needed in schools and hospitals, and federally funded programs for language and occupational training are needed, as well as summer programs and part-time jobs for Asian American youths.

The magnitude of the problem is not recognized by the Federal, state, or local government, by private foundations or corporations, or by the public at large. In all too many cases, Asian Americans are not even regarded as a minority in need. They are often considered ineligible for loans for minority businesses, ineligible for scholarships and fellowships for minority students, and are overlooked when private businesses wish to increase the number of their minority employees.

Administrators tend to think of minorities as black and Spanish-speaking people, but not Asian Americans. Asian Americans are therefore relegated to a never-never land, where they are neither majority nor minority. As a matter of fact, all too often Asian Americans are even thought of not as Americans, but as foreigners.

One prominent Asian from Hawaii, for example, has said:

"A third generation American, why must I always be asked how I like living in this country? As if this country can never be my country."

Asian Americans are told by private employers that they already have too many foreigners on the payroll, while white Canadian newcomers find acceptance without question.

Asian Americans, even the American-born, are constantly asked—by acquaintances and total strangers—whether they come from China or Japan and are complimented on their ability to speak English, and asked when they are going to return to their "own" countries. These questions and remarks reflect the fact that, in the minds of a great many people, Asian Americans do not really belong here and are not really Americans. In terms of employment, many Asian Americans are still relegated to low-status and low-income occupations such as waiters, laundry workers, and houseboys. Those who work in industry tend to be involved in research, where there is little need for personal contact.

Asian Americans are often thought of as Asians first and people second. White Americans, on meeting an Asian, often tend to ask which Chinese restaurant serves the best food, no matter if the person involved is a professor, an engineer, a cook, or a scientist. In advertisements and commercials, Asians are increasingly being used, in part because of the renewed American interest in Asia, especially in things Chinese. But even here Asian models are frequently used for background and atmosphere, to give an exotic effect. Moreover, many advertisements and television commercials that feature Asians actually advance derogatory stereotypes of Asians.

Even in greeting cards, Asians are made fun of, both in their physical appearance and sometimes in their accents. Thus a popular card shows a caricature of a Chinese wishing "rots of ruck" to a "Number One Son."

Part of the reason why Asian immigrants are not given the assistance they require is their small number. Nothing on the scale of what is being done for Spanish-speaking people, for example, is being done for Chinese-speaking immigrants. But the reason why there are so few Chinese is that they were not permitted to increase. It is ironic that the product of one injustice should be used to justify a further injustice.

A generation ago Japanese and Chinese in the United States often viewed each other antagonistically, mainly because of developments in Asia. Today, Asian Americans, especially the young, are developing a keen sense of identity and solidarity. The Asian American movement, which emerged on the West Coast in the late 1960's as an outgrowth of the black movement and the civil rights movement, has spread across the country.

Asian American studies—which are similar in concept to other forms of ethnic studies—have been developed at major universities, and Asian Americans at smaller colleges have banded together to request one or more introductory courses on the Asian experience in America. These courses seek to raise the student's consciousness, and to reconstruct Asian-American history, which is more often than not ignored in white history books; to instill a sense of pride and purpose, to deepen one's understanding of the past and to clarify what needs to be done in the future.

As a result of these efforts, various organizations have been formed—mainly on the East and West coasts, where the Asian Americans are concentrated—whose purpose is to further the cause of Asian American communities, to fight anti-Asian discrimination and prejudice, to express Asian American viewpoints on domestic and foreign affairs, to combat racism and bigotry in all their manifestations.

Aside from Japanese and Chinese, among the Asian Americans are to be included Koreans, Hawaiians, Indians, Bengalis, Pakistanis, and the Filipinos, who are the most numerous after the Japanese and Chinese.

Obviously, the adjustment that different immigrant groups had to make varied with the background of the people involved, with their time of migration, and with their motivations. There were different waves of Asian immigration, and therefore various Asian American nuclei have undergone different experiences of acculturation and assimilation. The Chinese were the first to arrive, coming in the mid-1800's, first to work in the gold mines, then as railroad workers, farmers, and industrial workers. The earliest Japanese also came as laborers. They went to Hawaii to work in the sugar refineries in the late nineteenth century, at a time when Hawaii was not yet part of the United States. They came to the mainland United States in the 1900's to work on farms, in mines, and in canneries. The Filipinos came in growing numbers after 1924. They worked on ranches, took jobs as elevator operators and bell boys, waiters and hotel attendants, and as seamen. Unlike the Chinese and the Japanese, the majority of Filipino Americans are foreign-born. Large numbers have been migrating here since the immigration law was changed in 1965.

For the most part, Asian Americans have remained in the West, where they or their forefathers first arrived. Thirty-eight percent live in California alone, while twenty-seven percent are in Hawaii. Only the Chinese have dispersed eastward in significant numbers. More than 115,000 Chinese-Americans live in the Northeast, with the vast majority living in New York City.

Census Bureau data show that 90 percent of all Asian Americans live in urban areas, and more than 54 percent live in inner cities. Of these urban dwellers, half live in just three metropolitan areas—Honolulu, San Francisco-Oakland, and Los Angeles-Long Beach. Their median family income is rising, and is higher than the national median. Such figures, however, do not take account of the fact that, for many, such an income is achieved only by having two or more members of the family employed, and frequently the working hours may be 10 or 12 hours a day, six or seven days a week, as is the case with many laundry and restaurant workers.

In spite of their relatively small numbers, Asian Americans have made impressive contributions to the United States in politics, business, science, and the arts. Many of the successful Asians have been from Hawaii, the one state where Asians constitute roughly half the population, and where career opportunities have been least restricted.

One of the most successful Asians in Hawaii is Senator Hiram Fong, the first American of Asian ancestry to be elected to the United States Senate. Senator Fong, a Republican, is the son of an immigrant indentured laborer who went to Hawaii from

Kwangtung Province, in southern China, to earn $12 a month. His son, the Senator, is a millionaire lawyer who is president of a Honolulu finance and investment institution.

His was a Horatio Alger story and, appropriately enough, in 1970 Senator Fong received the Horatio Alger Award, joining such notables as Dwight Eisenhower, Herbert Hoover, Ralph Bunche, and Bernard Baruch.

Hawaii's other Senator is also an Asian American—Daniel K. Inouye, a Democrat. In 1962 Mr. Inouye, at the age of of 38, became the first Japanese-American to win a seat in the United States Senate. Two years before that, he had become the first Nisei—or second-generation Japanese-American—to take a seat in the United States Congress. In both cases, he was elected by the largest number of votes cast for a candidate for public office in Hawaii's history.

During the Watergate scandal, Senator Inouye achieved widespread publicity as a member of the Senate's Watergate committee. But even his distinguished career has not made him exempt from anti-Asian bias. He was called a "little Jap" by John Wilson, attorney of John D. Ehrlichman, who, adding insult to injury, said he would not feel insulted if he were called a "little American."

Another legislator from Hawaii is Representative Patsy Mink, who in 1972 was a candidate for the Democratic Presidential nomination. Mrs. Mink, who is of Japanese descent, is the most prominent woman politician in Hawaii. She was unsuccessful in her effort to gain the nomination in the 1959 Congressional primaries, but won it in 1964. In the election, she easily defeated the Republican candidate and was re-elected in 1966 by the highest margin in Hawaiian Congressional election history.

Still another Hawaiian Asian American legislator is Spark M. Matsunaga, a Democrat. Mr. Matsunaga received his elementary, secondary and college education in Hawaii. After graduation, he attended Harvard University Law School, receiving his degree in 1951. In 1962 he was elected to the House of Representatives.

Mr. Matsunaga campaigned vigorously to have Congress repeal a law that permits the Government to put suspected spies into detention camps. It was fitting that the move to repeal the law should have been led by a Japanese-American, whose people had been so grievously wronged during World War II, when the United States Government labeled them enemy aliens and put them in detention camps.

Two Asian Americans have been especially outstanding in the field of architecture. One is Minoru Yamasaki, a Seattle-born Japanese American. Mr. Yamasaki designed the United States science pavilion at the Seattle World's Fair, and it was hailed as a masterpiece by many critics. He has designed buildings all over the world. Yamasaki won the first honor award of the American Institute of Architects several times—in 1956 for the St. Louis airport terminal, in 1959 for the McGregor Memorial Community Conference Center at Wayne State University in Detroit, and in 1961 for the Reynolds Metal Company regional office building in Southfield, Michigan. Another of Mr. Yamasaki's triumphs is the World Trade Center in lower Manhattan, which he designed.

One of America's best known architects is I. M. Pei. He was born in Canton in 1917, the son of a Shanghai banker. He came to the United States in 1935. His buildings include the John F. Kennedy Library at Harvard University and the East Building of the National Gallery of Art in Washington. In New York, he designed the $40-million National Airlines terminal at Kennedy International Airport.

Two of this country's foremost physicists, both Nobel Prize winners, are of Chinese ancestry, Dr. C. N. Yang and Dr. Tsung-Dao Lee. The two men shared the 1957 Nobel Prize for physics. Dr. Yang, Albert Einstein Professor of Physics at New York State University, Stonybrook, was born in Hofei, Anhwei Province, China, in 1922. He arrived in New York by way of India in 1945, after having received bachelor's and master's degrees in China. He earned his doctorate from the University of Chicago in 1948.

Dr. Lee, like Dr. Yang, was first educated in China. He was born in Shanghai in 1926. Dr. Lee received his doctorate in 1950, also from the University of Chicago. At the age of 29, he became the youngest full professor on the faculty of Columbia University.

Another Chinese physicist performed tests to prove the Yang-

Lee theory that led to their Nobel Prize. The physicist is Dr. Chien-Hsiung Wu of Columbia University. Born in 1903 in Shanghai, Dr. Wu received a bachelor's degree from National Central University in Shanghai and a doctorate from the University of California at Berkeley. During World War II, Dr. Wu worked on the Manhattan Project at Columbia University, helping to invent and develop the atomic bomb. In 1958, she was the first woman to receive Princeton Universitys' honorary doctorate in science. She also was the first woman recipient of the Cyrus B. Comstock Award of the National Academy of Sciences, given every five years for the most important discovery in electricity, magnetism, or radiation. Dr. Wu in 1973 was named to fill the recently created Pupin chair in physics at Columbia.

Another scientist is Dr. Choh Hao Li, a biochemist. In 1962, he was named winner of the Albert Lasker Medical Award, one of the highest recognitions in basic medical research in this country. Dr. Li, who is with the University of California, is the world's foremost authority on the pituitary gland. He has isolated in pure form six of the hormones of the gland. In 1947 he received the Ciba award in endocrinology. In 1948 he was a John Simon Guggenheim Memorial Foundation fellow. He was the first to receive the American Chemical Society's California section medal in 1951. In 1955 he won the Francis Emory Septennial Prize of the American Academy of Arts and Sciences.

S. I. Hayakawa is another educator. For some twenty years, Mr. Hayakawa has been provoking comment with his lectures, books, articles, and television talks on language habits in relation to the common phenomena of contemporary civilization. His book *Language in Action*, published in 1941, became a Book of the Month selection. Dr. Hayakawa was catapulted to national attention in 1968, when he was appointed acting president of San Francisco State College, at a time when the campus was racked by student violence. He called in the police to forcibly suppress student rebels, thus creating a national controversy. At the time Dr. Hayakawa took over San Francisco State, the campus had been shut down because of arson, bombings, and police raids. He devised a hardline strategy of keeping a strong police force on hand at all times.

Asian Americans have also contributed to society in the artistic realm. One of the best known artists is the American-born Dong Kingman, who is of Chinese ancestry. Born in 1911 in California, Mr. Kingman returned at the age of five to live in Hong Kong, where he studied painting under Szeto Wai, his only art teacher. He came back to the United States and in 1954 lectured for the State Department's international cultural exchange program. He did the water color prelude to the film "Flower Drum Song." His work has been shown at international exhibitions and his paintings hang in major galleries.

An artist of a different sort is Ming Cho Lee, a set designer. Born in Shanghai in 1930, he came to the United States at the age of 19. Mr. Lee studied art at Occidental College in Los Angeles and did graduate work at U.C.L.A. He has also taught set design at the Yale University drama school. The principal set designer of the New York Shakespeare Festival and the Juilliard School Opera Theater, he has been widely acclaimed for his imaginative set designs.

Still another kind of artist is Isamu Noguchi. Mr. Noguchi is an abstract artist, a sculptor who works in wood and stone. Since 1935 he has been making stage sets for Martha Graham. Born in Los Angeles on November 17, 1904, Mr. Noguchi's father was a poet and an authority on art while his mother was a writer. He was taken to Japan at the age of 2 and, at the age of 13, was sent back to the United States to finish his education. Before turning to sculpting, Noguchi attended medical school at Columbia University in New York for a while. In 1927 he went to Paris on a Guggenheim fellowship and met the abstract sculptor Brancusi. Later he went on to Peking, and back to Japan, working and studying. Samples of his work can be found at Yale University. One of his works is a bridge that he designed in Peace Park, Hiroshima. To some, his sculpture is esthetically fragile. He himself has explained his works by saying that they are intended as "images of moods—moods of flowers, of the vegetative and nonvegetative aspects of nature."

In the field of cinematography the reputation of James Wong Howe is unsurpassed. He was born near Canton and, when still a small boy, his family emigrated to Pasco, Washington, where his father became quite prosperous as the owner of two restaurants, a grocery store, and a hardware store. While still a youth, he decided to become a cameraman and, in spite of discrimination against his Chinese origin, he became the most sought-after cameraman in Hollywood. Some of the outstanding movies that are a product of his handiwork are "Come Back Little Sheba," "The Old Man and the Sea," "The Rose Tattoo," and "Hud." At one time, while filming a boxing scene, he put on a pair of roller skates and had himself pushed around the ring while using a hand-held camera so he could achieve close-up shots of the boxers, yet avoid jerky movements.

Aside from the superstars, there are a host of distinguished Asian Americans who have made significant contributions in their various fields of endeavor. Tommy Kono, of Sacramento, California, was an Olympic weight lifting champion, who set and broke world records. Chin Ho, born in Hawaii, built a financial empire on the island of Oahu. Joe Shoong and his family created the National Dollar Stores, Ltd., and he became one of the wealthiest Chinese in the country and an outstanding philanthropist. K. C. Li created an important tungsten operation in the United States. His company, Wah Chang Company, in 1953 built the world's largest tungsten refinery. Harry Low in 1966 became the first Chinese American to serve in the San Francisco municipal court. Wing F. Ong, a former laundryman, was elected a state legislator in Arizona in 1946. Worley K. Wong, born in Oakland in 1912, has become a successful California architect and won a competition to design a new California governor's mansion. Tetsuo Toyama, who went to work in the sugarcane fields of Hawaii in 1906 and stayed on to become a publisher, died in 1971 at the age of 88. Pat Suzuki is a singing and recording star. Tomi Kanazawa, a Californian, became the first Nisei to appear in a leading role with the Metropolitan Opera Company and was widely known as a concert performer. Harry A. Osaki of Pasadena, California, is a silversmith whose work is widely displayed and who has traveled in U. S. State Department shows in Europe. Norman Mineta was elected mayor of San Jose in 1971. Ken Nakaoka was elected mayor of Gardena, California, and Frank Ogawa has served on Oakland's city council.

In addition to contributions by individual Asian Americans, one should also keep in mind those that required long days of back-breaking labor and received no honors and little publicity. In this category are the thousands of Asians who worked in gold mines, on the railroads, as farm hands, in restaurants and laundries and as houseboys and as gardeners. Finally, in spite of the instances of outstanding success, one ought to remember those Asian minorities—especially the recent arrivals who have not "made it" in American society. Large numbers of them still live in substandard housing, in ghettos that they cannot leave because of language and cultural barriers.

SELECTED BIBLIOGRAPHY

BARTH, GUNTHER. *Bitter Strength: A History of the Chinese in the United States, 1850–1870.* Cambridge, Mass.: Harvard University Press, 1964.

COOLIDGE, MARY. *Chinese Immigration.* Reprint ed., New York: Arno, 1969.

DANIELS, ROGER. *The Politics of Prejudice.* Berkeley, California: Peter Smith, 1972.

GULICK, SIDNEY LEWIS. *The American Japanese Problem.* New York: C. Scribner's Sons, 1914.

ICHIHASHI, YAMATO. *Japanese in the United States.* New York: Arno, 1969.

KAVER, RICHARD. "The Workingman's Party of California," *Pacific Historical Review,* XIII (1944).

MACARTHUR, WALTER. "Opposition to Oriental Immigration," *Annals of the American Academy of Political and Social Science,* XXXIV (September, 1909).

McCLELLAN, ROBERT. *The Heathen Chinese: A Study of American Attitudes toward China, 1890–1905.* Athens, Ohio: Ohio State Univesity Press, 1971.

MILLER, STUART CREIGHTON. *The Unwelcome Immigrant: The American Image of the Chinese, 1785–1882.* Berkeley, California: University of California Press, 1969.

SANDMEYER, ELMER C. *The Anti-Chinese Movement in California.* Urbana, Illinois, University of Illinois Press, 1973.

SAXTON, ALEXANDER. *The Indispensable Enemy: Labor and the Anti-Chinese Movement in California.* Berkeley, California, University of California Press, 1971.

IX

The McCarran-Walter Act and the Conflict over Immigration Policy During the Truman Administration

By PHILIP C. DOLCE
Bergen Community College

THE McCarran-Walter Immigration and Nationality Act of 1952 was the first major immigration law to emerge from Congress in twenty-eight years and was a source of controversy until revised in 1965. Hence, it is a focal point of over forty years of immigration history. It reflected long-term attitudes toward newcomers as well as contemporary fears and frustrations. The McCarran-Walter Act also was an attempt by Congress to regain control over immigration policy in the face of constant encroachment by the executive branch of government.

Once the movement to restrict immigration began to gain momentum in the late nineteenth century, Congress became a champion of the cause. Gradually overcoming resistance from the executive branch, Congress managed to assert its own authority and by 1930 enjoyed a virtual monopoly in the field of immigration policy. Motivated primarily by domestic concerns, Congress enacted the national-origins quota system into law in 1924, and this was designed to establish the basic immigration policy of the nation as one of limited entry and favored treatment toward the countries of northwestern Europe.

The depression decade of the 1930's was the first test of the new law, and most Americans agreed that immigration had to be curtailed during this period of economic collapse. Due to a series of internal disputes, Congress was unable to enact new legislation and executive action began to influence immigration policy. This trend, reluctantly begun by Herbert Hoover, continued with only one serious interruption in the 1950's. It represented a significant shift in decision making and reflected in part a general growth of presidential power at the expense of Congress. In time, the wider perspective of presidential leadership would shift immigration policy from its narrow domestic base and use it as an important tool of United States foreign policy.

In 1930 President Hoover began to restrict immigration by strict administrative enforcement of existing law. U. S. consular officials, using a clause in the 1917 immigration law prohibiting the admission of persons likely to become a public charge, began excluding all but the most prosperous European immigrants. This method drastically cut European immigration, and its success stalled any action by Congress while establishing a base for executive leadership in immigration policy. Franklin Delano Roosevelt continued the public charge policy and seemed to be fulfilling the wishes of Congress, but at the same time he also was building a base for executive leadership which would reach fruition in the 1940's.

This can be seen in the attempt to deal with refugees fleeing Hitler's Europe. The ideal of asylum for persecuted people has a long tradition in America. However, it was never substantially written into the immigration statutes, and therefore refugees were given few privileges under the law. While there were many attempts to liberalize immigration regulations on behalf of these victims of tyranny, none received serious consideration in Congress.

Those seeking to aid the refugees looked to Roosevelt for governmental assistance. While his efforts on behalf of the refugees may be judged controversial, he did at least assume a role of moral leadership in the rescue attempt. By various means, he tried to demonstrate a sympathetic understanding of the problem. Roosevelt's policy was circumspect at best, yet there is no doubt that he was mainly responsible for the limited actions taken on behalf of refugees by the United States. Despite the fact that this country managed to absorb more refugees than any other nation in the world, there are those who believed that the Roose-

velt administration could have done much more for these persecuted people. The problem was that aid to refugees was purely
a humanitarian gesture. Stronger advocacy on their behalf would
have met firm resistance on the domestic front. Furthermore,
there were no gains to be made in foreign policy. Yet Roosevelt's limited intervention in the refugee problem combined
with the larger demands made on the administration, both
pointed to the expanded potential of presidential leadership in
immigration matters.

This potential became even more apparent in the 1940's when
our immigration policy began to reflect international rather than
domestic concerns. Earlier in this century, presidents ranging
from Theodore Roosevelt to Calvin Coolidge had been aware of
the grave international consequences that a restrictive immigration policy would cause but were either unable or unwilling to
prevent it. For instance, when the movement to exclude the
Japanese was gaining momentum in the early 1900's, Theodore
Roosevelt tried to soften the blow by diplomatic means. In the
"Gentlemen's Agreement" of 1908, Japan voluntarily restricted
immigration to the United States and thus avoided the humilia-
tion of congressional restriction. Roosevelt's action, motivated
by a concern for international affairs, did not reverse the tide
toward restriction but only delayed it. Even the inept Calvin
Coolidge was well aware of the international crisis which the
national-origins quota system would cause but was unwilling to
defy congressional demands for restriction.

Clearly, a restrictionist immigration policy was premised on
the primacy of domestic affairs over international concerns,
and presidential influence was minimized by circumstances.
World War II helped to reorder these priorities and thereby
enhanced presidential power. This can be seen by the gradual
change in our immigration policy which took place under presidential direction. During World War II, President Roosevelt
pressured Congress to break the bonds of Asian exclusion and
enact a Chinese quota provision. Obviously, our alliance with
China during the war was the main reason for altering immigration policy, and it was the President who forced the change
to reflect the nation's international obligations. Similarly, a quota
for India was enacted under strong administrative pressure.

During World War II and the Cold War which followed, the President came to be viewed as the leader of the free world. As our international obligations mounted, immigration more and more reflected executive-directed foreign policy. While changes in our immigration policy theoretically conformed to the existing national-origins quota system, in reality they represented a departure from the intent of the legislation passed in the 1920's. Nowhere was this more evident than in the administration of Harry S. Truman.

World War II had displaced millions of people from their traditional homelands in Europe. The Yalta Conference established procedures for the repatriation of these displaced persons, but the beginning of the Cold War and the establishment of Communist regimes in eastern Europe disrupted these agreements. Approximately one million displaced natives from eastern European countries refused to return to their homelands, and the pressure of millions of Germans expelled from behind the Iron Curtain complicated the problem.

President Truman sought to solve part of the nation's foreign policy problems by altering the immigration system. Moving cautiously at first, Truman announced in 1945 that he was inaugurating a new program of granting European displaced persons preferential treatment under the existing immigration laws. By reserving half the quotas of European countries for displaced persons, Truman remained within the limits of immigration statutes, but his action clearly showed executive independence from congressional restraints.

Since this proposal was inadequate in meeting the problem, Truman announced in 1946 that he would ask Congress to admit displaced persons outside the quota limits set by law. After a long debate, the displaced persons legislation as enacted in 1948 and amended in 1950 was a clear victory for the President. Though the law conformed to traditional immigration policy by charging displaced persons against future quotas of their country of origin and limiting this mortgage to fifty percent of the quota for any one year, it was restrictive more in form than in practice. Actually, displaced persons were allowed to enter immediately as nonquota immigrants and charge their entry against some future quota.

At the time, the mortgaging feature was seen as a harsh price to pay, but in reality it was a debt which could not be collected. The mortgaging of quotas, thought to be a guarantee of existing law, became absurd in practice. At one point, Latvia's quota was mortgaged until the year 2274, Greece's until 2013, Poland's till 1999, and Romania's until 2001. The more important point about the displaced persons legislation is that Congress was unable to sustain its effort to make the law conform in some way to the national origins principle. In 1948 the Displaced Persons Act was heavily weighted toward people from the Baltic area and agricultural workers and deliberately set early deadlines which excluded Jews. However, when the law was amended in 1950 the deadline was advanced, the Baltic and agricultural priorities were eliminated, and the selection of displaced persons was to be made without regard to their race, religion, or national origin. In four years (1948–52) approximately 400,000 displaced persons were admitted under this legislation, many of whom would have been ineligible under standards established in the 1920's.

The displaced persons legislation of the 1940's marked a high point of executive leadership in immigration matters and clearly established that immigration was an instrument of our foreign policy especially in the Cold War. While immigration policy was still governed by the major legislation enacted in the 1920's, executive leadership and foreign policy considerations had altered it substantially.

As long as the national focus remained on the external threat posed by Russian aggression, immigration policy could continue to be liberalized under presidential direction. However, once the fear of Communism became an internal problem, domestic priorities were restored and congressional attempts to restrict immigration were thus strengthened. President Truman had been able to overcome congressional resistance and manipulate immigration policy because the American people felt that the main danger to the United States came from abroad. However, in the early 1950's, the Truman administration was crippled by charges of communist subversion at home which at times reached hysterical proportions. The internal fear of Communism when combined with traditional hostility to certain immigrant groups and congressional attempts to regain power from the chief executive led directly to the enactment of the McCarran-Walter Act.

Although Representative Francis Walter had introduced the House version of this legislation, the moving spirit behind the bill was Senator Pat McCarran of Nevada. The seventy-five-year old McCarran was the son of Irish immigrant parents who was first elected to the Senate in 1933. He soon became a power within the chamber, especially after he was selected as chairman of the Judiciary Committee. An advocate of greater congressional power and strongly anti-Communist in attitude, McCarran viewed immigrants, especially those from areas outside northwest Europe, as a potential source of danger to American society.

The McCarran-Walter bill represented the first complete American codification of immigration and naturalization laws in modern times. It was a highly complex and technical measure which was over 300 pages long and contained 400 sections covering all aspects of immigration and nationalization. It replaced or amended previous laws and merged countless treaties, executive orders, proclamations, and regulations in the field. In fact, five years of congressional study preceded the final enactment of the bill.

This legislation contained a number of good features. It permitted Asian immigration and stopped sexual discrimination by allowing alien husbands of citizens to enter the country as nonquota immigrants. The bill continued to exempt nations in the Western Hemisphere from the quota system and clarified previous legislation pertaining to the admission of former members of totalitarian political parties. Most important of all, the McCarran-Walter bill recognized the need to codify all existing immigration statutes.

Yet, despite these features this bill was basically an attempt by Congress to regain control of immigration by restoring the restrictive policy it had established in the 1920's. In fact, it can be said that the McCarran-Walter bill was actually a restatement by Congress of traditional policy in light of the Cold War. The principal feature of the McCarran-Walter bill was that it retained the national-origins quota system which was first introduced in the 1920's. This system had a twofold purpose. It reduced the volume of immigration by establishing a numerical limit for all countries and made the selection of the immigrant's nationality automatic by providing a fixed limit for each country. The bill provided for the entry of approximately 154,000 persons a year based on the proportions of the United States population in 1920 which were attributable to various national origins. In other words, the McCarran-Walter bill retained, almost exactly, the same low total of immigration allowed under the 1924 law and, more importantly, used the 1920 census instead of a more recent one for proportioning quotas.

By using these figures, eighty-five percent of the European quota was assigned to the countries of northwestern Europe, principally Great Britain, Germany, and Ireland. In fact, these three countries were assigned almost two-thirds of the entire yearly immigration quota for the world. The underlying intention, as in 1924, was to preserve the ethnic composition of the nation by selecting immigrants whose traditions, language, and culture were thought to be nearly the same as that existing in the United States. The national-origins quota principle was deemed to be so important that the McCarran-Walter bill continued the policy of charging refugees admitted under emergency legislation to future quotas.

The bill also specified preferences within each national quota. Fifty percent of each national quota was reserved for applicants possessing special abilities or economic skills needed in the United States, while relatives of citizens and resident aliens had a priority on the remaining places. Non-preference applicants received consideration only when these priorities remained unfilled.

Advocates of the McCarran-Walter bill proclaimed that it ended racial discrimination in immigration policy. However, this was only partially true. The bill ended the exclusionary policy toward Orientals by allowing immigration from twenty-one countries or quota areas in the so-called Asia-Pacific Triangle which included all continental Asia and the islands of the Pacific. Most of these areas were given a minimum quota of 100. However, there was a permanent overall limit on immigration from the Asia-Pacific Triangle so that quota allotments for most nations would be reduced if new areas were granted immigration privileges. Asia and the Pacific islands were the only area with a permanent overall limit on immigration.

In addition, race was an important feature of Asian immigration. The McCarran-Walter bill provided that immigrants whose parentage was Oriental or even half-Oriental would be charged to the country of their ancestry, not their country of residence. For instance, a person born in France with a French father and a Japanese mother would be charged to the Japanese quota, even though he was a French citizen. This racial stigma only applied to Orientals because it was feared that the United States might be inundated by thousands of Asians who were citizens of Latin American or European nations. The provisions for Oriental immigration were designed to end the need for piecemeal quota allotments, such as the ones granted to India and the Chinese, and reflected the Cold War concern for Asia. Yet the racial nature and permanent limit on Asian immigration insured that it would not unduly upset the national-origins quota system favoring northwestern Europe.

Even if a person had the right national, racial, and economic background to gain a quota number, he was not assured easy entry into the United States. The McCarran-Walter bill established hundreds of separate grounds for the denial of visa papers. Consular officials were able to deny a visa if it only appeared to them that the alien was ineligible. No concrete grounds were necessary, nor were judicial safeguards provided.

These strict provisions in part exhibited congressional concern over subversion. So urgent did Congress consider the issue of alien subversion that in 1950 it enacted the Internal Security bill over President Truman's veto. This legislation, sponsored by Senator McCarran, provided for the registration of Communist or Communist-front organizations, internment of Communists during national emergencies, and the absolute prohibition against the entry of aliens who had ever been members of totalitarian organizations. Therefore, it is not surprising that the new immigration bill should be filled with hundreds of safeguards against "unfit" aliens.

In reality, the McCarran-Walter bill reflected the era in which it was proposed while striking a responsive chord in the nation's past. Proponents of this legislation believed that domestic tranquility demanded a largely homogeneous population. They believed that northern Europeans could best assimilate into American society and also maintain the nation's traditions and culture. Moreover, Americans have long lived in fear of being contaminated by some alien ideological disease. From the earliest history of our nation, we have worked on the assumption that there was an innate connection between foreigners and radicalism. If every foreigner was not a radical, every radical was in some way thought to be foreign and that was un-American.

At Senate subcommittee hearings on immigration, the theory was constantly expounded that Communism was an alien doctrine imported by foreigners. There also was a general belief that Communists tended to come from certain countries more than from others. Therefore, it is not surprising that at the height of domestic concern over the Cold War a movement to restrict immigration should occur. The McCarran-Walter bill combined the traditional motivation of immigration restriction, which was to preserve the racial and cultural heritage of the nation, with the Cold War fear of subversive foreigners. In other words, those who favored the McCarran-Walter bill basically believed that immigration was a potential source of danger to the nation and therefore should be as stringent as possible.

There were those who opposed this view and believed that immigration laws should be liberalized. Ethnic considerations, theories of racial harmony, humanitarian concerns, efforts at international cooperation, and America's role as the leader of the free world all influenced those who opposed the McCarran-Walter bill. In addition, an important factor was that many of the opponents of the McCarran-Walter bill looked upon immigration as an instrument of foreign policy and favored the flexible approach achieved under presidential leadership. They rejected the rigid regulations and theoretical formula of the new legislation which was regarded as more reflective of the 1920's than of the contemporary age.

Opponents, such as Senator Herbert Lehman, objected to basing the national-origins quotas on the 1920 census, thus continuing to grant two-thirds of the total annual immigration quota to Great Britain, Germany, and Ireland. This was especially true in light of the fact that since 1929 these countries did not use half the quota numbers allotted to them. Lehman and others objected to the racial discrimination against Asians, Blacks, and southern Europeans contained in the bill as well as the arbitrary provisions to exclude subversives and other undesirables. They maintained that the McCarran-Walter bill was a denial of the ideals and principles upon which the nation was founded.

Liberals in the Senate rallied behind the Humphrey-Lehman bill sponsored by Senator Hubert Humphrey of Minnesota and Senator Lehman of New York. This was designed to be an alternative immigration bill to that sponsored by McCarran. The Humphrey-Lehman bill would have based quotas on the 1950 census, and this would have granted greater quotas to southern and eastern Europeans. It would have permitted pooling all unused quotas each year and granting the additional numbers to countries that needed them. The Humphrey-Lehman bill also would have eliminated racial quotas for Asia and modified exclusionary provisions so that they were based on factual evidence instead of opinion.

While these provisions offered marked improvements, the opponents of the McCarran-Walter bill had made a serious error in judgment. The Humphrey-Lehman bill retained the national-origins quota system which was the very basis of existing immigration inequities. Liberals such as Humphrey and Lehman felt that a direct assault on the national-origins quota system would not work, so they compromised and tried to modify but not change existing policy. In doing so, they were seeking accommodation in an age which demanded absolute values. Furthermore, they could not focus attention on the main flaw in our immigration policy. McCarran exploited this weakness by constantly pointing out that his opponents accepted the basic necessity of a national-origins quota system and only differed in detail.

When the vote was finally taken in the Spring of 1952, the McCarran-Walter bill was passed overwhelmingly. Congress' action was motivated by several obvious factors. No doubt, theories of racial superiority, though unspoken, moved many congressmen to support the McCarran-Walter bill. During the middle of the Cold War, attempts to limit potential subversive elements were popular with both Congress and the people. In addition, many in Congress were unwilling to alter what they considered a time-tested method of immigration.

Beyond this there were less obvious reasons for the bill's passage. A study of both the McCarran-Walter bill and the Humphrey-Lehman bill concluded that "each of them contains over 400 sections. The interrelationships of these sections are highly complex. It is doubtful that anyone fully understands them." Members of Congress, who are undecided, usually vote for the bill which received committee endorsement. In the case of these complex pieces of legislation, no doubt some votes were cast for the McCarran-Walter bill out of sheer bewilderment.

The only remaining hope to defeat the McCarran-Walter bill was if the President vetoed it. Although Truman was against the bill, he was in a difficult position. He had not taken a leadership role while the McCarran-Walter bill was under study or during the debate in Congress. Lack of executive leadership was in part caused by the fact that the Truman administration was constantly on the defensive during the period 1950–52. Wild charges of being soft on Communism and harboring subversives in government hurt the administration. The stalemated Korean War, the conviction of Alger Hiss for perjury, and the sensational Rosenberg trial, all seemed to give credence to the charges of demagogic leaders, such as Senator Joseph McCarthy, that Truman was unable to check the Communist menace, especially on the home front. In addition, a series of scandals were revealed within the executive branch of government which shocked the nation. Public outrage over corruption in the Bureau of Internal Revenue, the Reconstruction Finance Corporation, and the Tax Division of the Justice Department not only weakened the administration but reinforced the concern over domestic issues.

Truman's initial response to the immigration question was not made until March, 1952, well after the debate on the McCarran-Walter bill had begun and the Humphrey-Lehman bill had been drafted. The President requested that Congress approve emergency legislation to allow 300,000 European refugees to enter the United States over and above quota limitations. In reality, this was an attempt to extend the displaced persons program which was scheduled to end that year.

The aim of the President's proposal was to relieve the over-population in Western Europe and thereby keep the Communists from gaining political ground, especially in Italy. The foreign policy goals of this plan were apparent, and a presidential aide, David D. Lloyd, pointed out that "The proposals in the President's Message are similar in their popular appeal to the Displaced Persons Bill, with the added advantage that they are anti-Communist and an important part of the cold war." There was another advantage to this approach which was that the President again would be able to direct immigration policy to his own ends through the use of temporary or emergency legislation. Thus he could continue to emasculate the immigration laws without confronting Congress over the basic issues. However, Truman's proposal was not only too late but ill-conceived. Congress was in no mood to put off formulating a basic immigration policy, nor to enact further temporary legislation.

Truman's late entry into the immigration struggle had other serious drawbacks. The White House, according to the President's Special Counsel, had "admittedly imperfect and limited knowledge" of the McCarran and Walter legislation even after the bills had passed Congress. This, of course, hindered effective efforts to block congressional action. Moreover, lack of presidential direction had allowed his own administration to become openly divided on the McCarran-Walter bill. The White House staff, the Department of Labor, the Director of Mutual Security, and the Bureau of the Budget, all urged Truman to veto the bill. However, the two agencies most concerned with immigration policy, the State Department and the Justice Department, both approved of the impending legislation.

The President seemed to have lost control over some agencies within the executive branch of government. The Justice Department at times had advanced legislation which even contradicted White House policy. Certain of these agencies had openly advised McCarran on immigration legislation and seemed more loyal to Congress than to the President. The divided counsel of his advisors only complicated matters. As one frustrated White House aide put it:

We already have trouble in the field of immigration policy because the Visa Division in the State Department . . . plays "footsie" with McCarran and is practically outside the control of the Secretary of State. In the same way, the Immigration and Naturalization Service in the Department of Justice tends to become independent of Executive control, and to look more for guidance to Congress than it does to the Attorney General.

The controversy over the McCarran-Walter bill exhibited the basic contradiction which existed within the Truman administration. The President and members of his administration had emphasized the extreme dangers of Communism and internal subversion, but seemed unwilling to oppose either too strongly. At one point, Attorney General J. Howard McGrath had warned that "the Communist conspiracy—at this very moment—is endeavoring to accomplish [its purpose]. They are busy at work—undermining your government, plotting to destroy the liberties of every citizen, and feverishly trying, in whatever they can, to aid the Soviet Union." If the threat to national security was as acute as McGrath and other administration sources said it was, then the McCarran-Walter restrictions on immigration could be viewed as essential and not excessive. Moreover, by highlighting the internal threat of Communism, the Truman administration unwittingly reinforced the domestic concerns over immigration. When it seemed that the administration could not adequately cope with this internal threat to our security, a movement to restore a restrictive immigration policy would be hard to resist.

Despite these damaging contradictions, Truman tried to regain control of the situation. Invoking the Bible and the Constitution, he vetoed the McCarran-Walter bill. Truman's veto message focused major criticism on the retention of the national-origins quota system. He stated:

The basis of this quota system was false and unworthy in 1924. . . . It is incredible to me that, in this year of 1952, we should again be enacting into law such a slur on the patriotism, the capacity, and the decency of a large part of our citizenry.

While Truman's remarks were valid, they were politically inappropriate at this late date. His relative silence on the national-origins quota system throughout his term of office and the debate in Congress made the veto message seem oddly inconsistent. Furthermore, his veto message was out of line with the fact that the State Department and the Justice Department had accepted the bill. In addition, he attacked the very part of the McCarran-Walter bill which congressional liberals accepted, thus dividing the opponents of this legislation. Driven by lapses of leadership and circumstances beyond his control, Truman was responding to events and not initiating them. Congress overrode the veto and the McCarran-Walter bill became law.

Two months after his veto had been overridden, Truman established the President's Commission on Immigration and Naturalization which was designed to study the impact of the McCarran-Walter Act on the nation. The Commission held hearings in major cities throughout the nation and out of the 634 statements it obtained, only 87 approved of the legislation. In fact, few except Senator McCarran would actively defend the law. When the Commission issued a highly critical report on his legislation, McCarran stated the new law was:

tough, very tough, on Communists, as it is on criminals and other subversives, and, that is why they are squealing. It is a tragic fact that the out-and-out Reds have ready colleagues in this fight: The "Pinks," the well-meaning but misguided "liberals" and the demagogues who would auction the interests of America for alleged minority-bloc votes.

While McCarran's charges were almost hysterical in nature, they did contain one element of truth. In an election year, Truman's veto message was as much aimed at attracting ethnic voters to the Democratic party as it was toward aiding immigrants. A number of his aides privately pointed out the political advantages of vetoing the McCarran-Walter bill, and his strong message in part reflected that view. In addition, Truman could have established a commission to study immigration earlier when it might have done more good. The fact that he waited until after the McCarran-Walter bill had been enacted probably reflected political as much as humanitarian concerns.

The authors of the McCarran-Walter Act had reasserted Congress' prerogatives in immigration matters and restored the national-origins quota system to full vigor. Domestic concern over the Cold War and a crippled chief executive provided the necessary background for the passage of the law. Yet for all the hundreds of clauses and details, the McCarran-Walter Act ultimately failed to achieve its purpose. Despite its attempt to force emigration from northwestern Europe, major sources of immigration sprang from other areas. Western Hemispheric nations, which were exempt from any quota, sent more immigrants than anyone envisioned. Nonquota immigrants and refugees admitted under special legislation also served to distort the national-origins quota system.

Presidential leadership and foreign policy considerations again became influential in formulating immigration policy and both ultimately undermined the McCarran-Walter Act. Dwight D. Eisenhower's election reinvigorated the presidential office. Inheriting none of Truman's liabilities, Eisenhower was in a stronger position to use executive power. In addition, the domestic fear of Communist subversion was alleviated because it was generally believed that the new administration could adequately deal with the problem. Almost immediately, immigration policy began to reflect these changes.

Since Eisenhower accepted the basic Truman foreign policy, it was not surprising that he would also use immigration as a tool in the Cold War. Therefore, Eisenhower's administration marked the resumption of the piecemeal destruction of the national-origins quota system. Using the same tactics Truman had employed in the 1940's, Eisenhower and liberal members of Congress circumvented the immigration law without challenging its central tenets. Within two months of his inauguration, Eisenhower requested additional refugee legislation, and in August, Congress passed the Refugee Relief Act of 1953 which admitted approximately 200,000 persons, most of whom were escapees from Communist nations. During the remaining period of his administration, five other acts were passed for the admission of nonquota immigrants. One of these, the Refugee Escapee Act sponsored by Senator John F. Kennedy, not only relaxed exclusionary practices and enlarged nonquota immigration but also dropped the mortgages against national quotas.

In addition to emergency legislation, the McCarran-Walter Act also was eroded through administrative action. The Act had vested broad authority in the Justice Department to waive many restrictions which excluded aliens, and it did so in thousands of cases.

In the thirteen years that the McCarran-Walter Act was in force, the overwhelming majority of immigrants were classed as nonquota and entered without restriction. The President by administrative direction, and Congress by legislative exception, had all but abandoned the national-origins quota system without repealing it outright. The Immigration Act of 1965, first introduced by President Kennedy and subsequently enacted under the administration of President Johnson, finally achieved that goal. Briefly, this law ended the national-origins quota system and instead established an overall annual quota of 170,000 which was open to all countries of the world excluding the nations of the Western Hemisphere. Aside from preferences reserved for relatives and applicants possessing special abilities or economic skills, the entire quota generally was available on a first come-first serve basis with the stipulation that no more than 20,000 immigrants could be admitted from any one country in a given year. The law also established the first quota ceiling on immigration from the Western Hemisphere which was fixed at 120,000 immigrants a year.

There was an unsuccessful attempt to grant the president almost independent authority to set aside up to twenty percent of the total annual quota and reallocate it to refugees whom he considered to be in need of special treatment. This provision was not written into the 1965 Immigration Act because it afforded too much power to the president. Yet its mere consideration is evidence of how important presidential direction of immigration policy had become. The basis of presidential power in immigration stemmed from a focus on foreign affairs, especially during the Cold War. This is not to deny that genuine humanitarian concerns and ethnic political considerations were not also at work. Yet these were not the paramount reasons for the transformation of our immigration policy. Immigration was never purely humanitarian, and in the twentieth century domestic considerations, despite the potency of the ethnic vote, usually worked in favor of restriction rather than liberalization of our immigration laws. It is generally assumed that the lack of controversy in immigration matters since 1965 resulted from the fairness of the new law. This is true, but another important factor is the growing detente with Russia. Presidential directed foreign policy is now aimed at peaceful coexistence with the Soviet Union and minimizing conflicts between the two great powers. In an era of detente, there are few gains to be made by aiding victims of Communist tyranny.

SELECTED BIBLIOGRAPHY

Manuscript Sources

David D. Lloyd Files, Harry S. Truman Library, Independence, Missouri

Official Files, Harry S. Truman Papers, Harry S. Truman Library

Other Sources

BENNETT, MARION T. "The Immigration and Nationality (McCarran-Walter) Act of 1952, as Amended to 1965," *The Annals of the American Academy of Political and Social Science*, 367 (Sept., 1966), 127–36.

BRUCE, J. CAMPBELL. *The Golden Door: The Irony of Our Immigration Policy*. New York: Random House, 1954.

CHASE, HAROLD W. *Security and Liberty: The Problems of Native Communists, 1947–1955*. Garden City, N. Y.: Doubleday, 1955.

COCHRAN, BERT. *Harry Truman and the Crisis Presidency*. New York: Funk & Wagnall, 1973.

DIMMITT, MARIUS ALBERT. "The Enactment of the McCarran-Walter Act of 1952." Unpublished Doctoral Dissertation, University of Kansas, 1970.

DIVINE, ROBERT A. *American Immigration Policy, 1924–1952*. New York: DaCapo edition, 1972.

ECKERSON, HELEN F. "Immigration and National Origins," *The Annals of the American Academy of Political Science*, 367 (Sept., 1966), 4–14.

FEINGOLD, HENRY L. *The Politics of Rescue: The Roosevelt Administration and the Holocaust, 1938–1945*. New Brunswick, N. J.: Rutgers University Press, 1970.

GOLDBLOOM, MAURICE J. *American Security and Freedom*. Boston: American Jewish Committee, 1954.

HAMBY, ALONZO L. *Beyond the New Deal: Harry S. Truman and American Liberalism.* New York: Columbia University Press, 1973.

JONES, MALDWYN ALLEN. *American Immigration.* Chicago: University of Chicago Press, 1960.

KENNEDY, EDWARD M. "The Immigration Act of 1965." *The Annals of the American Academy of Political and Social Science,* 367 (Sept., 1966), 137–49.

NEUSTADT, RICHARD E. "Congress and the Fair Deal: A Legislative Balance Sheet," *Public Policy,* 5 (1954), 351–81.

NEVINS, ALLAN. *Herbert Lehman and His Era.* New York: Charles Scribner's Sons, 1963.

O'BRIAN, JOHN LORD. *National Security and Individual Freedom.* Cambridge, Mass.: Harvard University Press, 1955.

PHILLIPS, CABELL. *The Truman Presidency: The History of a Triumphant Succession.* New York: Penguin, 1969.

Public Papers of the Presidents: Harry S. Truman, 1945–1953, 8 vols. Washington, D. C., 1961–1966.

SCHLESINGER, ARTHUR M., JR. *The Imperial Presidency.* Boston: Houghton Mifflin, 1973.

THEOHARIS, ATHAN. *Seeds of Repression: Harry S. Truman and the Origins of McCarthyism.* Chicago: Quadrangle, 1971.

TRUMAN, HARRY S. *Memoirs,* 2 vols. New York: Doubleday, 1958.